CAMPANULAS

CAMPANULAS

THEIR CULTIVATION
AND CLASSIFICATION

BY

H. CLIFFORD CROOK

1951

THEOPHRASTUS
SAKONNET
1977

First Edition 1951
(*London*: Country Life Limited, *2-10 Tavistock Street,
Covent Garden, W. C. 2*)

First Reprint by Theophrastus Publishers 1977
(*Sakonnet*: Post Office Box 458, Little Compton,
Rhode Island 02837)

Library of Congress Cataloguing in Publication Data

Crook, H. Clifford. 1882?-1974?
CAMPANULAS.

    Reprint of the 1951 edition published by Country
Life, *London.*
    Includes index.
    1. Campanula.   I. Title.
[SB413.C2C7   1977]   635.9'33'57   76-46561
ISBN 0-913728-18-7

Printed in the United States of America

CAMPANULAS

CAMPANULA THYRSOIDES VAR. CARNIOLICA

CAMPANULAS

THEIR CULTIVATION
AND CLASSIFICATION

BY

H. CLIFFORD CROOK

LONDON
COUNTRY LIFE LIMITED
CHARLES SCRIBNER'S SONS
NEW YORK

First published in 1951
by Country Life Limited
2-10 *Tavistock Street, London,* W.C.2
and in the United States of America
by Charles Scribner's Sons
597 *Fifth Avenue, New York,* 17
Process engraving by
Charterhouse Engraving Co. Ltd
*London, E.C.*3
Set in Imprint and Perpetua
and printed in Great Britain by
Robert MacLehose and Co. Ltd
University Press, Glasgow

CONTENTS

ILLUSTRATIONS

7

FOREWORD

IN the present volume an attempt has been made to collect descriptions of every known or recorded species of Campanula whether it is, or ever has been, in cultivation in this country or not. No similar attempt has been made since 1830, when De Candolle published in Paris his *Monographie des Campanulacees*, and descriptions of species discovered since that date have to be searched for in works dealing with the flora of restricted areas or in the periodical publications of scientific societies or botanical gardens throughout the world.

Wherever possible descriptions have been compiled from the living plant, but in the case of species which are not in cultivation and which grow in parts of the world not readily accessible, recourse has been had to the original published description supplemented by additional details from later authorities and, in many cases, herbarium material has, of necessity, had to be relied on.

On the question of nomenclature, all specific names have been written with a small letter in accordance with the latest views of the Kew authorities. The name of the authority responsible for a name has been added (in accordance with general botanical practice) only in those cases where a name has been used by different authors for different plants and it is essential to make it clear whose plant has been accepted as justly entitled to the name.

To facilitate reference, species have been arranged in the body of the work in alphabetical order. Little or no attempt has, however, been made to deal with the sub-species, forms, or varieties into which the more widespread or naturally variable species have been divided by certain botanists.

Hybrids are dealt with in a separate section and the extensive synonymity has been relegated to pages at the end of the book.

No attempt has been made to include a systematic key to the genus—a task for the trained botanist—but in the chapter on classification, some indication has been given of the lines on which such a key might be constructed and the species have been very roughly grouped. In the descriptions, however, sufficient botanical details have, it is believed, been given to make identification certain.

My thanks are particularly due to the authorities and staffs of the Royal Botanic Gardens at Kew and Edinburgh, and of the Royal Horticultural

Society at Wisley and Vincent Square; and to Messrs. David Wilkie and Robert M. Adam, of Edinburgh, Mr. W. G. Mackenzie, of Chelsea Physic Garden, and Mr. Stuart Boothman of Maidenhead, for permission to use a number of their excellent photographs.

A short bibliography is appended, but clearly cannot be regarded as comprehensive.

BIBLIOGRAPHY

1737.   LINNAEUS, *Genera plantarum.*

1753.   LINNAEUS, *Species plantarum.*

1785.   LAMARCK, *Encyclopaedia.*

1786.   VILLARS, *Histoire des plantes de Dauphiné.*

1806.   SIBTHORP AND SMITH, *Prodromus florae graecae.*

1819.   ROEMER AND SCHULTZ, *Systema vegetabilium.*

1825.   SPRENGEL, *Systema vegetabilium.*

1830.   A. DE CANDOLLE, *Monographie des Campanulacees.*

1861.   WILLKOMM AND LANGE, *Prodromus florae hispanicae.*

1872-5. HOOKER, *Flora of British India.*

1875.   BOISSIER, *Flora orientalis.*

1878.   ASA GRAY, *Synoptical Flora of North America.*

1883.   POST, *Flora of Syria, Palestine and Syria.*

1888.   BATTANDIER AND TRABAT, *Flore de l'Algerie.*

1902.   HALACSY, *Conspectus florae graecae.*

1903-7. FOMIN, *Flora caucasica critica.*

1907.   BLAS LAZARO E IBIZA, *Compendio de la flora espanola.*

1913.   HEGI, *Illustierte Flora von Mittel Europe.*

1931.   HAYEK, *Prodromus florae peninsulae balcanicae.*

CHAPTER I

THE GENUS CAMPANULA

THE genus Campanula is one of the larger groups into which botanists have divided our flowering plants, and contains plants suitable for all sizes of gardens and for all types of gardeners. There are, in the genus, something like 300 distinct species but a more exact count is impossible because the botanists are unable to agree among themselves or even individually from year to year what really constitutes a distinct species, the number depending on whether the writer is a 'lumper' or a 'splitter'. An extreme instance of the latter group is provided by Witasek who a few years ago attempted to divide the very widely distributed *C. rotundifolia* into three separate series and thirty-two sub-species.

No complete monograph on the genus has appeared since 1830 when De Candolle admitted 137 distinct species, many of them with sub-species or forms, and added fifteen others which he regarded as being doubtfully within the genus rather than properly to be included in one or other of the various closely allied genera. In 1907 a list of 206 species was compiled by Col. Beddome and published in the Royal Horticultural Society's *Journal*, while a few years later Farrer, in *The English Rock Garden*, recognised and partly described at least 220.

Since that date more have been found and there seems no reason to think that the end has yet been reached, for *C. formanekiana*, one of the most distinct, was only discovered and introduced as recently as 1931.

The genus is the largest and most important of the larger family group of Campanulaceae, which also includes Adenophora, Symphyandra, Edraianthus, Wahlenbergia, and Phyteuma, together with a number of smaller and less important genera and, strangely enough, Lobelia, though some authorities make this a separate family—Lobeliaceae.

The essential characters of the family are that there should be five petals joined into a tube; the corolla thus formed is inserted on the inferior ovary and within the adherent calyx. Five stamens are inserted within the corolla at its base but are otherwise free from it. The seed capsule is divided into a number of many-seeded cells, which open by pores. All members of the family are herbs, have stems which bear alternate leaves without stipules and generally contain a milky sap.

For the genus Campanula itself the corolla must be regular, which eliminates Lobelia. In Symphyandra the anthers are connate or joined;

Phyteuma has only two or three cells in the ovary as compared with three or five in Campanula, while Adenophora has a cylindrical nectary surrounding the base of the style, and Edraianthus and Wahlenbergia have seed capsules dehiscing by pores at the apex, in fact *above* the calyx teeth. Some attempt has also been made to create a new genus—Asyneuma—in which the corolla is so deeply lobed that for all practical purposes it may be regarded as composed of five separate petals though actually joined at the base. The other associated genera are of less importance and it is unnecessary to go into the detailed differences here. To mark the limits of our subject it is here necessary to inflict on the reader a technical definition and to say that all members of the genus Campanula are:

'Herbs with alternate leaves without stipules; an inferior ovary divided into many-seeded cells to which the calyx, divided into five segments, adheres and persists. The corolla consists of five equal petals joined for more or less of their length into a tube and inserted on the ovary within the calyx with the segments of which the corolla lobes alternate. The five stamens are inserted on the base of the corolla but are otherwise free. The flowers are without nectaries. A cylindrical style divides into as many stigmata as there are cells in the ovary.'

The genus Campanula is confined strictly to the northern hemisphere and even of the closely allied genera only one or two, and those of little importance, and a number of species (mostly annual) of Wahlenbergia, have their homes south of the Equator. Further, with very few exceptions, the distribution of the genus is restricted to the temperate zone with its main centres in the Caucasus, the Balkans, and the Mediterranean basin. Members of the genus are found on high ground in Persia, a few in the Himalaya and in Japan; North America and Canada yield a few and, completing the world circuit, a rich field exists in the Pyrenees and Spain. The British Isles can show seven species (excluding the so-called *C. hederacea* now not generally recognised as properly within the genus) but none of them is a true endemic.

Many of the species have a very wide range within the area. For example, *C. rotundifolia*, the well-known 'bluebell' of Scotland, is abundant all over the British Isles, particularly perhaps in Northern England and Scotland; it is undoubtedly the commonest species throughout Europe and Russian Asia from the Mediterranean to the Arctic Circle and is also common in the northern parts of the United States and Canada. Not unnaturally it shows numerous minor variations such as degree of leafiness of flower stem, number of flowers on each stem, amplitude and lobing of corolla, or relative length and carriage of calyx segments, but there is an almost infinite gradation and no real evidence that the variations will persist or be reproduced from seed; and in any case large numbers of such variants can be found in any district by a careful search over a few square miles of the countryside. Similarly with a number of so-called species from the Himalayan area which Hooker (*Flora of British India*) suggests may eventually be merged in the generally distributed *C. colorata.*

In its altitudinal range the genus generally inhabits the meadow and sub-alpine regions, for though a few species, as for example *C. cenisia*, may be found up to 9,000 or even 10,000 feet above sea-level in Switzerland (*C. cenisia* itself rarely descends below 8,000 feet) these are the outliers of the race. Many others are dwellers in screes or are strictly saxatile, but they indulge their likings at more modest elevations. Higher elevations are sought by many of the Indian species but this is merely a compensation for the more southerly latitude.

Few genera can show the diversity of form and habit of Campanula. The giant *C. pyramidalis*, sometimes as much as 5 feet high, adorns the baronial hall (if such still exists) or large conservatory; while the Canterbury Bell (*C. medium*) is ubiquitous in the humblest cottage garden; the herbaceous border cannot afford to overlook *C. lactiflora* and many other erect growing species; rougher, coarser and more invasive species find a congenial home in the wild, or very wild, garden. Even the 'dog's grave' rockery of clinker and concrete can be beautified by two species with names which seem to match the surroundings, *C. poscharskyana* and *C. portenschlagiana*, while the genus provides gems which are indispensable for any serious rock garden, be it large or small; for, though there are some early flowering species, the vast majority flower during July and August when most of the other alpine genera are but a memory of early spring days.

The predominant colour of the genus is blue; not perhaps that perfect blue of Tyltyl's 'blue glass marble' or of *Anchusa italica*, *Gentiana verna* or *Eritrichium nanum*, for throughout there is some underlying pink pigment which results in purples, mauves, lavenders and lilacs. In fact, in a few species, notably *C. medium*, the blue is sometimes entirely suppressed and we have a pure pink form which can, indeed, be reproduced from seed, and in at least one species—*C. betulaefolia*—only forms with some pink colouration are known. White forms have been found, and are in cultivation, of most of the better known and widely distributed species and the number will almost certainly be added to as the native habitats of other species are more fully explored. Nevertheless, the general effect is in the blue range and, as this colour is not one of the most common, the genus provides really essential plants for borders or rock gardens as well as for the alpine house and conservatory.

Finally, though the genus as a whole presents little difficulty in cultivation, there are a few species, including some of the very best, which will tax the skill of the most expert cultivator and so provide amusement for those whose greatest ambition is to flower (and exhibit) plants which will arouse admiration and envy in the beholder.

CHAPTER II

CLASSIFICATION

I N a genus of this size some system of classification is essential if species
are to be readily identified and although this book is in no way intended
as a scientific study of, or monograph on, the genus, some indication
of the lines on which such system has been, or could be, founded will
doubtless prove of interest to many readers.

A very cursory acquaintance with a fair number of quite commonly
grown species will reveal at once that while some have three stigmata there
are others in which the style divides into five, and rather more detailed in-
vestigation shows that this is directly related, as would naturally be supposed, to the number of cells in the seed capsule. This fact might well
give a first line of cleavage and has in fact been largely adopted, but it turns
out that the number of species with the style divided into five is comparatively small; in fact, out of the 137 species admitted by De Candolle only
thirteen come within this group and the proportion has not been materially
changed by later discoveries.

In much the same way—and to much the same extent—another group
could be made from species in which the petals are joined for a short part
of their length only and the remainder so much reflexed that the corolla is
rotate, or star-shaped, instead of forming the usual bell.

A comparatively small group of species can be distinguished as annuals
in the strictest sense of that term, namely as plants which make their growth
from seed to seed in an unbroken sequence and without any intermediate
stage such as the formation of rosettes of basal leaves, but this is the only
characteristic many of them have in common and is only of very secondary
value for purpose of identification.

It will be remembered that one of the essential characters of the genus
is that the seeds should be freed from the capsule through pores. These
pores are situated at different places on the capsule in different species,
being sometimes at the bottom, sometimes in the middle and in other cases
at or near the top, and this fact has been relied on by some botanists as a
line of classification. The first two groups are difficult to separate satis-
factorily and as a main line of division it suffers from the same defect as
that based on the number of stigmata, as in a very large majority of the
species dehiscence takes place somewhere in the lower half of the capsule and
the number of species with the pores definitely near the top is quite small.

A rather more careful examination of the flower structure will show that while some species have five quite normal calyx segments there are a number which bear growth developments between the segments, which at first glance resemble a second set of segments always more or less reflexed, and quite commonly closely adpressed to the calyx tube itself. Closer scrutiny, particularly of the venation and often of the degree and direction of rolling of the edges, shows clearly that they are developed on the calyx segments themselves rather than separate segments. This is particularly noticeable in species like *C. sarmatica* where the calyx segments are not separated completely to the base and the development between them is quite small. These growth developments between the calyx segments are, accordingly, referred to as calyx appendages. Within this group De Candolle includes 46 (out of his total of 137) species—a much nearer approach to a fair division of the genus. It is also a fact that this group includes all the species with five stigmata, there being no species having five cells in the capsule which do not also bear appendages on the calyx. Further, all the species with calyx appendages dehisce through pores at the base of the capsule. Difficulty certainly arises from the fact that in a few species the appendages are so small as to be scarcely noticeable, thus making it a matter of opinion in which section the species should be put (unless perchance it also has a five-partite style) but, on the whole, this gives the best main line of division.

In order to identify any particular species, therefore, it is necessary in the first place to ascertain whether the calyx is provided with appendages. If it is, the question of importance is whether the style is divided into three or five. In the case of the ex-appendiculate section of the genus, groups of species with rotate flowers, or of annual duration, can be segregated but further subdivision may perforce have to rely on the position of the capsule pores. A more detailed key of the genus must, however, await the production of the scientific monograph which is now much overdue.

As a preliminary division this would give us:

Section I—Calyx furnished with appendages (botanically *Sectio Medium*).

(*a*) capsule with five cells:

betonicaefolia, bordesiana, bourdiniana, crispa, laciniata, longestyla (sometimes only 3-celled), lyrata, medium, mollis, mykalaea, orphanidea, pelviformis, reiseri, rupestris, saxatilis, tubulosa.

(*b*) capsule with three cells:

affinis, alliariifolia, allionii, alpina, andia, atlantica, atlantis, *autraniana, axillaris, *balansae, barbata, bayerniana, betulaefolia, calamenthifolia, calcarata, *camptoclada, candida, choziatowskyi, constantinii, daghestanica, *dichotoma, dolomitica, dulcis, edulis, embergeri, engurensis, erucifolia, esculenta, filicaulis, fondervisii, formanekiana, gilliatii, grossekii, gumbetica, heterophylla, *hierosolymitana, hypopolia, imeritina, incanescens, incurva, jacobaea, kachethica, karakuschensis, kemulariae, kolenatiana, komarovii, lanata, leucoclada, leucosiphon, ligularis, lingulata, longestyla* (sometimes 5-celled), *macrostyla, malacitana, makaschvillii, massalskyi, microdonta, mirabilis, monodiana, oliveri, orbelica, oreadum, papillosa, pelia, petrophila, pilosa, *propinqua, punctata, quartiniana, raddeana, radula, *reuteriana, rigidipila, *rimarum, rupicola, sarmatica, sarmentosa, sclerotricha, serpylliformis, sibirica, speciosa, *stellaris, stricta, *strigosa, suanetica, sulphurea, teucrioides, thessala, tridentata, vayredae, velata, violaefolia.*

Section II—Calyx without appendages (botanically *Sectio Eucodon*).

(a) corolla rotate:

aparinoides, cymbalaria, elatines, elatinoides, floridana, fragilis, garganica, michauxioides, parryi, piperi, poscharskyana, velenovskyi, versicolor, waldsteiniana.

(b) capsule with pores near the apex:

*abietina, aizoon, albertii, americana, aristata, arvatica, aurita, beauverdiana, calcicola, chrysosplenifolia, compacta, crenulata, *diekii, epigaea, *erinoides, *expansa, *fastigiata, fulgens, *ghilanensis, grandis, herminii, *kotschyana, lasiocarpa, *loefflingii, mairei, olympica, peregrina, *phrygia, *ramosissima, rapunculus, *retrorsa, scouleri, *sidonensis, silenifolia, *singarensis, sophiae, *sparsa, spruneriana, stefanoffii, steveni, uniflora, verruculosa.*

The remaining species, being without calyx appendages and with capsules which dehisce at the base, require more botanical details for their classification.

* Indicates an annual species.

CHAPTER III

CULTIVATION

T HE genus as a whole presents few difficulties in cultivation. Any decent garden soil will grow most of them, with the usual recipe of 'a good medium loam' as the ideal. With the exception of a very few which are definitely lime-hating, a limy, alkaline medium is preferable and, generally speaking, good drainage is essential. Naturally this is of fundamental importance with species which are by nature scree dwellers or saxatile, and these, as well as the lime haters, are clearly indicated in the detailed description of each species in the later part of this volume. Again, as a general indication, those species with soft woolly or hairy leaves need some sort of protection from heavy winter rains.

All strictly annual species must, of course, be raised from seed and this should be sown where the plants are to bloom, for they do not transplant well. Most of the annual species (except the Himalayan ones) are quite hardy and make better plants and flower earlier if sown in autumn, provided the soil is on the light side, but it must be admitted that as a matter of fact very few of them are worth growing. Exceptions to this rather sweeping condemnation are *C. ramosissima* (or *C. loreyi*), *C. drabaefolia*, and (quaint rather than beautiful) *C. macrostyla*, which are very useful in places on rock gardens which are occupied by early flowering bulbs. Certainly some purists object to annuals on rock gardens, but nature should be the best guide and her rock garden contains large numbers of annual plants. The true criterion should be that the species used are in harmony with the rest of the scheme and that care is taken to avoid the introduction of rampant, half-hardy, or lowland plants among the hardy mountaineers with which the rock garden is normally furnished. All these annual species, if left to their own devices, will reproduce themselves year after year from self-sown seeds.

Then there is the group of true biennials, of which the Canterbury Bell (*C. medium*) is the best known. Others which are well worth growing— and they can be used in a mixed border—are *C. longestyla*, *C. sibirica*, and *C. patula*. They are easily raised from seed sown outdoors in May, transplanted when large enough and placed in their flowering quarters in autumn or spring. Here again, self-sown seedlings are commonly produced and if these can be left undisturbed exceptionally sturdy plants generally result.

Intermediate between the biennials and the true perennials which con-

stitute the bulk of the genus are those species correctly described as monocarpic. Like biennials they form basal growths or rosettes in their first year
of growth but defer the production of flowers to a later season. Many of
them will, in fact, behave like ordinary biennials and flower in the second
year but others will produce additional rosettes or increase the size of the
rosette formed in the first year. *C. laciniata* indeed has been known to grow
for four years—increasing in size each year—before flowering. After flowering, monocarpic plants die but generally produce plenty of seed. The
majority of the species with this habit are from Greek and Balkan areas
and among the best are *C. rupestris*, *C. sartori*, and *C. formanekiana*. They
are as easily raised from seed as the true biennials but, possibly because of
their hot-country origin, are more satisfactory if given cold-frame cultivation in pans or boxes until ready for their permanent positions. Unlike
the true biennials these species are not suitable for borders because all the
plants in a batch cannot be relied on to flower in the same season. Further,
they are generally speaking less vigorous and cannot hold their own with
more robust or stronger growing neighbours. But the group includes some
of the most attractive members of the genus which are almost ideal for
planting in large or small clumps in the rock garden, for in addition to their
flowers many of them produce really handsome rosettes of basal leaves in
their early years. Many people indeed find more beauty in the rosettes of
species like *C. formanekiana* than in their flower spikes, desirable as the
latter may be. Most of them have thick, fleshy roots and even where more
than one rosette is formed there is only a single collar or crown so
that division is not practicable and seed provides the only means of
increase.

Coming then to the perennial group, general cultivation directions depend on the habit of the particular species and great diversity exists among
them. The tall, erect-growing species will thrive in any ordinary border
and are not particular as to soil given reasonably good drainage. They are,
however, rather intolerant of drought and some of them are inclined to be
brittle, breaking away from the base, so require early and adequate support
if in exposed positions. Some of them, for example *C. lactiflora* and *C.
alliariifolia*, have thick fleshy roots like most of the monocarpic species
but, unlike them, form a number of crowns and can be divided in autumn
or spring. The practice, however, is not recommended, as it is almost impossible to lift a plant without seriously damaging the thick root, and the
transplanted portions take some time to re-establish themselves. Nor should
it be necessary, for they are easily raised from seed and can be put into their
permanent positions while still quite small, and will generally flower in their

second year and increase in size and beauty annually thereafter. On the other hand, those with a running, or stoloniferous, habit, such as *C. persicifolia* or *C. grandis*, can be divided with impunity to almost any extent and in fact are better if so treated at least every other year. Either autumn or spring is a suitable time for this work. Perennial species of medium height, such as *C. glomerata*, *C. carpatica* and *C. rotundifolia*, are very effective in fairly large patches at the front of mixed borders. As a rule they can readily be increased by division either in autumn or spring, with a slight preference for the latter period particularly on the heavier soils, and this is equally true of the stronger growing of the dwarfer species such as *C. portenschlagiana*, or those with a mat-forming style of growth, such as *C. cochleariifolia* (popularly, but erroneously, called *C. pusilla*), which are very effective as edgings.

Many of the really dwarf, or more strictly alpine, species present greater difficulties. Some of these, like *C. cenisia* and *C. allionii*, do not so much form mats as throw out a number of underground runners from a central carrot-like root, each runner terminating in a rosette of leaves which is rather slow to form roots and start life on its own. If plants of these species are required to form new colonies (or to give away or exchange with friends) these rosettes must be detached with a short length of the runner and treated as cuttings. Inserted in a very sandy compost and placed in a close frame they will generally form roots within a few weeks. Others, including *C. caespitosa* and *C. zoysii*, form an increasing root crown from which the shoots are produced and in such cases a few of the non-flowering growths may be carefully detached when an inch or so long and treated as cuttings in the same way. Then there are a few species with an intermediate habit, for example, *C. hercegovina* and *C. petrophila*, which, while increasing at the root crown also occasionally throw out one or two runners. Either of the above methods of increase may be adopted with these, but it is probably safer to use the runners rather than cut at the crown, while seed is safer than either. Finally, there are the strictly saxatile species, of which *C. tridentata* and its close kin and *C. saxatilis* may be taken as typical, which, like the monocarpics, are crown growers only and, though steadily increasing in size and in the number of rosettes produced, produce these rosettes direct on the rootstock without any semblance of a stem and thus do not provide material for cuttings. Here, therefore, seed must be relied on.

As a matter of fact seed-raising is in general to be preferred to vegetative propagation. Seed of species, even if not of particular colours or forms, can fairly confidently be relied on to come true, for hybridisation occurs very rarely in nature despite the wide distribution of the genus and the extensive overlapping within any area of distribution, and artificial hybrids are not secured without difficulty. At one time it was believed that the genus relied on self-fertilisation and that, in fact, this took place before the flowers opened. More modern views, however, suggest that, in view of the proved advantages of cross-fertilisation in most plants, this is very unlikely, particularly in a genus characterised by a corolla with the petals fused into a tube and by the wide prevalence of blue as the flower colour— both of which are generally considered to indicate an advanced stage in the development of our flowering plants. Nevertheless it is clear that the pollen is shed before the flower opens and is collected on hairs on the outside of the style and when, a day or so after the flower opens, the stigmata recurve and roll back on themselves there would seem to be a very good chance of self-fertilisation taking place if cross-fertilisation has not already been effected. All known hybrids are dealt with in a later chapter and reference thereto will show how comparatively few there are for a genus of this size. As with practically any plant there is a certain amount of natural variation in a large batch of seedlings, an occasional seedling being more (or less) vigorous with perhaps larger flowers or with those of a slightly modified shape. Some colour variation may also be expected for, as already noted, practically all the widely distributed and well known species have white forms which, more often than not, come true from seed. Any specially desirable form must, however, be reproduced by cuttings or division, while where the habit of growth makes this method impracticable there is no alternative to taking the chance that seed saved from the desired form will breed true.

With comparatively few notable exceptions, the members of the genus do not take kindly to pot culture. True, numbers of the smaller and rarer species seem to call for the extra care and attention they can thus obtain; the few really difficult species are so much more under the cultivator's control; cultivation in pots (or pans) does facilitate protection against that arch enemy of the genus, the slug, whose tastes invariably run to the best; and those species with woolly or hairy leaves (and these are mainly natives of warmer, drier climates than our own) appreciate the protection from winter rains which it is the main function of an alpine house to afford. For, be it fully understood, there are few members of the genus which are not fully hardy, or which will not withstand any degree of cold which they are likely to have to suffer in any part of these islands, always assuming that they are not at the same time expected to put up with excessive moisture round the crowns or on the leaves. And, being essentially hardy subjects, they will not respond to, or even tolerate, anything in the way of forcing, the immediate result of which is sappy, straggly growth with few and small flowers and a plant quite divorced from its true character.

Details of cultivation will depend, naturally, on the species it is desired to grow. The giant *C. pyramidalis* which chooses a richer soil than most in its native haunts will fully repay a rich diet in cultivation and given such treatment and regularly repotted as the roots fill their allotted space, will often call for a nine- or ten-inch pot in which to flower. At Kew, many such plants are grown every year and, assisted by moderate feeding when the buds are forming, grow to a height of five or even six feet and are always a centre of attraction when brought into the conservatory during August. The Canterbury Bell also makes a first-class subject for conservatory decoration and here too a fairly rich medium and some feeding will not come amiss. But, of the erect growing species, the palm must undoubtedly be awarded to *C. formanekiana*. Only the pen of a Farrer (and, alas, he never saw it) could do justice to this superlative plant. Whether in its rosette of pale grey velvety leaves or its eighteen-inch spire of white bells, it is unsurpassed. Not for *C. formanekiana* the plebeian crowds of flowers and somewhat bloated form of *C. medium*, nor the almost ostentatious splendour of *C. pyramidalis*; here is no garish display, no striving after effect, but detachment and poise, the quiet dignity of the true aristocrat. This, however, unlike the species just mentioned, does not need, and will not tolerate, an over-rich soil. Naturally a crevice plant, it seems to be happiest when thrusting its root fibres among rocks and stones in search of food and moisture and though, where this thrusting is confined within the limits of a pot, a rather richer medium is necessary than in the open, the greatest measure of success may be looked for where the soil contains a large admixture (50% by bulk is not too much) of stone chippings, which should by preference be limestone.

Most of the other tall growing species are too coarse for satisfactory pot culture, though the lighter growing ones, such as *C. sibirica*, *C. longestyla*, and, above all, *C. divaricata*, will add interest to the alpine house if only by breaking the rather flat effect of the pans of dwarf plants with which such structures are generally furnished.

Passing then to the dwarfer species, our main concern in considering cultural details must be the root. Some indication of soil requirements is given as regards many of the species in later pages and these should be kept in mind when preparing the soil mixture for potting, as well as the general requirement of the genus as a whole for impeccable drainage. But however much care is given to the preparation of a suitable soil you cannot expect

CAMPANULA ABIETINA

CAMPANULA AFFINIS

25

CAMPANULA ALLIARIIFOLIA

CAMPANULA ALLIONII

27

CAMPANULA ALPINA

CAMPANULA
ARGYROTRICHA

28

a plant which makes a long taproot to be a success in a shallow pan, nor can you expect the running roots of a spreader to be happy if compelled to go round and round in circles in a small pot. Some of the most successful plants of the *tridentata* group I have ever seen were growing in pots fifteen inches deep, yet only six inches across the top (facetiously, but not inaptly, described as 'chimney pots') and even then the roots grew out through the drainage holes at the bottom. One may venture to doubt whether the use of such contrivances can properly be described as 'pot culture'.

C. cochleariifolia which, in its various varieties, makes most attractive ten- or twelve-inch pans, soon begins to 'go back on you' if not frequently divided and repotted. *C. cenisia* and *C. excisa* are notorious ramblers which, even at home, never seem to come up in the same place a second year but stray off to fresh territory, and when grown in pans seem to need repotting every other year. In fact all the species with running roots appear to exhaust the soil very quickly and are not really happy within the confines of even a large pan.

The greatest measure of success must be looked for among the rosette-forming species. Most of these are, by nature, crevice plants and accustomed to having their roots confined, but it must be realised that these roots ramify to very considerable depths in their search for food and water, and to ensure fully developed plants nothing smaller than a five-inch or six-inch pot should be used, the former being reserved for the smaller species, such as *C. rupicola*, *C. oreadum*, etc. Always the soil must be well drained and kept open by a free admixture of coarse sand and stone chippings, while a surface layer an inch thick of unmixed chippings worked well in under the rosette and round the crown will protect the latter from excessive damp (and resultant rotting) and be generally appreciated as well as keeping leaves and flowers clean. All the *rupestris* and *lyrata* group make delightful subjects, preferring a pot, and a fairly deep one at that, to the more usual shallow pan. *C. heterophylla* too will give greater satisfaction than under outdoor conditions because its radiating flower stems are very brittle and easily broken away from the crown by a few hours of rough weather. But if *C. formanekiana* is the king of the erect growing species, *C. mirabilis* is the queen of the trailers, more particularly if the white form can be obtained. In its first year the large rosette of thick, glossy, bright green leaves is distinctly ornamental, while when, in a later year, the flower stem begins to lengthen no sticks should be used but the plant should be stood on a shelf or on an inverted pot and the stem allowed to droop naturally and gracefully. It seems to appreciate a fairly rich (if well-drained) soil, but the surface must be covered with a good layer of stone chips to ensure that no stagnant moisture remains round the thick crown or in contact with the fleshy leaves.

Lastly mention must be made of *C. isophylla* in any of its many forms for its value in furnishing hanging baskets or trailing over the sides of window boxes. Soil should not be too rich or there will be a development of leaf at the expense of flower, but otherwise it is not exacting in its requirements and has probably the longest flowering season of any, continuing in bloom for the greater part of the summer.

CHAPTER IV

THE SPECIES

C. aaronsonii. A species from Northern Palestine which forms a tuft of obovate, long-petioled leaves, from among which grow numerous ascendant leafy stems, some five or six inches long, terminating in a few-flowered cluster of long-stalked flowers. The stem leaves are similar in shape to the basal ones but sessile and all leaves are finely crenate. The calyx is rough with short, broadly triangular segments, quite erect and less than half as long as the corolla. The latter is small, about one third of an inch and straightly tubular with bluntly triangular lobes a third its length and not reflexed. The trifid style is as long as the corolla tube.

Very similar to *C. damascena* (and allied to *C. trichopoda* and *C. euclasta*) it is distinguished by its longer basal leaves on longer petioles, by its broader and relatively shorter calyx segments and by longer flower stalks, but the group as a whole is uninteresting (*C. euclasta* is probably the best) and the introduction of seed, which would be the only way of getting a stock, is clearly not worth while.

C. abchasica is sometimes given specific rank but more generally regarded as a variety of *C. collina* with more greyish leaves and broader flowers on longer footstalks.

C. abietina. An attractive species which is endemic to stony summit ridges in the Carpathians. It produces rosettes of narrow ovate-lanceolate leaves, sessile, finely crenate and of a brilliant green colour. The flowers are borne in loose few-flowered branching spikes on slender wiry stems, up to a foot high, which also bear a few lanceolate leaves. They are, in general, reddish purple in colour, about three-quarters of an inch across, and of an open star shape, the lobes extending to half the length of the corolla and being well reflexed. They are erect in both the bud and the developed stage. The awl-shaped calyx segments are fully half as long as the corolla and not reflexed. The stigma is trifid while the capsule is tri-locular and dehisces at the top.

Some years ago M. Savulescu, a botanist of Romania, endeavoured to trace the affinities of this group and gave cogent reasons for regarding *C. hemschinica* as the earliest type from which have diverged *C. olympica* (in Pontus and Bithynia), *C. steveni* (in Armenia, Cappadocia and the Altai region), and *C. abietina* (in the Carpathians). Shortly, the argument is that *C. hemschinica*, an essentially alpine but biennial species, widely spread over Asia Minor and the Balkan Peninsula, began to develop a perennial habit by the production of underground runners wherever increasing climatic severity made such perennial habit essential if the species were to survive. Changes in land and water configuration during and after the ice age segregated some of these groups and the line of development has since proceeded independently. In the result we have the occasional production of runners in *C. olympica*, the regular production of such runners in *C. steveni* (in Asia Minor) and *C. epigaea* (in the Balkans), while the runners have given place to a stoloniferous habit in *C. abietina* (in the Carpathians). In post-glacial times, after the retreat of the glaciers, the universal alpine type descended to the plains and gave rise to the very widely distributed *C. patula*, which is of biennial and often even of annual duration and never ascends to the alpine zone.

However this may be, there is no doubt that the perennial habit of *C. abietina* is not very marked. In fact it frequently dies after flowering and almost the only way of keeping a stock is to pinch out the flower spike from some of the plants at an early stage, thus almost compelling them to make growth rather than flower. Even so, annual division and replanting, in fairly rich soil, is necessary, though seed is sometimes freely produced.

The species obtained the Award of Merit as long ago as 1891.

C. acutiloba. A perennial from rock fissures in Kurdistan which may be called the Asiatic counterpart of the *C. garganica* group. It produces a number of spreading, curving stems some four inches long with ovate-cordate, deeply crenate-dentate leaves and racemes of flowers in stalked clusters of one to three in the leaf axils. The calyx tube is spherical with spreading linear-lanceolate segments which are only about a third as long as the corolla. The whole plant, including the outside of the corolla, is reported to be softly hairy, but it is at least possible that glabrous forms occur.

C. adsurgens. See p. 217.

C. affinis, R. & S. A Spanish species generally regarded as closely allied to *C. speciosa*, Pourr.

From a thick taproot it produces a number of ribbed unbranched stems covered with short recurving hairs. The stems have linear-lanceolate leaves, sometimes as much as four inches long, smooth and ciliate. The flowers are in bracted clusters of three or four and both terminal and axillary. The calyx has broad, ovate appendages and broad awl-shaped segments, while the large corolla, over an inch long, and fully twice as wide, is twice as long as the calyx segments.

In 1935 an Award of Merit was given to a plant under the name of

C. bolusii and the photograph on page 25 is of a plant raised from seed of the Award plant. The Kew authorities regard this as synonymous with *C. affinis*, with the latter as the prior name. The Spanish Flora of Blas Lazaro e Ibiza distinguishes them, the more marked differences being that *C. affinis*, R. & S., is perennial and has *solitary* axillary flowers, whereas *C. bolosii*, Vayr, is only biennial and bears its flowers in racemes of two to ten; *C. bolosii* too is a much taller grower, *C. affinis* not exceeding two and a half feet. Minor distinctions seem to be that *C. bolosii* has a less dentate leaf, shorter calyx segments and more acuminate appendages. Farrer suggests that *C. affinis* (or *C. bolosii*) is only a variety of *C. speciosa*, Pourr., but he cannot have seen the true plant, since he says that it carries its blooms erect.

The Kew plants form in their first year a rosette of long narrow rough scalloped leaves with distinctly undulate and hairy margins; in the second (or sometimes third) year a flower spike some two feet high is produced, unbranched and furnished with leaves similar to those of the rosette, diminishing gradually in size, and in its upper half with wide-open shallow semi-pendent bells, over an inch across, usually of a mid blue colour, in clusters in the leaf axils. The calyx segments are broad and not more than half the length of the corolla, while the trifid style projects to nearly double the length of the bell.

Whether one or two species, their native home is North-Eastern Spain, particularly Monserrat, which is also the home of the closely allied *C. speciosa*, Pourr., about which again there is constant dispute as to its perennial character.

The photograph shows clearly the sterile rosettes which develop at the base of the flowering stem and form the foundation for the following year's flower spikes, but while this apparently perennial character and the height favour *affinis*, the clustering of the flowers is given as a definite characteristic of *bolosii*, and the correct name remains uncertain.

C. aizoon. A rare biennial or monocarpic species from Southern Greece which forms rosettes, about three inches across, of numerous smooth, strap-shaped, crinkled or undulate, leaves. These leaves have a cartilaginous margin and often terminate in a sharp, stiff point giving the plant an almost unique appearance.

The erect flower stem, some twelve to eighteen inches high, rigid and ridged, is freely branched from the base with many stiff lateral branches well spread from the main axis, bearing a few sessile lanceolate-acute leaves, each branch terminating in anything up to five flowers, the whole inflorescence forming a thyrsoid panicle.

The calyx, which is without appendages, is smooth with triangular segments only about a quarter the length of the rich purple campanulate corolla. The latter, which is held stiffly erect, is fairly large, half an inch or more across, but the lobes are only short. The globose capsule dehisces near the top, thus showing a near relationship to species like *C. patula.*

In its native haunts it is a crevice plant; it needs a similar position in the rock garden and must be raised from seed, but, though a really attractive plant, it is strangely rare in cultivation as, indeed, it is in nature. Apart from its scarcity, it is not at all easy to cultivate successfully for, though seed germinates, the plants frequently refuse to grow beyond the seedling stage.

C. ajugaefolia, Sestini. A plant from Galatia with rough oblong leaves coarsely crenate-dentate, hairy on the undersides and drawn out into a petiole. A simple erect stem bears sessile leaves and terminates in a dense axillary spike of sessile flowers. Vatke says it is a distinct plant but the corolla does not spread out and it cannot be compared with any other Campanula and considers it very doubtful whether it should be included in the genus. The plant is not in cultivation and no further information is obtainable.

C. alata. A rather coarse Algerian species, generally perennial, which forms a tuft of smooth, broadly lanceolate, irregularly dentate and wrinkled leaves on short petioles or sessile and sends up an unbranched, angular, stem three to five feet high, bearing sessile lanceolate leaves, rough on all nerves, and, near the apex, a few sessile flowers, the upper ones being condensed into a head. The individual flowers are of good size being well over an inch across, broadly campanulate with broad ovate lobes well displayed. Calyx segments are linear-lanceolate and slightly hairy and only about half as long as the corolla. The tripartite style is shorter than the corolla and dehiscence is basal. There are no appendages.

If obtainable, seed provides the most satisfactory means of increase; it is freely produced and germinates as freely. In some ways the species resembles *C. primulaefolia* and *C. peregrina,* either of which species is rather more showy and easier to obtain.

C. albertii. A perennial from sub-alpine rocks in the district of Tashkent, which produces numerous erect thin and unbranched stems up to a foot in height. The stems bear a few almost grassy denticulate leaves, the lower ones diminishing to short petioles, and terminate generally in a single fairly large flower, though there are sometimes two or three. The calyx segments are linear-lanceolate, acute and erect; the smooth corolla, deeply lobed, is nearly three times as long as the calyx segments; the style is trifid;

and the capsule, which is carried erect, dehisces nearly at the top. It does not appear to be in cultivation but should be an attractive plant if obtainable.

C. alliariifolia, Willd. A strong growing species from Asia Minor and the Caucasus, which may be described as a second-class border plant but very useful for a wild garden. It is completely herbaceous but a true perennial and in early spring produces a tuft of large, heart-shaped, coarsely serrate and hairy leaves on petioles as long as or longer than the leaves themselves. A noteworthy character is the way in which the edges of the leaves incurve in the young state. Later a number of erect or ascendant, more or less branched and leafy stems rise to a height of anything up to four feet. These stems are covered with a felt of greyish hairs and carry large numbers of long tubular white bells in a one-sided raceme, the individual drooping flowers being generally borne singly on short stalks in the leaf axils. The corolla, which is tubular-campanulate and somewhat inflated may be as much as two inches in length, the lobes, not more than about one sixth of the length and only slightly reflexed, ciliate on the margins and with characteristic tooth-like processes at the base of each sinus. The calyx segments are only one quarter to one third as long as the corolla; they are broadly triangular with revolute ciliate margins, are not reflexed and are furnished with almost circular, softly hairy appendages equal to, or longer than, the calyx tube. The style divides into three (sometimes four) stigmata.

Seed provides a ready (often too ready) means of increase.

A double form has been reported but does not sound very attractive. The type is pictured in *Bot. Mag.* at t. 912 as *C. macrophylla*.

C. allionii. This is now regarded as the correct name of the plant long known as *C. alpestris.*

A native of the western ranges of the European Alps, the species is far from easy in cultivation and emphatically demands scree treatment. It is one of the species for which a granitic soil is usually advised, but there is no doubt of its tolerance of limestone. It increases by underground stolons and requires plenty of room to ramble about, full sunshine, and a constant *underground* water supply during the growing season.

It forms small rosettes of narrow lanceolate, sessile, hairy leaves, from which the flower stems, carrying a single flower (occasionally two) rise to a height of one or two inches. The large fully-campanulate flowers are semi-erect, in shape like those of the Canterbury Bell and, in the type, about half the size though some forms grow up to an inch and a half long and as much across the mouth. These flower stems are furnished with a few narrow, sessile and ciliate leaves. After fertilisation the capsule assumes a drooping position. The calyx tube is small and glabrous; the segments which are linear, acuminate, more or less ciliate and much reflexed, are about half the length of the corolla, while the ovate-acute appendages are also ciliate and reflexed on to the calyx tube. The trifid style is about as long as the bell.

Generally of some shade of blue, white forms are not uncommon and a pink form has been found and named. It is a species which deserves a careful selection of the best forms when in flower from the point of view of both size and colour. A particularly large form has been dignified with the appellation *grandiflora* but many people will regard the blooms of this form as clumsy and too large for the size of the plant.

The runners may be detached and treated as cuttings, as described on p. 22, but seed provides a more certain means of increase except where special forms are required.

The white and pink forms (the latter under the varietal name Frank Barker) obtained the Award of Merit in 1930.

C. alpina. A native of Austria-Hungary and the Tyrol, where it frequents the highest mountains, this species, though claimed to be a true perennial, generally seems to die after flowering. It makes a long taproot surmounted by a single flat rosette of narrow ligulate leaves, generally glossy smooth and slightly dentate. The flower stem is short, seldom more than six inches high, and stiffly erect; it is more or less freely branched and as each branch carries, singly on long peduncles, anything up to ten large pendent or semi-erect lilac-lavender bells, the whole inflorescence forms a pyramidal raceme. As in *C. barbata*, to which species, in fact, it is nearly allied, the flowers are noticeably bearded. The narrow hairy calyx segments are noticeably longer than the bud and nearly as long as the fully expanded flower at which stage they are widely spreading and recurved. Appendages are so slightly developed as to be frequently unnoticeable. The corolla lobes are short and not noticeably recurved, making a blunt-ended flower. The style is shorter than the corolla and is divided into three filiform stigmata. If it is to prove its perennial character there is no doubt that it must be grown in poor stony soil, with a good admixture of lime and plenty of depth for its long taproot, but seed is produced very freely and germinates so readily that it is better, on the whole, to regard it as a biennial.

It is far from common in gardens although it was introduced as long ago as 1779 and illustrated in the *Bot. Mag.* at t. 957.

C. alsinoides. A small straggling species, seldom more than about four inches high, from the North-West Himalayas at 8,000 to 10,000 feet.

CAMPANULA ARVATICA

CAMPANULA AUTRANIANA

37

CAMPANULA BARBATA

38

It forms a woody root so should be perennial but generally seems to be little more than annual, at least in this country. From the root grow a number of thin zigzaggy stems which make a tangled mass and are patently hairy and furnished with small oblong-ovate, sub-petiolate leaves, softly hairy on both sides and obscurely toothed. The small tubular flowers, not above half an inch long, are whitish with purplish veining and are borne erect on slender stalks up to an inch long, singly in the leaf axils; the corolla is lobed to about a third of its length and the blunt lobes are well spread; the calyx segments, about two thirds the length of the corolla, are narrowly lanceolate. The style is trifid and dehiscence basal. It obtained the Award of Merit in 1932. See also p. 221.

C. amasiae. A perennial species from Asia Minor which has a thick carrot-like root and a simple angled erect stem about a foot high covered with short bristles and terminating in a compound raceme. The basal leaves die off as the flower stems elongate, while the stem leaves are oblong or oblong-lanceolate, sessile and more or less finely dentate. The flowers, in groups of one to three on short footstalks have awl-shaped calyx segments and an obconical campanulate corolla half as long again as the calyx segments and divided nearly to the middle into narrow triangular lobes. It is said to be very similar to *C. lanceolata*, Lapeyr (which itself can scarcely be distinguished from *C. rhomboidalis*) but to differ in the shape and length of the calyx segments and in the longer lobing of the corolla.

C. americana, Linn. A stiff and not very interesting species which is widespread throughout the United States of America and adjacent parts of Canada.

The rootstock, a short-lived perennial, but more often no more than biennial, produces a tuft of rough, ovate-acute, sub-cordate, serrate leaves on petioles longer than the blade. Erect, angled stems follow, which may reach a height of five or six feet and are sometimes branched at the base. They bear a number of oblong or lanceolate leaves which have gradually shorter petioles and ultimately become sessile, the upper part of the stems bearing numerous flowers in a long leafy spike, composed of one to three flowers in the axil of each leaf or bract. The calyx is elongated and smooth, with long, acuminate, reflexed segments, while the corolla, light violet, is campanulate-rotate, under an inch across, only slightly longer than the calyx segments and carried erect, the pedicels being short or absent. The style is considerably longer than the corolla and tripartite, while the capsule dehisces at, or near, the top.

In general appearance it is quite unlike other members of the genus; so much so that one American botanist has proposed transferring it to a

c

new genus of its own, as Campanulastrum. This, however, has not been generally accepted.

Farrer describes it as 'coarse, rank and worthless' but this is something of an exaggeration. It is easily raised from seed, but I have found difficulty in bringing it on to the flowering stage. It is doubtful whether seed can now be obtained in this country—but why bother?

C. amorgina is nothing but a small form of *C. heterophylla.*

C. anchusiflora. See p. 218.

C. andorrana. A plant from limestone screes in Andorra for which specific rank is claimed though it appears to be nothing more than a local form of *C. cochleariifolia.* The distinctions on which the claim is based are that the stem leaves, oval and slightly dentate, are similar all the way up the stems instead of becoming very narrow near the top as in the type, and that the calyx segments are much larger, broader and spreading. These variations, which are quite common throughout the genus, do not seem sufficient to justify specific rank.

C. andrewsii. See p. 218.

C. angustiflora. An annual from America which is not universally distinguished from *C. exigua,* Rattan. As described it is a stronger, more branched plant, sometimes reaching eighteen inches in height, but the flowers are smaller and less conspicuous with calyx segments almost as long as the corolla. It has been suggested that these small annual Campanulas (which are inconspicuous and grow in out-of-the-way places) may be more common than is supposed and may vary a good deal among themselves. How many of them really deserve specific rank is still very uncertain but, in any case, very few of them are of any interest to anyone but the botanist.

C. aparinoides. A North American species with weak ascendant stems up to a foot high rambling about among the grass of the meadows though it sometimes occurs in thickets and swamps where it grows rather taller and takes on almost a climbing habit. The bristly stems bear a few scattered leaves which are obovate or linear-lanceolate with rough edges and backs, and terminate in a few small erect campanulate flowers, deeply lobed and not more than half an inch long. They are whitish in colour. The calyx is without appendages and has short triangular segments. The thin trifid style is shorter than the corolla. Dehiscence is basal and the species is of annual duration only.

C. arenaria. A perennial from Bosnia which is very near *C. hercegovina,* but a generally smaller plant. It is said to produce only a single stem which is branched from the base with spreading or ascendant branches bearing leaves scattered along their whole length. The leaves are ovate-rotund, sessile and more or less crenate and ciliate near the base, becoming gradually narrower and ultimately bluntly lanceolate and amplexicaul. Flowers are produced from the upper axils, usually solitary, nodding and on fairly long stalks. The calyx is smooth and ribbed, thus providing one of the distinctions from the better known species, while the smooth calyx segments are linear, twice the length of the calyx tube itself and only about a third as long as the campanulate corolla which is lobed almost to the middle. There are no calyx appendages and the style is trifid.

C. argentea. A perennial species from Armenia which forms close rosettes of small thickish linear-obovate leaves, not more than an inch long, with wavy margins and covered with silvery down.

The erect velvety stems are about three inches high and shortly branched. They bear a few oblong acuminate entire leaves, silvery like the basal ones, and a few flowers terminating each branch, the flowers being very shortly stalked and carried erect. The velvety and markedly angular calyx has short triangular segments but no appendages, while the narrowly tubular corolla, three times as long as the calyx segments, has rather short lobes which do not recurve. The trifid style is the same length as the corolla and the turbinate capsule remains erect after fertilisation and dehisces at the base.

It does not seem to have been in cultivation in this country, though the description makes it appear to be a very desirable species.

C. argyrotricha. A Himalayan species with most of the characteristics of other species from the same area, such as a strongly developed calyx broader than the corolla tube, and an unfortunate tendency to produce a number of small cleistogamous flowers. Still further, its hardiness and perennial character are not above suspicion.

The root gives rise to numerous procumbent, hairy, thread-like stems, dichotomously branched, furnished with nearly sessile leaves which are thin, broadly ovate, only very slightly toothed, silvery-green in colour and softly hairy. The blue flowers, on long pedicels and usually solitary, are half to three-quarters of an inch long and hairy outside. While generally tubular in shape there is considerable variation in the form, some varieties having full-bell shaped flowers rather wider than long. In any case the lobes are well reflexed but the colour is rather too pale and indeterminate to give a showy flower. The hairy calyx segments are short, not more than one-sixth the length of the corolla and not reflexed. Although the flowers are carried more or less erect, the capsule is pendent. It is included in the larger section of the genus in which the style is trifid and dehiscence is basal.

So far it would seem to be the best species India has given us, being more attractive than either *C. alsinoides* or *C. cashmiriana*, but none of them is particularly distinguished, though they provide interest and relief on the rock garden with their low-toned and restful colouration at a time when the hues of high summer tend to become almost garish.

Seed, if procurable, provides the only means of increase.

The Award of Merit was given to a plant under this name in 1932.

For the relationship between this species and its allies see p. 221.

C. aristata. A species from Northern India, Kashmir and Tibet at elevations of 11,000 to 16,000 feet, which is probably not hardy in this country.

It forms a thickish root crowned with tufts of lanceolate-acute, undulate leaves, an inch to an inch and a half long, on petioles of equal or greater length. From these rise numerous thin, smooth, erect, unbranched flower stems three to four inches high (Blatter says eight to twenty-four) with narrowly linear, sessile leaves and small terminal solitary semi-pendent flowers. The narrow calyx segments are long, awl-shaped and erect, while the corolla, little more than half the length of the calyx segments, is funnel-shaped, and divided into five short acute lobes. The style, about the same length as the corolla, divides into three long stigmata which recurve considerably. The most usual flower colour is a pale blue. The narrowly oblong capsule is carried erect and dehisces at or near the top.

C. arvatica. A native of Northern Spain, this species grows in the narrowest of limestone crevices, but in cultivation runs about freely in any light soil, forming mats of rosettes of a few small long-stalked leaves which are rotund-cordate, usually entire but sometimes with jagged edges and always quite smooth. From each rosette springs a single stem up to three or four inches in height furnished with a few oval or rhomboid leaves from the axils of which spring violet star-shaped flowers always held boldly erect. The flowers are perhaps on the small side but their widely expanded shape makes them conspicuous and showy. The awl-shaped calyx segments are longer than the corolla tube and the species belongs to that section of the genus in which appendages are absent. Dehiscence takes place in the upper half of the capsule. Easily increased by division, by cuttings in early spring, or by seed which is freely produced and germinates readily, this is among the most attractive of the dwarf species. Considerable doubt has been thrown on the correctness of the name, which De Candolle knew not, but the latest Kew Hand-list agrees with Farrer in repudiating *C. acutangula* in favour of the name here used, under which the species was figured in the *Bot. Mag.* at t. 8431. Although a species with its native habitat in Europe, it is of comparatively recent introduction; it was not included in the list of known species compiled by Beddome in 1907 and the earliest reference I have been able to trace puts the date of introduction as 1915.

A white form has been found and received an Award of Merit in July 1937. There is also a form known as Bevan's variety which appears to differ from the type in having rather larger flowers, together with a looser habit of growth and less tendency to run underground and is in many ways an improvement on the type.

Given a light limy soil it presents no difficulty in cultivation, but in heavier soils it is liable to go off in the winter.

C. aspera, Moench. A rough biennial plant with erect, angled and unbranched stems up to three feet in height and stiff, oblong-obtuse, crenate leaves, the basal ones being petiolate and the upper ones sessile. The flowers are borne in a loose terminal raceme, the lower ones being on short stalks usually in clusters of three. The calyx segments are lanceolate-acute, dentate and somewhat shorter than the corolla which is showy and has ovate lobes. The style divides into three (or, sometimes, four) stigmata but the capsule has three cells. It is ex-appendiculate.

C. atlantica. A small perennial species from Algeria which forms a tuft of oblong, sinuate leaves from among which spring erect, rigid, unbranched stems. The small flowers, only about half an inch across, are exceeded in length by the calyx segments. It is included in that section of the genus which has appendages on the calyx though they do not appear to be much developed in this species.

Battandier says the correct name is *C. afganica*, Pomel, but abandons that name lest it be thought that the species is a native of Afghanistan. In any case it does not seem to be worth bothering about. Clay describes it as having decumbent stems clothed with small hairy leaves terminating in one or more small campanulate flowers with long narrow lobes.

C. atlantis. A perennial species which grows among limestone rocks of the Great Atlas at an altitude of about 9,000 feet. It has a branched woody rootstock, the branches ending in rosettes of oblong-spathulate or lanceolate leaves which diminish to short petioles. The leaves are ashy green due to a layer of soft hairs, blunt ended and only very slightly denticulate. Prostrate or ascendant flower stems, four or five inches long, grow out from beneath the rosettes and are slightly branched at the apex, each branchlet terminating in a single flower. The leaves on these stems are oblong and sessile. The calyx is roughish with linear-lanceolate segments and the appendages are so short that they are sometimes reduced to mere knobs. The corolla is campanulate, with broadly ovate lobes, smooth externally and usually of a whitish-violet colour with darker veins. The style is white and shortly trifid.

It is probably only a local variant of *C. malacitana*.

C. aucheri. See p. 210.

C. aurita. A perennial from tablelands in the neighbourhood of the Yukon River, Alaska. It produces a tuft of oblong-lanceolate leaves, about an inch long, sessile and generally entire, though sometimes there are a few coarse teeth. A number of erect slender stems, ten to twelve inches high, bear a few leaves and terminate in a single semi-pendent flower. The calyx segments are lanceolate, each with a pair of erect teeth at or near the base; the violet corolla is about three-quarters of an inch long and cleft for rather more than half its length into lanceolate widely-spreading lobes. It may well be nothing more than a local form of *C. uniflora*.

C. autraniana. A Caucasian species which produces a tuft of smooth, broadly ovate, sub-cordate, regularly crenate leaves on long petioles. Among these rise, to a height of eight or nine inches, slender sub-erect, unbranched flower stems furnished with a few narrow leaves and terminating in one to three large flowers. The calyx is wider than the base of the corolla; it is smooth with short linear triangular reflexed segments not more than a third the length of the corolla and with edges which recurve slightly; the appendages are so small as to be scarcely noticeable and, indeed, are often absent. The corolla is large, tubular-campanulate, with broad reflexed lobes about one third of its length and generally of a deep rich purple colour with a white base. The style is rather shorter than the corolla and the stigma is tripartite; the filaments are bluish and the pollen almost white. The whole plant is glabrous. After flowering the capsule is pendent.

Its nearest allies are *C. betulaefolia* and *C. suanetica* which are, in general, rather larger plants and frequently have stems which branch towards the extremities, each branchlet carrying up to three flowers.

The species seems to present no difficulties in cultivation and is readily raised from seed. In a light soil it increases by short underground runners, soon forming a fair sized clump which is susceptible of division, preferably when new growth is commencing in the spring.

C. axillaris, Boiss. Described by Farrer as 'a large and stalwart border plant, with toothed leafage and flowers in their axils almost stemless' this native of Cilicia is closely related to *C. grossekii* and *C. sclerotricha*, differing from the former in having appendages which are only about a third the length of the calyx tube and from the latter in having much shorter calyx segments, these being only about a third the length of the corolla. It grows about two feet high but does not seem to be in cultivation.

C. balansae. This annual species from the lower alpine regions of Cappadocia is a dwarf spreading plant not more than four inches high with a rough stem branching from the base with oblong-ovate entire leaves, sub-petiolate near the base but reduced to little more than bracts in the upper portions. Both main stems and branches terminate in small tubular flowers the smooth lobes of which are scarcely recurved; the calyx has spreading lanceolate segments and triangular appendages nearly equal to the corolla tube in length; the nodding capsule dehisces at the base.

C. balfouri. A form of *C. dichotoma* from Socotra which differs from the type in having smaller flowers and appendages.

C. barbata. This species is common throughout the European Alps and seems to be indifferent to its surroundings for it occurs in open pastures and in light woodland and though it probably reaches its finest development on granitic soils it is not by any means confined thereto. It does not occur in the Pyrenees or Jura, but has been reported from Norway.

It forms, from a long taproot, a rosette or cluster of rosettes, of ovate-lanceolate rough leaves, often undulate at the edges and narrowing into a very short petiole. Each rosette gives rise to a practically leafless, unbranched stem a foot or so in height bearing a one-sided shower of a few comparatively large hanging bell-shaped flowers. The usual colour is lavender-blue, but the shade varies considerably. Many very pale, almost white, forms will be found but, apart from the true albino which is far from common, all these have a darker zone at the base of the bell. The lighter forms and the albinos seem to be restricted to the non-calcareous soils. The specific name is derived from the fringe of hairs which edges the corolla being more conspicuous in this than in other species similarly adorned, the corolla lobes being sufficiently reflexed to show off this feature to advantage. The calyx segments are triangular acuminate and not reflexed and only about one third the length of the corolla. The calyx bears short reflexed ovate and hairy appendages. The style, rather longer than the corolla, divides into three filiform stigmata. It is not generally very long lived, though a true perennial, but seeds so freely that it is quite easy to retain a stock; in fact self-sown seedlings may generally be relied on. On account of its deep rooting habit it demands a deep soil and any transplanting that is necessary must be done while the plants are quite small. It is a most attractive plant and being so easy to please should be found in every rock garden.

Occasionally a strong growing plant will produce a branched flower stem and at higher altitudes a single flowered form occurs, but this is invariably mixed with forms with two or three flowers and is not entitled to the specific rank which is sometimes accorded to it as *C. firmiana*. The same applies to a form with erect flowers, which is sometimes referred to as *C. strictopedunculata*.

C. barbeyi. See p. 217.

C. bayerniana. From rocky alpine and sub-alpine regions of Armenia and Persia at elevations of 6,000 to 10,000 feet. A branched creeping root gives rise to tufts of minute leaves and dwarf thin flexible few-flowered stems, smooth or slightly rough and not rising more than two or three inches above the ground. The leaves are sub-coriaceous, those of the basal tufts being reniform or ovate-cordate, coarsely and irregularly dentate, with hard waved ciliate margins and long petioles; those of the stems are smaller, ovate, on shorter petioles and with five to nine sharp dentations. The small flowers are shortly stalked and bracted; calyx segments are long, triangular, acuminate and, like the leaves, with hard waved ciliate edges; the appendages are very short. The narrowly campanulate corolla is smooth externally but bearded within and four or five times as long as the calyx segments; the trifid style is shorter than the corolla. Forms with hairy leaves and flowers have been reported.

C. beauverdiana. A species which occurs in dry mountain meadows at elevations between 2,500 and 10,000 feet throughout Transcaucasia where it develops a thin, creeping perennial rootstock and numerous erect or ascendant stems about a foot high, each bearing one, two or three flowers on longish stalks. The leaves have membranaceous margins and the lower ones are broadly ovate or oblong-acute with bluntly crenate margins and long thin footstalks, while the upper ones are linear-lanceolate, acute and sessile. The calyx segments are narrowly lanceolate and acuminate and not more than half as long as the corolla, while the latter is quite smooth and open-campanulate. The calyx tube bears a number of whitish excrescences and dehisces at the apex. The trifid style is shorter than the corolla. The species is not easily distinguished from *C. steveni*.

C. bellidifolia. See p. 210.

C. betetae. A plant from Spain for which specific rank is claimed. In general outline it resembles *C. rotundifolia* but the basal leaves are ovate with three or four very distinct teeth on each side and have hairy petioles. The lower stem leaves too are fairly broadly lanceolate, distinctly dentate and hairy near the stem. The main distinction seems to lie in the length and shape of the calyx segments which are lanceolate or even ovate-lanceolate and only about one fifth the length of the corolla.

CAMPANULA BETULAEFOLIA

CAMPANULA BONONIENSIS

CAMPANULA CAESPITOSA

CAMPANULA CALAMENTHIFOLIA

48

CAMPANULA CARPATICA

CAMPANULA CASHMIRIANA

C. betonicaefolia, S. & S. A native of Bithynia and Mount Olympus which is biennial with a single, erect, leafy, angular, slightly branched stem twelve to eighteen inches high. The large basal leaves are elliptic-oblong or ovate-acute, regularly crenate-dentate, paler on the undersides, downy, and gradually diminishing into the petioles. Flowers are borne terminally and in the leaf axils on peduncles which are generally three-flowered. The calyx is hairy with broad, ovate-acute segments and with appendages much the same shape reflexed on to the tube; the corolla is rather small, barely an inch long but two or three times the length of the calyx segments, and is tubular with short recurved ovate-obtuse lobes. The white style is as long as the corolla and there are normally five stigmata.

Seed provides the only means of increase, but it is doubtful whether the species is at present in cultivation in this country—or whether it is worth growing.

C. betulaefolia. Very recently introduced into cultivation from rock crevices in Armenia, this species forms a clump of sub-cordate, pointed wedge shaped leaves which are smooth, sharply dentate and on long slender petioles. A number of stems from six to eight inches in length are produced which at first are upright and, while some may remain so, the majority tend to flop as the flowers expand. These stems, which have a few small ovate and petiolate leaves, are more or less freely branched and carry a loose cluster of erect full bell-shaped flowers in groups of three or four. The corolla lobes are pointed and not more than one fifth the length of the corolla, and as the peduncles vary in length the whole inflorescence tends to become an umbel. The calyx segments are pointed, wedge shaped and acuminate and are not reflexed; they are not more than a quarter the length of the corolla while the triangular appendages are very small and somewhat hooked at the ends. The style is white, equal to the corolla in length and trifid. The whole plant is glabrous.

In the type the flowers are white, but the plant to which an Award of Merit was given at Chelsea in 1937 had pale pink flowers; in either case, the exterior of the buds is a deep pink, or even wine-red, colour.

In the wild state it is found growing in fissures of the rocks and a similar position in the rock garden should suit it, though it succeeds well in the scree if given a fairly rich subsoil and an ample supply of moisture. The stems, however, are somewhat fragile and to see the flowers at their best it well repays the protection of the alpine house in exposed districts, though the plant itself is perfectly hardy.

A sound perennial, readily raised from the abundantly produced seed.

C. bolosii. See *C. affinis.*

C. bononiensis. A species of very wide distribution throughout Europe which is of no interest to the rock gardener and is, indeed, only suited to the more extensive of wild gardens.

It forms a woody rootstock which produces a tuft of stalked, ovate-lanceolate, sub-cordate leaves, irregularly serrate and more or less roughly hairy. Simple or slightly branched rough flower stems, leafy in the lower half, rise to a height of some three or four feet, the leaves being sessile or sub-amplexicaul and becoming gradually narrower and more pointed until the upper half of the stem bears flowers only. The inflorescence is between a spike and a raceme, the rather small semi-pendent flowers being in twos and threes on very short peduncles. The calyx is covered with bristly hairs and the segments are short, triangular-lanceolate and not reflexed, while the smooth funnel-shaped, usually blue, corolla, with rather short, reflexed and pointed lobes, is four or five times as long as the calyx segments. The cylindrical style is the same length as the corolla, trifid at the apex.

As may be imagined from its wide distribution, the species has no particular likes or dislikes and reproduces itself very readily from seed. It is of biennial duration only.

C. bordesiana. A species from uplands in the Central Sahara which has a thick spreading rootstock, the short branches of which terminate in rosettes of oblong-ovate or sub-spathulate leaves diminishing to short more or less winged petioles. The leaves are softly hairy and crenate. From below the rosettes emerge numerous flexible ascendant stems sometimes reaching a length of two feet, bluntly angled, covered with long stiff hairs, furnished with bluntly lanceolate sessile leaves and freely branched in the upper half, each branchlet terminating in a single long-stalked flower which is erect in the bud stage but gradually becomes pendent. The calyx segments are narrowly triangular, pointed and ciliate and there are ovate-lanceolate appendages with hairy margins longer than the calyx tube. The campanulate corolla, varying in colour from violet to lilac, is about half an inch long and divided half-way into broadly ovate spreading lobes. The style divides into five stigmata which are distinctly revolute.

In its general habit the species resembles *C. filicaulis* but the five-partite style and broad corolla lobes provide clear distinctions.

C. bourdiniana. Given specific rank on the authority of Gandoger, this seems to be nothing more than a form of *C. medium* with much rougher stems and, possibly, a more branching habit. I cannot see that the upgrading is justified.

C. caespitosa, Scop. This species appears to have one of the most uncertain names in the genus. It is a native of the Eastern European Alps, being found in quantities in the Dolomites. De Candolle says it cannot be distinguished from *C. pusilla*, Haenke, which should suffice to banish the latter name for ever, for the true *C. caespitosa* is one of the most easily recognisable of the smaller species if by no other characters than the noticeable constriction of the bell and the shape of the rosette leaves. It is tap-rooted and forms an ever-increasing tuft of smooth, broadly lanceolate leaves, about an inch long, pointed at both ends but scarcely becoming petiolate and with two or three sharp teeth on each side. From among these, thin angled stems arise, sometimes reaching a height of eight inches but usually not more than half this. These stems carry a number of linear leaves which are entire and sessile and much crowded at the base of the stems, and terminate in a number of hanging blue bells, mostly confined to the upper part of the stem, markedly constricted at the mouth and strongly ribbed outside. The calyx segments are linear and erect and about two thirds the length of the corolla. The corolla lobes are short and not markedly reflexed. A further means of distinguishing the true species from others with which it is often confused is that the anthers are rose coloured and the pollen red or violet.

In general appearance it is not unlike *C. cochleariifolia* but it does not run at the root like that species and is generally rather taller.

The species requires a position in full sun and thrives in any light well-drained soil or in a limestone scree, even though it is not quite so easy to keep as some other dwarf species. It is easily raised from seed but is rare in cultivation, due, no doubt, to the confusion which has so long reigned as to its identity.

C. calamenthifolia, Lam. A perennial, but short lived, species from Crete and other of the Greek Islands which produces rosettes of small, ash-coloured leaves, sub-spathulate, crenulate, and diminishing into short petioles. Numerous slightly branched, decumbent stems are emitted from between the rosette leaves; they grow to a length of six or eight inches and bear entire, sessile, obovate to lanceolate leaves and solitary, shortly pedicelled, erect flowers terminally and in the upper leaf axils, forming a loose raceme. The whole plant is softly downy and greyish.

The calyx has erect lanceolate acute segments with revolute margins and bears short, rather rounded appendages. The cylindrical corolla is nearly four times as long as the calyx segments and has well displayed ovate-obtuse lobes. The style is equal to the tube of the corolla in length and terminates in three short filiform stigmata.

Its nearest affinities will be found in *C. mollis*, L. from which it differs in its more dentate basal leaves and three (not five) stigmata, and *C. heterophylla*, which has entire, smooth basal leaves and is much more reliably perennial.

In view of the brittle nature of the flowering stems it is much more suited for alpine house culture than for the open rock garden, but given such treatment it makes a most ornamental plant.

In var. *olivieri* the stem leaves are orbicular or orbicular-ovate and the flowers on shorter stalks.

C. calavrytana. Another Grecian species (if entitled to specific rank) which, on general appearance, would go into the *rupestris* group. It has the long calyx segments and short appendages which characterise *C. celsii* but has thinner and more-branched stems than any member of the group. It is, however, definitely excluded by the fact that the style divides into three stigmata only, and I am quite unable to find sufficient evidence to justify the idea advanced by one Swiss botanist that members of this group may have three, four, or five stigmata indiscriminately.

C. calcarata. A perennial species from the woody regions of the Southern Caucasus, this species has a running root which forms rosettes of smooth or slightly hairy leaves, ovate or oblong-cordate, on long petioles and doubly crenate-dentate, the teeth being mucronate. Thin leafy ascendant flower stems are produced, bearing leaves gradually diminishing in size and becoming sessile. The stems terminate in a few-flowered raceme of medium sized bell-shaped flowers generally singly on longish footstalks. The calyx segments, which are quite smooth, are triangular lanceolate and one third to one half the length of the corolla, while there are awl-shaped appendages, bent down into a hook at the ends, longer than the calyx tube. The style is as long as, or even longer than, the corolla and trifid, while the ripe capsule is pendent.

C. calcicola. A species from dry limestone cliffs in Tibet and Yunnan, at 10,000 to 11,000 feet, which is not now in cultivation in this country. It received an Award of Merit in 1925, but Kingdon-Ward points out that it grows 'in association with Primulas of the *Amethystina* and *Rotundifolia* sections and other plants which have not proved amenable to cultivation under English conditions'. It is a perennial which forms mats of small petiolate reniform or kidney-shaped leaves, cordate, obscurely undulate, crenate and rounded at the apex, olive green in colour with paler veinings and covered with a soft white down. From among these mats rise a number of flexible erect stems two to four inches high which are unbranched and covered with long white spreading hairs, bear a few leaves similar to the basal ones though becoming lanceolate in the upper part, and terminate in few-flowered clusters of large nodding flowers, deep violet in colour and about the size and shape of *C. rotundifolia*. The corolla is much longer than the calyx and divided to a third of its length into ovate lobes; the linear-lanceolate calyx segments are not reflexed; the ripe capsules are carried erect.

C. camptoclada. An annual species from fissures of rocks in the Anti-Lebanon where it lies out in the sun and the flexible roughish, repeatedly divided stems shape themselves over the stone and often reach nearly a foot in length. The lower leaves, drawn out into short petioles, are ovate or oblong, while the upper ones are smaller and acute. The narrowly tubular-campanulate flowers have well spread lobes and are borne throughout the upper parts of the stems on more or less long pedicels and are twice as long as the calyx segments; the latter are awl-shaped and pointed and the rather rough calyx also bears ovate-obtuse appendages. The capsule is pendent and dehiscence is basal.

Growing eight to ten inches high the species is closely allied to *C. strigosa*, but its leaves are shorter and broader and the flowers less tubular; it would appear to be almost worth growing if obtainable.

C. cana, Wall. An Indian species from the temperate Himalaya at 6,000 to 8,000 feet which, from a running rootstock, forms dense tufts in clefts of the rocks. The leafy pubescent stems are decumbent, six to nine inches long; bear numerous sessile sub-lanceolate, acute and denticulate leaves, pilose above and ash-coloured below; and terminate in a single shortly stalked and rather large pendent flower. Both calyx and corolla are more or less hairy, the segments of the former being acute, serrate and about half the length of the corolla; the latter is broad funnel-shaped with narrow, well-reflexed lobes and hairy on the outside. The style is rather shorter than the corolla, and trifid, while the short obconical capsule dehisces at the base.

How far this can be regarded as a distinct species is discussed on p. 221, and it is uncertain which of the forms is still in cultivation in this country, though a plant under the name of *C. cashmiriana* (see p. 57) was not uncommon a few years ago. In any case the species is short-lived, though of a perennial character, and must be raised from seed if and when obtainable. Hooker says that *C. cana*, Hook f. & T., is a 'Kashmir and West Tibet plant with fine large blue flowers which Wallich probably never saw'. Can this be Kingdon-Ward's *C. calcicola*?

C. candida. A perennial species whose home is in Turkistan and Western Persia which makes a thick root with a tuft of obovate or spathulate, sub-entire leaves about one and a half inches long with petioles about the same length, from among which rise numerous erect, unbranched stems up to six inches high, leafy in the upper part, the leaves being ovate, crenate and shortly petiolate. The flowers are borne singly, terminally and in the axils of the upper leaves. The calyx is softly hairy and, like the leaves, greyish with erect and entire segments and small appendages. The corolla is funnel-shaped, up to three-quarters of an inch long, and divided for half its length into acuminate lobes. The trifid style is shorter than the corolla. It is similar to *C. calamenthifolia* and its variety *olivieri*, differing from the former by its *less* dentate leaves and its petiolate basal ones, and from the latter by its larger and *more* dentate leaves, laxer stems and generally whiter appearance.

C. cantabrica. A species from sandy and gravelly wastes, with a turnip-shaped root producing numerous thin stolons which terminate in tufts of small orbicular or broadly oval leaves and thin erect flexible stems sometimes reaching six inches in height each bearing a single erect flower. The leaves on the stems are ovate or lanceolate with entire revolute margins and crowded towards the base. The calyx segments are broadly triangular, pointed and erect and about half the corolla in length; the latter is narrowly funnel-shaped, with broadly triangular spreading lobes about a quarter of its length. In general outline it resembles *C. cochleariifolia*.

C. carniolica. Though regarded as a form of *C. thyrsoides*, this is a most distinct plant, the inflorescence being lengthened into a tapering spike, the flowering portion being up to eighteen inches in length and the flowers less closely packed.

C. carpatica. Coming, as its name implies, from the Carpathians, this is among the best known of the dwarf species of the genus and was introduced as long ago as 1774. It has been taken in hand by some of our florists and, by selection from batches of seedlings, a number of improved forms have been obtained, some of which have been named, and several of these named forms have been given the Award or Merit.

The type forms a large clump of smooth, rotund or ovate, cordate leaves, irregularly dentate and on long petioles. From the clump spring erect wiry stems up to twelve or eighteen inches high, slightly branched, and bearing, on long leafless peduncles, large saucer-shaped flowers in white or varying shades of violet, blue or purple. The calyx tube is obconical and the acute, sub-dentate segments are wide at the base, nearly half the length of the corolla and reflexed to a position at right angles to the flower stems. The tripartite style is very prominent and much divided.

It is one of the easiest to grow, is soundly perennial, has a longer flowering season than many others of the genus and has no fads as to soil or situation apart from a desire for the fullest amount of sunshine. It is easily raised from seed, which, however, cannot be relied on to come true to any particular colour, but division in spring presents no difficulty and enables special forms to be increased.

Two plants frequently offered as distinct can only be regarded as forms of this species. The first is the so-called *C. turbinata*, which should be rather dwarfer than the type, with slightly hairy foliage and unbranched, *one-flowered*, stems. The other masquerades as *C. pelviformis* (though there is a very distinct species which rightly bears this name) and seems to be characterised only by a rather flatter flower than the type.

Its near relations are dealt with more fully on p. 212.

C. cashmiriana. Of comparatively recent introduction, it has yet to be proved that this species is reliably hardy in the average English winter, though, as it is reported to occur up to an altitude of 12,000 ft. in its name country, there is room for hope on this point, particularly from seed collected at the highest elevations, but in any case it is certainly short-lived. It certainly survived the winter of 1943/1944 at Edinburgh, outdoors and with no protection, and started into growth, breaking freely from the base, but was killed by later frosts. It forms a woody rootstock which penetrates deeply into rocky crevices and from this are emitted a number of stiff zigzaggy but often trailing growths bearing a few sessile light green, oblong, slightly dentate leaves about an inch long, covered with grey hairs. These stems are freely branched and carry numerous fairly large bells generally of a pale-blue, which are inclined to droop. The calyx lobes are broad and incurving, as with so many of the Himalayan species, and form a kind of saucer in which the flower sits. They are softly hairy and only about a quarter the length of the corolla. The trifid style is slightly longer than the corolla and the pendent capsule dehisces at the base.

Seed is produced with fair freedom and germinates without difficulty.

An illustration of the plant in its natural surroundings appeared in the *Gardeners' Chronicle* for 7th March 1936.

A plant under this name received the Award of Preliminary Commendation from the Royal Horticultural Society in 1939 and an Award of Merit in 1947.

For the relationships between this and other Himalayan species see p. 221.

C. celsii. See p. 218.

C. cenisia. What a pity this species is so difficult to please, for few can give such a thrill when seen growing in wide mats in nature. Absolutely calcifuge, it selects shaly screes of the highest Alps where the rock is of a slaty or flaky character, never descending below about 8,000 feet, and its thread-like runners travel long distances from the central taproot between the flat stones, pushing up the unmistakable rosettes through every crack. Its favourite situation is among the detritus at the edge of glacier torrents and always in full sun.

The rosettes are composed of small, sessile, rounded leaves, smooth and bright green. Short one to two inch flower stalks bear a few small ovate, entire and sessile leaves and terminate in single erect wide-open starry or short funnel-shaped flowers of a remarkable slaty-blue colour. The calyx is noticeably hairy and the erect, linear-lanceolate segments are more than half as long as the corolla: the species belongs to the ex-appendiculate section of the genus. The style, which equals the corolla in length, terminates in three blunt stigmata. A noticeable character is the colour of the pollen which is reddish violet and contrasts boldly with the corolla colour. A white flowered form has been reported but I have never seen it, though it obtained an Award of Merit in 1914.

The root structure makes it almost impossible to collect or move except in the very young stage, and seed, if and when procurable, forms the best means of securing a stock. The best hope of success in cultivation rests in planting quite young seedlings in a non-limy, very loose scree, keeping them nearly dry in winter and providing a constant supply of underground water throughout the growing season. For pot cultivation, success has been achieved by placing about an inch of peat at the bottom of a fairly deep pot and, after seeing that the end of the main root reaches this, filling the pot with coarse chips unmixed with soil or sand. It is occasionally possible to treat non-flowering rosettes as cuttings in the way advised for *C. allioni* (see p. 22), though the present species is even less amenable to such treatment.

C. cephallenica. See p. 217.

C. cervicaria. A biennial species which is widespread throughout Southern and Temperate Europe. From a tuft of large rough lingulate or lanceolate leaves, sometimes as much as six inches long with petioles which may be as long as the blade, rise simple, erect, hairy and angular stems to a height of one or two feet furnished with linear, acuminate amplexicaul leaves diminishing in size towards the top. The flowers are borne in a terminal spherical head, while smaller heads of flowers are sometimes produced, sessile, in the axils of the upper leaves. Each head of flowers is surrounded by a number of ovate acute bracts slightly shorter than the flowers themselves. The calyx is smooth apart from a few bristles on the

CAMPANULA CENISIA

CAMPANULA
CHOZIATOWSKYI

CAMPANULA COLLINA

CAMPANULA COCHLEARIIFOLIA

CAMPANULA CRENULATA

ribs and a ciliate margin, while the campanulate corolla, though little more than half an inch long, is half as long again as the calyx segments and has short ovate acute reflexed lobes. It is smooth inside but hairy externally. The style is as long as the corolla or rather longer and is trifid. It is a much less attractive species than *C. glomerata* which in general appearance it resembles, having coarser, rougher leaves and stems but substantially smaller flowers. Specific differences are the shorter, more bell-shaped corolla and the rather longer style; its merit that it is only biennial. Propagation is, of course, only possible from seed.

C. choziatowskyi. Growing among rocks in the mountainous parts of Russian Armenia this species is smooth throughout or, at least, only very slightly rough. A thick creeping rootstock forms a tuft of small leaves and emits a number of ascendant flexible stems. The leaves are thickish, the basal ones being ovate-cordate, deeply and sharply dentate on long petioles; the stem leaves sub-cordate or rotund, sharply dentate with shorter petioles, those near the apex ovate-lanceolate and sub-sessile. The medium-sized flowers are on thin stalks with very short bracts.

The calyx is wider than the corolla; the calyx segments are triangular-acute and widely spreading; the appendages are very short and the corolla, tubular-funnel shaped and contracted at the base, is smooth externally but densely bearded within. The trifid style is shorter than the corolla tube.

With its small neat leaves and numerous erect flowers the species is distinctly attractive. It comes freely from seed and can be divided without much difficulty, but appears to be short-lived though soundly perennial. It was fairly widely grown up to 1939 but is difficult, if not impossible, to procure at the present time. Its reintroduction is much to be desired.

C. chrysosplenifolia. A Chinese species from mountain regions of Yunnan which has a thick carroty root and smooth, erect, filiform stems, simple or branched, the branches being one-flowered. The rosette and basal leaves are small, ovate or orbicular with seven to nine small teeth and covered with white hairs; the stems carry a few linear subulate leaves. The calyx has lanceolate-subulate erect segments, longer than the bud; the corolla, about half an inch long, rather longer than the calyx, is divided to a third of its length into triangular acute lobes. The ovate capsule is pendent and dehisces near the middle.

C. cinerea. A Balkan species, probably biennial, with grey-hairy leaves and stems. The leaves are crenate, the lower ones being obovate with short slender petioles, the upper ones ovate-acute, rounded at the base and sessile. A number of unbranched, flexible, decumbent stems are produced carrying stalked flowers singly in the leaf axils. Calyx segments

D

are ovate, acute and softly hairy, and there are small linear appendages. The campanulate corolla is usually pale blue in colour and more than twice as long as the calyx segments. It is closely allied to *C. lanata* from which it differs mainly in the shape of the calyx segments and appendages and in the upper leaves being not cordate.

C. cissophylla. A small grey and velvety plant from cracks in calcareous rocks of Kurdistan. It forms a thick woody root with a tuft of small petiolate leaves, reniform-cordate in shape and margined with five to seven sharp teeth. In the case of the lower leaves the petiole is actually longer than the leaf itself but this condition is reversed in the case of the stem leaves. The stems themselves are erect but thin and flexible and carry up to five flowers on long footstalks. The flowers are very small, narrowly funnel-shaped, while the narrow spreading calyx segments are only a third as long as the corolla. The calyx is without appendages and the style is trifid. I cannot trace that it has ever been in cultivation and it seems to be too insignificant to be worth bothering about.

C. clisophylla. A small plant which appears to be near to *C. portenschlagiana*. The flower stems bear rotund, sub-cordate and regularly serrate leaves on petioles about as long as the leaves themselves and terminate in a small cluster of campanulate flowers held erect on short footstalks. The calyx is slightly hairy but the segments are smooth, lanceolate and erect and about half as long as the corolla; the latter is lobed to about a third its length with well spread rounded lobes. The trifid style is much exserted.

C. cochleariifolia, Lam. (formerly *C. bellardii*, All.; *C. pumila*, Curt.; *C. pusilla*, Haenke). Authority has spoken and this is the name by which henceforth we must know the daintiest, easiest and one of the most widely distributed of the dwarf Campanulas. No longer may we call our 'Fairies' Thimbles' *C. pusilla*, or *C. pumila*, or *C. bellardii*, for Lamarck got his name in a year or two earlier than anyone else and the rules of botanical nomenclature are rigid. One other name which is sometimes attached to this species—*C. caespitosa*—must also be mentioned, for that name is appropriate to a species distinct in every way (see p. 53).

The species occurs generally throughout the mountain regions of temperate Europe, though it is not recorded from Greece or Great Britain. The thin fibrous rootstock runs freely in cracks in the rocks, forming a mat of small rosettes of little shining oval (almost circular) cordate leaves with a small number of prominent teeth (usually three) on each side and fairly long petioles, and pushes up numerous thin wiry erect stems, some three or four inches high, bearing two to six flowers on long pedicels. The sub-erect flowers are of a full rounded bell shape with short, rounded and scarcely reflexed lobes, the bell being normally as wide as it is long. They range in colour from white through all shades of lilac, lavender and blue, but the species varies so considerably in size and colour of flower that many forms have been selected and given varietal names, the best known being var. Miranda and var. Miss Willmott. The last named obtained an Award of Merit in 1915, while var. Miranda received a similar award in 1920, to which was added the Award of Garden Merit in 1925.

The calyx is quite smooth and the linear-lanceolate segments, less than half the length of the corolla, are not reflexed. There seems, however, to be some variation in this character and also in the form of the bell, for there are varieties with longer reflexed calyx segments and a corolla at least half as long again as wide and this may one day lead to botanists splitting up the species and, perhaps, restoring one or more of the other names.

Propagation is easy by simple division and the only objection which the plant seems to have is to a situation which is both hot and dry.

C. colettae appears to be merely a form of *C. radicosa* with basal leaves somewhat more pointed and crenulate rather than minutely toothed.

C. collina. An Armenian species which, from a running rootstock, produces masses of long pointed-ovate, cordate leaves on fairly long petioles. These leaves are regularly serrate and softly downy, while among them rise the erect flower stems to a height of nine to fifteen inches bearing an unilateral raceme of flowers, well spaced on the stem, and a few leaves similar to the basal ones but becoming smaller and sessile as they near the top.

The flowers are large, fully campanulate and semi-pendent and of a rich purple-blue colour; the lobes are nearly half the length, broad, acuminate, hairy on the margins and well reflexed. The calyx is only slightly hairy and the segments, which are not reflexed, are fairly broad but pointed suddenly and barely one third as long as the corolla. The species is without appendages (though Boissier says that there *may* be *very* short reflexed ones). The style is rather shorter than the corolla and the stigma is tripartite.

As Farrer says 'it is one of the most gorgeous Campanulas we have'. It is easy to propagate by division or seed, and easy to grow in any decent soil, though with me it does not flower freely until well established. In nature it is said to choose granitic soils but in cultivation does not seem to be particular, though it does not like drought.

Vatke reports a *major* form, illustrated in *Bot. Mag.* at t. 927.

C. colorata. An annual species from woods and hedges in shady places throughout the Himalayan foothills, up to 10,000 feet. It has an erect branched and hairy stem with lanceolate, crenate-dentate, sessile leaves and axillary and terminal flowers on short stalks. The hairy calyx, like so many of the Indian species, is broader than the corolla and has broad, acute, slightly dentate and ciliate segments about half the corolla length. The latter is small (a quarter to half an inch long) and cylindrical with pointed triangular lobes well reflexed, making a starry flower with a prominent exserted trifid style. While the flowers are generally more or less erect, the capsule is invariably pendent.

It was first flowered in this country at Kew in 1850 but though seed is sometimes offered, it is scarcely worth the space and trouble required.

C. compacta, Boiss. A small, softly hairy, perennial which forms rosettes of narrowly obovate or linear-spathulate leaves, obtuse or acute and sub-denticulate. From the rosettes grow numerous simple leafy one-flowered stems one to three inches high, the stem leaves being narrowly linear and acute. The calyx tube is very short with lanceolate segments twice its length, while the smooth corolla, twice the length of the calyx segments, is divided almost to its base into narrowly oblong spreading lobes. The exserted style divides into three stigmata. The capsule is borne erect and dehisces just below the apex. The deeply divided corolla suggests that the plant should more properly be included in the genus Asyneuma.

C. conferta. A species from Cappadocia which appears to be very similar to *C. spicata* and has even been suggested to be merely a dwarf form thereof. On the other hand, however, it is said to be perennial. It forms a short thick root and rosettes of spathulate shortly petioled leaves from which rise simple erect angular and hairy stems nine or ten inches high. These stems bear a number of ovate-acute leaves, sub-sessile to sub-amplexicaul, and, in the axils, clusters of three to five small almost stalkless flowers interspersed with ovate dentate bracts shorter than the flowers. The latter are funnel-shaped, somewhat hairy externally, lobed to a third their length and with an exserted trifid style. The calyx has ovate, rough and spreading segments; is without appendages and dehisces at the base, the capsule being carried erect. Both rough and glabrous forms have been reported.

C. constantinii. A biennial from mountain rocks in Euboea which forms a rosette of softly hairy leaves on long winged petioles, the limb being elliptic-oblong and irregularly crenate. These leaves disappear at flowering time when many decumbent or erect branched stems nine to twelve inches long are produced. These stems have a few leaves similar to the basal ones, though becoming smaller and sub-sessile towards the ends and the branches carry the flowers in one-sided short stalked racemes. The flowers, about half an inch long, are tubular, inflated at the base and noticeably longer than the calyx which has triangular acuminate ciliate segments and ovate appendages longer than the calyx tube. The exserted style divides into three stigmata which gives a clear distinction from the *C. rupestris* group with which, superficially, the species might be grouped, though the exserted style brings it near *C. reiseri*.

C. corymbosa is now generally regarded as synonymous with *C. pelviformis*, differing in producing only a single stem which is stiffer and more erect.

C. crenulata. A species from Yunnan which would appear to be attractive. It is a smooth dwarf plant with rosettes of broadly ovate, fleshy leaves slightly crenate and on long footstalks. The thin graceful ascendant stems carry a few small linear leaves and terminate in a single flower. The calyx segments are narrowly awl-shaped, erect, and considerably longer than the bud, while the deep-blue corolla, half to three-quarters of an inch long, is broadly campanulate with short triangular acute lobes. With a capsule dehiscing near the top it is allied to *C. uniflora*, but has flowers which are considerably larger than those of that species.

A few plants, from seed collected by Forrest, reached flowering size at Edinburgh in 1911. Seeds from a further collecting flowered in 1926 and obtained the Award of Merit in that year, but efforts to establish the species in cultivation have so far been unsuccessful and reintroduction is awaited.

C. crispa. A species from Armenia, said to be perennial but which, from its near relationship to *C. rupestris*, is more likely to prove monocarpic. In fact, Fomin (in *Flora caucasica critica*) says definitely 'biennial'. The leaves are glossy smooth, paler on the undersides, cordate and irregularly crenate-dentate or with a laciniate, crisped edge, up to two or three inches in length, the basal ones with long winged petioles, the wings themselves being few, short, alternate and irregular. The stem leaves are smaller, becoming sub-sessile towards the ends of the branches and broadly ovate-acute. The erect, generally unbranched flower stems are six to twelve inches high and bear the flowers in a pyramidal raceme in the upper half, the flowers themselves being borne singly in the leaf axils on short stalks. The calyx is rough with short awl-shaped segments with revolute margins and small toothlike appendages much shorter than the calyx tube. The widely open campanulate corolla is as much as an inch across and deeply cut into ovate-acute lobes with mucronate tips; it is smooth internally but often more or less hairy on the outside. The style is short, not longer than the corolla, and divides, for the greater part of its length, into five revolute stigmata. Like all this section it is strictly saxatile and seed, if obtainable, would form the only method of propagation. Being smooth leaved it would probably prove easier in cultivation than many of its near allies.

C. cuatrecasasii. A Spanish species which, from a woody root, produces a number of smooth prostrate stems which are simple or sometimes slightly branched and terminate in clusters of anything up to five long-stalked flowers. The lower leaves are ovate-cordate and on long petioles while the upper ones are linear-lanceolate, acute, and merely narrowed towards the base. The calyx is without appendages and has short, broadly lanceolate acute segments about half as long as the tube of the corolla; the latter, narrowly campanulate and usually of a good purple colour, is divided for only about a fifth of its length into obtuse lobes. It is nearly allied to *C. malacitana,* though ex-appendiculate, and, in nature, grows in crevices of shady calcareous rocks.

C. cylindrica is now regarded as merely a poor form of *C. crenulata*; it is *not,* as thought at one time, a species of Wahlenbergia.

C. cymbalaria. A small species from fissures of rocks in alpine and sub-alpine Lebanon, which is doubtfully perennial. From a tuft of ovate, coarsely and sharply toothed leaves on long petioles rise a number of thin branched decumbent stems six to twelve inches long furnished in the lower part with leaves similar to those of the basal tuft, though with shorter petioles, and, in the upper part, with minute sessile leaves little more than bracts and short branches bearing one to three flowers on thin stalks. The flowers are bell-shaped with widely spread lobes about a third their length, while the awl-shaped spreading calyx segments are about half as long as the corolla. It is without appendages and has a trifid style. Although somewhat loose and perhaps even weedy in growth, the large number of bright flowers make quite an attractive plant and even if it does die out after flowering, a few self-sown seedlings can generally be found, or, of course, seed may be saved and sown.

C. daghestanica. A perennial from rocky regions of its name country with a thick woody root from which spring a number of simple or branched ascendant hairy stems. The basal leaves are spathulate and petiolate, the stem leaves oblong and petiolate near the base of the stems, smaller and sessile above; all are softly hairy and have bluntly crenate and undulate edges. Flowers are of medium size and stalked, the corolla being tubular and generally smooth, while the smooth triangular-lanceolate calyx segments are a quarter to one third the corolla length. The calyx is furnished with appendages which are obovate, edged with a row of stiff hairs and shorter than the calyx segments. The style, which is shorter than the corolla, divides into three stigmata.

C. damascena. An uncommon perennial species from Syria, which makes a woody root and a rosette from which a few thin, but rigid, ascendant stems, two or three inches high, are produced. The basal leaves are ovate or obovate, acute, entire or slightly subdentate, narrowing to the base or sub-petiolate. The stems bear a few similar but smaller leaves and a few small pedicelled flowers, often only one, on more or less long footstalks.

The calyx is ovoid, with erect, pointed awl-shaped segments and no appendages, while the corolla, twice the length of the calyx, is cylindrical and has erect, acute lobes. The style is about the same length as the corolla tube and divides into three short stigmata, while the three-celled capsule is carried erect and dehisces at the base.

The whole plant, including calyx and corolla, is softly hairy.

It is closely allied to *C. argentea*, differing mainly in the shape and size of the calyx and, like that species, might be worth growing if obtainable.

Seed appears to be the only means of increase.

C. davidovii seems to be nothing more than a form of the Bulgarian *C. transsilvanica* with smaller flower heads and, like that species, difficult to distinguish from *C. cervicaria*.

C. davurica. A name with no description to match and, accordingly, not valid.

C. debarensis. See p. 217.

C. delavayi. A Chinese species from mountain regions of Yunnan which appears to be the Far Eastern equivalent of *C. rotundifolia* or of *C. linifolia*, though there is no record of the carriage of the buds. It forms basal rosettes of cordate reniform or broadly ovate leaves with a few irregular dentations, on long petioles. The ascendant flower stems are thin, softly hairy near the base but otherwise smooth; they carry a few lanceolate or linear leaves and terminate in a loose raceme of open campanulate flowers having ovate acute lobes about half the length of the corolla. The erect linear-lanceolate calyx segments are half the length of the fully developed corolla. The ovate capsule is pendent and dehisces at the base.

C. delicatula. This annual species from the region of Caria in Asia Minor is a spreading plant under six inches in height and throughout rough and greyish. The thin stems are freely branched from the base and the ovate-obtuse leaves (acute in the upper parts) are entire or obscurely toothed and diminish to short petioles. Flowers are small and tubular and carried on short pedicels in the leaf axils and terminally. The roughish calyx segments are lanceolate-acute, well spread and almost as long as the corolla; there are no appendages and dehiscence is basal. The style is trifid and the species scarcely differs from *C. erinus*. It is at the best a weedy little plant.

C. dichotoma. A Grecian species of annual duration also reported from Algeria and the whole Mediterranean basin with erect dichotomously branched hairy stems, three to six inches high, and oblong entire sessile leaves. The shortly pedicelled drooping flowers are borne singly in the leaf axils and terminally. The corolla is tubular campanulate and smooth, the short lobes not being reflexed and the calyx segments, about two thirds the length of the corolla, are lanceolate, acuminate and produced backwards into small acute appendages. The style is shorter than the corolla and trifid, while dehiscence is basal.

C. diekii. A Spanish species which forms a tuft of numerous oval dentate, rough, undulate leaves, shortly petioled at the base of the plant, but sessile or sub-amplexicaul on the stems. These stems terminate in a small cluster of rotate flowers lobed almost to the middle. A character of the species is that the calyx is clothed with translucent hairs; it is ex-appendiculate and the capsule dehisces at the top. As an annual it does not seem to be of much interest.

C. dimorphantha. An annual species from Egypt where it grows on walls and dry banks. Spreading softly hairy stems, simple or slightly branched, do not exceed six inches in height. The leaves are membranaceous and dentate and the ovate, sub-petiolate lower ones often exceed an inch in length; the upper ones are smaller and linear-lanceolate, while the small flowers are borne solitarily on long erect pedicels in the upper leaf axils. The corolla is dull blue divided for half its length into ovate acute lobes, scarcely reflexed, while the hairy lanceolate calyx segments are erect and shorter than the calyx tube itself. There are no appendages, the style is trifid and the capsule dehisces at the base, but the species may be distinguished from many somewhat similar species by carrying its ripe capsule erect.

C. divaricata. A North American species of considerable charm, in fact one of the few from that part of the world that is worth bothering about. At home it grows on rocky banks in sun or half shade and reaches a height of eighteen inches or two feet.

The plant forms a cluster of rosettes of dark green oblong or linear-lanceolate leaves, acuminate at both ends, from which spring erect smooth

CAMPANULA CYMBALARIA

CAMPANULA DIVARICATA

CAMPANULA ELATINES

CAMPANULA ELATINOIDES

CAMPANULA EXCISA

73

CAMPANULA FILICAULIS

CAMPANULA
FORMANEKIANA

almost leafless stems which branch repeatedly forming a loose compound panicle of drooping, bell-shaped flowers, individually small but effective by reason of their number. The calyx is smooth and the short filiform segments are spreading but not reflexed. The species is ex-appendiculate and has a trifid stigma. A touch of almost fairylike grace is given by the long style which appears to be about twice the length of the light corolla owing to the degree of reflexing of the corolla lobes and the whole effect has been compared, not inaptly, with *Thalictrum dipterocarpum*. Seed is freely produced and forms a ready means of increase.

The plant described as *C. flexuosa*, Michx. is merely an alpine, dwarfed form of this species.

C. dolomitica. From stony sub-alpine meadows of the central Caucasus this species produces a tuft of reniform or orbicular-cordate leaves, slightly crenate, more or less hairy, and on long petioles. From among them rise slender ascendant stems to a height of one to two feet bearing similar leaves and a few large flowers on long stalks terminally and in the upper leaf axils. The calyx has reflexed ovate segments more or less hooked at the ends and arrow-shaped appendages longer than the tube. The broadly funnel-shaped corolla, one and a half to two inches long, is four or five times as long as the calyx segments, lobed to a third its length and bearded at the edges. The trifid style is shorter than the corolla.

It has been related to *C. alliariifolia* but while this may be true in a strictly botanical sense, in general appearance it is quite distinct and a most attractive plant which would be well worth introduction.

C. drabaefolia. This species, which is a native of Greece and the Isle of Samos, may be of use for filling gaps on the rock garden where early bulbs have died down, when it will produce a good patch of colour. It is, in fact, one of the most showy of the dwarf annual species and can be relied upon to reproduce itself year after year by self-sown seedlings. It makes a number of dichotomously branched, slightly hairy stems, erect or ascendant, bearing elliptic-oblong leaves which are coarsely dentate and sessile, the upper ones being smaller and gradually becoming linear. The erect, stalked flowers have a softly hairy calyx and no appendages, and a somewhat inflated campanulate corolla which is violet-blue with a white throat. The style is comparatively short and trifid.

Similar to *C. erinus*, it is distinguished from that species by its larger flowers which are also stalked instead of being sessile. Farrer, wrongly, makes it synonymous with *C. ramosissima*, from which it differs in many respects, mainly in the fact that its capsule dehisces at the base whereas in *C. ramosissima* the dehiscence occurs near the top of the capsule.

C. dulcis. Growing in vertical cracks among the rocks of Mount Sinai, this species is a small tufted plant some six inches high, all woolly grey and perennial. The basal leaves are ovate, obtuse, sinuate and sessile and from among them grow short brittle branching stems with a few sub-amplexicaul leaves and, in the upper axils and terminally, small, solitary flowers on thin footstalks. The calyx has lanceolate spreading segments nearly as long as the corolla and small ovate-acute appendages. The corolla itself is tubular and whitish and under half an inch long, while the style is trifid. I am unable to trace that it has ever been in cultivation, but it is an insignificant plant at best and seems to be closely allied to the equally uninteresting *C. edulis* which is a native of the same part of the world.

C. edulis. A somewhat doubtful Arabian species which has thin, erect stems, which are rough and ribbed and about six inches high. They bear sessile ovate-lanceolate leaves, not more than half an inch long, rough and sub-crenulate, and terminate in a single flower. The calyx has lanceolate segments and ovate-acute reflexed appendages the same length as the segments. The small tubular corolla is no longer than the calyx segments. The type is pale blue with violet veins but a white form has been recorded; the root is said to be edible, whence the specific name. It is regarded as closely allied to the annual *C. strigosa*, but is itself perennial.

C. elata is a more or less hairy form of *C. pyramidalis* in which the flowers are borne singly, and does not seem to deserve specific rank.

C. elatines. Native of the hot cliffs of the Cottian Alps, this species forms a thick fat rootstock surmounted by numerous basal rosettes of small ivy-shaped leaves, cordate at the base, with sharply scalloped and crimped edges and long petioles. The whole plant varies considerably in the degree of hairiness, being either quite grey with down or perfectly smooth. In either case the plant sends out numbers of long brittle flower stems branched at their ends. These hug the face of the rock, never rising more than about a couple of inches and are covered with a profusion of flat star-shaped flowers of a deep violet blue, the long lobes being sharply pointed. The flowers are borne either singly or in small panicles and are carried erect. The calyx tube is spherical and the narrow lanceolate reflexed segments are not more than half as long as the corolla. It is characteristic that one of the segments is often longer than the other four. There are no appendages. As in almost all species with a rotate corolla form the style is noticeably exserted and is trifid.

It is a true saxatile and requires a warm well drained crevice in light loam; in nature it avoids lime. While strictly perennial and hardy, it often fails to survive the winter wet, particularly if a hairy form is grown, unless the position is exceptionally well drained, as, for example, in the face of a retaining wall, or it is given the protection of a sheet of glass. Seed provides the easiest means of increase.

The true species is distinctly rare in cultivation being commonly confused with *C. elatinoides*, a coarser, stronger growing plant. It is closely allied to *C. garganica* which, however, is also stronger growing and is a more leafy plant with flowers less intense in colour.

It was given an Award of Merit in 1933.

C. elatinoides. A perennial saxatile species from a small district in the Maritime Alps which is closely allied to *C. garganica*. It makes tufts of greyish tomentose leaves, broadly ovate-cordate and sharply dentate on fairly long petioles. Hugging the rocks are a number of decumbent leafy stems which produce in the leaf axils throughout almost the whole of their length, many-flowered clusters of stalked flowers building up a long compound raceme. The flowers themselves are deeply lobed and rotate, about half as long again as the awl-shaped calyx segments, both calyx and segments being noticeably hairy. As usual with this form of corolla the trifid style is much exserted.

It is much less showy than others of the group, the flowers being generally smaller (though it makes up in numbers much of what it loses in size) and the habit of growth looser, and for general use it cannot challenge comparison with a good form of *C. garganica* itself, though in large gardens it forms a good successor to that species, being considerably later in its flowering period.

It can be fairly easily divided and cuttings of young growth in spring root easily, particularly if given the help of a closed cold frame. It also comes readily from seed and, as a young plant, makes an attractive alpine house specimen.

C. elegans, R. & S. This name refers to an alleged species of which very little is known. Reported in 1819 as a Siberian plant it was described as perennial with linear-lanceolate, entire leaves, the lower ones broader and sub-petiolate and with weak simple pubescent stems a foot or more high terminating in a short spike. It has not, apparently, been found since and later authorities who mention it at all refer to it as a 'doubtful' or 'uncertain' species.

C. embergeri. A perennial from sub-alpine rocks of the Great Atlas which spreads into a mat of rosettes, the leaves of the rosettes being spathulate reduced gradually to a petiole. Thin flexible stems are produced up to about a foot long, more or less prostrate and sometimes branched in the upper half. They carry leaves similar to those of the rosettes but becoming smaller and sub-sessile and a few, generally solitary, flowers on long hairy stalks. The calyx is hairy, particularly on the margins, and has erect triangular-lanceolate, obtuse segments and narrow acute appendages rather shorter than the calyx tube. The broadly cylindrical corolla is not more than a quarter of an inch long and is lobed to a third of its length, while the style is trifid.

It is related to *C. filicaulis* but can be distinguished by its smaller flowers which are less lobed than in the other species and by its shorter appendages.

C. engurensis. Another of the many perennial species from the Caucasus. Its leaves are green above, glaucous below with densely pubescent margins, sharply and unequally bidentate; the basal ones on long petioles, ovate-lanceolate or ovate, sub-cordate at the base and narrowing to an acute apex. They may be as much as three inches long and one and a half inches broad. Numerous thin stems, grey-green with small pellucid hairs, spring from the root and bear ovate leaves on short petioles or sub-sessile. They terminate in sub-corymbose, few-flowered inflorescences, the flowers being on short erect peduncles and based by lanceolate or linear-lanceolate bracts, entire or dentate. The calyx is broad with a very short hairy tube and triangular-lanceolate segments, a quarter to one third as long as the corolla; the appendages also are very short, indeed almost inconspicuous. The tubular corolla, about an inch long, is hairy outside and lobed to about one fifth of its length, while the trifid style is shorter than the corolla. Its relationship appears to be with *C. suanetica*, *C. kemulariae* and *C. betulaefolia* and, if obtained (it does not appear to have been in cultivation in this country) it should lend itself to propagation by division.

C. eo-cervicaria. Hailing from Bosnia, this species has a number of stiff erect stems nearly two feet high terminating in clusters of sessile flowers in a sub-globose head. The stems bear sessile amplexicaul leaves, the lower ones ovate-oblong and acuminate, the upper ones shorter and less pointed; all are irregularly crenate-dentate and, like the stems, covered with whitish hairs. The calyx is smooth, with long acuminate segments which have revolute, ciliate edges. The corolla is nearly an inch long, funnel-shaped and divided for a third of its length into ovate-acute lobes, while the trifid style is shorter than the corolla. It is very closely allied to *C. cervicaria* but is regarded as differing by reason of its much broader leaves, its shorter style and its cylindrical, rather than angular, stems.

C. epigaea. A root with short stolons makes a close mat of leaves which are shortly petiolate to sub-sessile and gives rise to stems some nine inches high which are simple or sometimes with a few long single-flowered branches. The wide funnel-shaped corolla, fully an inch long, is deep violet and rather longer than the narrowly lanceolate calyx segments. It is a native of alpine and sub-alpine meadows of Bulgaria and Macedonia and Hayek regards it as a sub-species of *C. patula*, giving a still less distinct form the name of *C. velenovskyi*, which has basal leaves on long petioles and the flowers on shorter footstalks.

The question of its relationship to its nearest allies is referred to under *C. abietina* (p. 31).

C. erinoides, Linn. From Southern Spain, this annual species has a simple erect stem four to six inches high terminating in a loose cluster of small erect flowers. The few leaves are linear-lanceolate, smooth, crenate and under half an inch long. The calyx, which is ex-appendiculate, is smooth with long acuminate segments, reflexed from, and about the same length as, the corolla, which is funnel-shaped and slightly inflated. The style is included and divides into three filiform stigmata, while the erect capsule dehisces at the top.

C. erinus. A species of annual duration generally distributed about the shores of the Mediterranean with erect thin dichotomously branched stems, making a bushy plant about six inches high. The leaves are obovate to oblong and dentate, shortly petioled when basal but sessile in the upper parts of the plant. The flowers are very small, terminal and axillary and practically sessile, with a corolla tubular in shape and little longer than the calyx segments which are without appendages. Dehiscence is basal. The whole plant is softly hairy. The colour is usually white in the tube and very pale mauve in the lobes which are not more than a quarter the length of the corolla. A *bright* blue form is also on record, but even so it is not worth space in the garden.

C. erucifolia. From fissures of rocks in the Eastern Mediterranean. A biennial species (or monocarpic) with few-flowered woolly stems up to eight or nine inches high, with flowers on short stalks. The leaves are white with down, the lower ones being ovate-oblong, deeply lyrate-pinnatifid, the lobes being ovate-lanceolate. The upper leaves are lanceolate-lyrate, the lyrations being linear. The calyx is also downy, with triangular segments and ovate-rotund appendages, while the corolla is broadly funnel-shaped, lobed for half its length, slightly hairy on the outside and about three times as long as the calyx segments. See also p. 218.

C. esculenta, Nob. A perennial from rocky places in Abyssinia with a creeping rootstock and hairy ascendant branches about nine inches high. The leaves are obovate, oblong or sub-spathulate, more or less thick and crenate and narrowing gradually to the base. The undersides are covered with stiff hairs. The flowers are borne singly at the ends of leafless branches. The calyx segments are lanceolate, acute and ciliate; the appendages short and acute; while the corolla has oval-acute lobes one third its length. It is closely allied to *C. rigidipila* but differs in its blunt, almost spathulate leaves, and its short calyx segments and appendages. The smooth (not hairy) corolla suffices to distinguish it from *C. edulis*, another closely allied species. So far as I know it is not in cultivation in this country and its native habitat would throw some doubt on its hardiness.

C. euclasta. A Syrian species from hot sunbaked rock crevices near Palmyra, which, from a small tuft of obovate, obtuse, more or less notched and petiolate leaves throws up brittle but stoutish stems some six inches high bearing oblong sessile or sub-amplexicaul leaves. The small flowers are dirty white in colour, not more than half an inch long, nearly sessile and borne at the apex either singly or in a cluster of three or four. The whole plant is softly hairy and is reputed to be a good perennial. So far as I know it is not in cultivation in this country, but we have *C. damascena* and *C. trichopoda* which are so closely allied to it that they may all prove, on further experience, to be merely forms of one species. According to Clay (*The Present Day Rock Garden*) this is the best species (or form) of the group.

C. excisa. Strictly confined to the Monte Rosa and Simplon districts of the European Alps this species is far from common or easy in cultivation. In its native haunts it rambles about among the stones as freely as *C. rotundifolia*, pushing up through every crevice its thin wiry stems each three or four inches high with narrow smooth-edged leaves and terminating in a single pendent blue bell-shaped flower with the curious punched out hole between the lobes from which it derives its name. The narrow reflexed calyx segments are comparatively short, not more than one third the length of the corolla; the latter is lobed to about one third of its length, but the ovate-acute lobes are not particularly recurved. The style, not more than half the length of the corolla, is trifid. The capsule is obconical and, like the flower, pendent. The whole plant is, generally speaking, glabrous, but a certain hairiness of the calyx may sometimes be found.

The rocks among which it grows are invariably granitic and it is fairly safe to say that where a plant of such free growth is only found on such formations, its objection to lime in any form must be recognised and studied if success in its cultivation is to be achieved, but it is only fair to add that various authorities report it as flourishing on limestone moraines. One characteristic it certainly seems to possess—a reluctance to remain in the same place for any length of time, preferring to ramble to fresh territory every year and territory which is not exposed to too much sun. It can be propagated readily from division or raised from seed.

It obtained the Award of Merit in 1933.

C. exigua, Forman. As there is another species which bears this name the present plant ought to be renamed to avoid confusion. The present is a dwarf annual plant from the sterile sub-alps of Peristeri, which is closely allied to *C. expansa.* It forms tufts of rotund leaves shortly petiolate and entire, from among which rise ascendant stems branched near the base and furnished with amplexicaul leaves which, as is not uncommon, become smaller and narrower towards the top. The flowers are solitary, or occasionally in threes, on fairly long footstalks; the calyx segments may be smooth or rough, narrowly awl-shaped in form, prominently nerved and nearly as long as the broadly funnel-shaped corolla.

C. exigua, Rattan. From ridges of the coastal range of California at elevations of between 2,000 and 4,000 feet, this annual species makes a small much-branched plant not above six inches high with obovate, linear, or awl-shaped leaves. Flowers are produced both terminally and from the leaf axils of all the branches; they are quite small (about a quarter of an inch across) and carried erect. The urn-shaped calyx has narrowly awl-shaped segments twice as long as the tube itself and dehisces just above the middle. Two forms of style are reported, one rather short with three revolute stigmata, the other longer, conspicuously club-shaped and merely notched at the apex.

C. expansa. A very variable species from the woods of Mount Olympus in Thessaly, but also occurring through large tracts of Bulgaria, Serbia and Greece, with tall hairy and leafy stems branching into a loose spreading panicle. The soft leaves, glabrous or more or less hairy, are oblong-lanceolate, crenate, and sessile, the upper ones being sub-amplexicaul and ultimately linear. The ex-appendiculate calyx has smooth awl-shaped segments, sometimes with a few small teeth, much longer than the short capsule and well spread. The corolla is small, campanulate, lobed to one third its length and about twice as long as the calyx segments. Ex-appendiculate and with a trifid style, the capsule dehisces at the apex, showing a marked affinity with *C. patula* and, like that species, it sometimes shows a biennial habit, though usually only annual.

It much resembles *C. sparsa,* but the flowers are smaller—not above half an inch across—and the calyx segments are more spreading.

C. sphaerothrix is now regarded as merely a form of this species, smaller in all its parts and less spreading in habit.

C. fastigiata, Duf. An annual, native of Spain and reported from uncultivated fields in Transcaucasia, with dichotomously branched stems about three inches high. The stems bear obovate, sessile leaves which are smooth edged except for a few coarse teeth at the apex, ornamented with a fringe of shiny hairs and, like the rest of the plant, rather greyish in colour. The branches terminate in small erect almost sessile flowers, the corolla being only about half as long as the calyx segments which, being erect, almost enclose it. Ex-appendiculate, the erect capsule shows apical dehiscence.

C. fedtschenkiana. A species of little or no importance which has a number of thin, fragile stems about eight inches high furnished with numerous small ashy-grey rounded ovate and serrate-dentate leaves, the lower ones with thin petioles, the upper ones sessile. The stems end in a loose narrow raceme confined to the topmost third, the flowers being not more than half an inch long and nodding on short footstalks. The calyx has linear-lanceolate segments and is without appendages, while the corolla, twice as long as the calyx segments, is tubular campanulate in shape, shortly lobed and hairy on the outside. The style, which is shorter than the corolla, divides into three stigmata and the capsule, like the flowers, is pendent.

C. fenestrellata. See p. 217.

C. filicaulis. From forest clearings and rocky wastes in Algeria and Morocco, at elevations between 2,500 and 10,000 feet above sea level, this species forms a thick fleshy rootstock and a rosette of dull green oval oblong leaves narrowing at the base. In due time there are produced a few flexible angular stems which hug the surface of the ground and grow sometimes to a length of twelve to fifteen inches. They bear a few leaves similar to those of the rosette and branch at their ends, the branches carrying a few starry flowers of a rather washy blue colour with a greenish reverse, in one or three flowered panicles. The calyx segments are pointed linear, broader at the base, and hairy; the calyx bears small triangular appendages, shorter than the calyx tube itself. The corolla, which is cut to the middle into five oblong lanceolate lobes, is fully rotate. The slightly exserted style is trifid and the capsule pendent when ripe.

Clay, in *The Present Day Rock Garden*, refers it to *C. malacitana*, but it is clearly distinguished from that species by the corolla form which in true *C. malacitana* is, at most, *sub*-rotate, while the present species also has a much looser habit of growth. The typical plant in which the leaves are entire appears to be restricted to Algeria, but minor variations occur as the species passes into Morocco, some of which have even been given varietal rank and one of which is almost certainly *C. maroccana*, Ball.

CAMPANULA FRAGILIS

CAMPANULA GARGANICA

83

CAMPANULA GLOMERATA

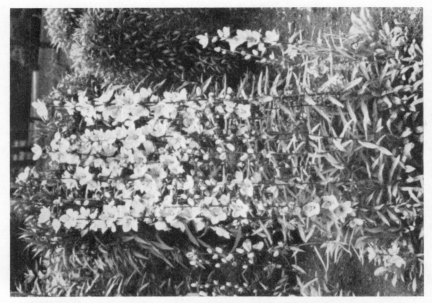

CAMPANULA GRANDIS

CAMPANULA GROSSEKII

85

CAMPANULA HAWKINSIANA

CAMPANULA HEMSCHINICA

86

which seems to differ from the type *C. filicaulis* only in having a very slightly dentate leaf.

C. reboudiana, Pomel. seems to be a form from lower elevations.

C. flaccidula. From Mount Singara, this species has thin spreading stems which may reach a length of ten to twelve inches and are thinly covered with hairs. The stems are freely branched and furnished with ovate irregularly crenate leaves on thin petioles. The small flowers, little more than a quarter of an inch long, are borne on long hairlike stalks both terminally and in the leaf axils, and are erect both before and after flowering. The smooth capsule is obconical, without appendages and with linear-lanceolate acuminate segments longer than the corolla. An annual.

C. floridana. A more or less prostrate perennial from Florida, where it occurs mainly in swamps and marshes. The leaves are oblong to linear-lanceolate, remotely serrulate, almost sessile and about half an inch long. The stems are filiform, simple or sparingly branched and about nine inches high, the few flowers terminating the stems and branches. The five-partite, somewhat rotate, corolla is usually violet with ovate-lanceolate lobes equalled by the slender, lanceolate-linear, smooth and spreading calyx segments. Seed would provide the only means of increase but, with its small flowers, the species does not appear to be particularly attractive.

C. foliosa. A species from the Central Apennines where it grows in woods between 4,500 and 5,500 feet above sea level, and from parts of Greece. The basal leaves are ovate-acute, sub-cordate and crenulate and on long, more or less winged, petioles. The smooth, or softly hairy, stems are about a foot high and erect, carry a few ovate acuminate leaves paler in colour on the undersides, with short winged petioles and terminate in a crowded globose head of sessile flowers surrounded by ovate acuminate coarsely serrate bracts almost as long as the flowers themselves. The calyx is smooth with long erect acuminate ciliate segments, while the tubular corolla is somewhat longer than the calyx segments, lobed halfway, but the lobes do not reflex, smooth externally but bearded within. The style is slightly longer than the corolla tube, but can scarcely be said to be exserted, and divides into three filiform stigmata.

It can scarcely be distinguished from *C. glomerata* and might, in fact, be regarded as only a form of that very variable and widely distributed species. Botanically it seems to differ from that species solely by being larger in all its parts and in the possession of something in the way of wings on the petioles.

C. fondervisii. A Caucasian species which forms a loose mat of rosettes and prostrate flexible bare stems, the latter having thin ascendant branches,

E

rising to a height of some six inches, almost leafless at the ends and terminating in loose few-flowered racemes. The ovate crenate basal leaves have petioles rather shorter than the blade while the stem leaves are ovate-lanceolate and sessile. Calyx segments are linear-acute and only about a quarter the length of the corolla while the appendages are so small as to be hardly noticeable. The corolla is smooth and narrowly campanulate. The whole plant is softly hairy and is allied to *C. petrophila*, though it is a larger plant than that species and generally has more flowers to a stem.

C. formanekiana. This species, a native of Northern Macedonia, was introduced by Dr. Giuseppi in 1931, thereby showing that Europe can still provide the observant plant hunter with novelties. In its native habitat it grows in rocky crevices and forms a very handsome rosette, sometimes seven or eight inches across, of crinkled grey-downy leaves which are pressed close to the ground. The individual leaves are lyrate, the terminal lobe being the largest, almost circular and regularly serrate, in fact in some leaves the lyrations on the petiole are scarcely noticeable. From this rosette rises the tall stem, up to two feet in height, bearing a number of large, amply bell-shaped flowers, usually singly on long pedicels in the leaf axils. These flowers are usually white and very solid looking, though blue or pink tinted forms occur from time to time. The leafy calyx, wider than the corolla, has broadly triangular segments a quarter to one half the length of the corolla with a few sharp teeth about the middle and continued backwards into small pointed appendages. The corolla is fully campanulate, like a small Canterbury Bell, the rounded lobes being only one third the length and recurved. The style is shorter than the corolla, white and trifid. Decumbent basal stems are also produced on strong plants and in the result the whole inflorescence assumes a pyramidal form which makes the species a most attractive plant for pot culture, but deep pots are essential to secure the best results. It is monocarpic, sometimes taking several years to reach flowering size, but is easily raised from seed which is freely produced and is a species which can certainly be described as easy. Though some doubt has been raised as to its absolute hardiness this may well be a question of winter damp rather than cold and its downy leaves clearly suggest the desirability of the protection afforded by a sheet of glass during the winter months.

It has been suggested that this is really an old species rediscovered, having originally been known as *C. ephesia*, but that species as described has five cells to the capsule. See p. 218.

Award of Merit 1933.

C. fragilis. An attractive species from central and southern Italy, in particular from the neighbourhood of Naples.

The woody perennial rootstock gives rise to tufts of long stalked leaves which are rotund, sub-cordate, coarsely crenate and of a deep shining green. The stem leaves are similar but smaller, scattered and ovate lanceolate. Numerous branched and flexible prostrate flower stems, sometimes as much as a foot or eighteen inches long, are produced, each of which carries a number of large showy mid-blue flowers and hangs down loosely over the face of a rock. The corolla is campanulate-rotate in shape, being lobed for at least half its length with the lobes well spread, forming a flower an inch or more across. It shows a very close affinity with the better known *C. isophylla*, the main differences being that *C. fragilis* has firmer, more fleshy leaves and longer but narrower calyx segments. The calyx segments are linear-lanceolate and acuminate, not reflexed and nearly equal to the corolla in length. The species is ex-appendiculate and has an exserted, trifid style. The whole plant is as a rule smooth and almost glossy, though the existence of hairy forms has been reported, and even in the generally smooth forms the flower stems are often softly hairy in the young state. So far as I have been able to ascertain, no white form of the species is known.

It does not seem to be possible to divide this species successfully, but spring cuttings usually root without much difficulty and seed can also be relied on. A position, fairly high up, in a good sunny retaining wall, with plenty of lime in the soil, provides an ideal situation, but the species is not too hardy and is frequently lost in severe winters. It is a good subject for hanging baskets in the same way as its near relative.

The plant sometimes listed as *C. barrelieri* is only a rather more vigorous hairy form of this species.

C. freyeri. A German plant figured by Reichenbach which has erect stems some six or eight inches tall clothed with linear-lanceolate leaves which are sessile and regularly serrate. The stems terminate in a raceme of shortly stalked flowers terminally, and singly in the upper leaf axils. These flowers are carried erect, are narrowly tubular-funnel shaped in form with short unreflexed lobes; the calyx is smooth and has triangular dentate segments which are very short and held against the corolla tube. The basal leaves are not shown in the figure, but the plant has the general appearance of *C. tommasiniana* except that the flowers are erect.

C. fulgens. An Indian species, possibly biennial, which occurs on grassy slopes and pastures at high elevations and produces an erect hairy stem a foot or more high, generally unbranched and clothed with shortly petioled leaves, hairy on both sides, lanceolate, acuminate and serrate, the basal ones often as much as two inches long and three-quarters of an inch wide and narrowed at both ends. The axillary, sub-sessile, semi-pendent flowers are borne singly or in threes, somewhat crowded towards the apex and forming a spike. The calyx segments are subulate, erect, entire and slightly hairy and are nearly equal to the corolla in length; the latter, which is quite smooth, is funnel-shaped or sub-rotate with narrow pointed lobes, leaving the club-shaped style very prominent. This divides into three stigmata and the capsule, which is prominently ribbed, dehisces at the top.

C. garganica. A species from the rocky coasts on both sides of the Adriatic forming evergreen tufts of ivy-shaped, sharply dentate leaves on fairly long petioles. Numerous decumbent flower stems are produced, sometimes branched, seldom more than five or six inches in length and furnished with a few leaves similar in shape to those of the basal tuft but sub-sessile or sessile. The flowers which are always held rigidly erect on their short footstalks are rotate, or star-shaped, in form and are very freely produced in small clusters in the leaf axils, so that in a well grown example the leaves are practically hidden. Strictly speaking the inflorescence is racemose, which may give a distinction from the rather paniculate inflorescence of *C. elatines*, but this is not very reliable. The calyx segments are spathulate (a rather unusual shape) and spreading and about two-thirds the length of the corolla. The species does not spread much at the root but increases in size by additional growths from the central crown. These growths produce adventitious roots and so provide an almost unlimited supply of 'Irishman's cuttings'.

The species is very variable, and while what may be regarded as the type has smooth leaves (and capsules), a hairy form is quite common and dignified as var. *hirsuta*. This form approximates to *C. elatinoides* and is indistinguishable from the plant sometimes offered as *C. istriaca*, but all forms of *C. garganica* are larger in all their parts than *C. elatines*. There is also a white variety and the variety listed as ' W. H. Paine ', in which the flowers are of a richer blue than the type and have a conspicuous white eye. This form received an Award of Merit in 1914.

One of the most generally grown and easiest, it reproduces itself freely from self-sown seedlings, while any particularly good form can be propagated by means of spring cuttings. It is among the earlier flowering species, being at its best in June, but keeps up a less profuse succession of flowers almost until stopped by frost. To flower freely it requires a place in full sun and a good supply of lime or chalk in the soil.

It is one of the few members of the genus to which the Award of Garden Merit has been given (1930) and is certainly one of those easy plants which should be in every garden.

For a note on the relationship between this species and its near allies see p. 217.

C. ghilanensis. An annual Persian species which has erect flexible striated stems nearly two feet high with long branches forming a loose panicle. The leaves, which may be as much as an inch and a half long, are membranaceous and oblong-lanceolate, slightly serrate and sessile, the lower sides bearing a few stiff light green bristles. The flowers, borne at the ends of the branches, are obconical in shape, divided into oblong lobes for a third part of their length and carried on short thin pedicels. The short calyx tube is smooth and the linear segments recurved. It is ex-appendiculate and, with apical dehiscence, shows affinity with *C. olympica*.

C. gilliatii. A species from Northern Persia which Clay says is 'very distinct'; other authorities place it with *C. stricta*, L. from which it is only to be separated by its dwarfer habit, broader leaves and much shorter peduncles. It is a perennial which forms a mat of rosettes of orbicular spathulate leaves, nearly an inch long, with a few sharp teeth and longish winged petioles. The thin flower stems only rise about a couple of inches from the ground and usually terminate in a single flower. The calyx has triangular-ovate, sub-acute and ciliate segments and very short, almost unnoticeable appendages, while the bell-shaped corolla, about three-quarters of an inch long, much exceeds the trifid style.

C. glacialis. A very doubtful species, being difficult to separate from *C. caespitosa* and *C. linifolia*. As described it differs from the first named in being nearly twice the size and having a shorter style, while from *C. linifolia* the distinctions must be found in the inflated corolla, borne more or less erect and nearly four times the length of the calyx segments.

C. glomerata. One of the few species which are indigenous to Great Britain, this species is widespread throughout Europe.

The basal leaves are rough and more or less hairy, ovate-oblong, sub-cordate and irregularly dentate and on long footstalks. The simple, smooth or slightly hairy, unbranched, angular flower stems may be anything up to two feet in height and bear a number of sessile, almost amplexicaul, ovate-acute leaves and, at the top, mixed with a few broadly ovate leaf-like bracts, a cluster of eight to twenty or more sessile or sub-sessile erect flowers deep violet in colour and funnel-shaped, the corolla lobes being about half the length and not much reflexed except in bright weather. In strong plants, smaller clusters of flowers may be produced in some of the leaf axils particularly towards the upper part of the flower stems. The calyx tube is smooth, the segments very narrow and more or less hairy on the margins; these segments are narrowly triangular, entire, acuminate and erect and not more than half (usually rather less) the length of the corolla. The species is ex-appendiculate and the style is shorter than the corolla with three revolute stigmata.

Although the colour of the flowers, particularly in selected forms, is distinctly attractive, the type has too much leafage in proportion to flower to be of use except for large and rather rough borders. Dwarfer forms are shown from time to time but it is doubtful whether the dwarfness is constant. A particularly good form, with larger and richer coloured flowers, is generally known as *C. glomerata dahurica*, and many would include this in a list of the best dozen plants for the herbaceous border. There are also pale blue and white forms which are not unattractive. Both the species and its forms run freely at the root and may be increased by division, preferably when growth is beginning in spring.

In view of its widespread distribution it is not surprising to find that it has a large number of synonyms, very minor and not persistent modifications in various parts of the plant having led botanists from time to time to regard as new species, and name accordingly, plants which do not, after the test of growing side by side, prove to be distinct.

C. grandis. This species is a useful, if rather coarse and stiff, border plant whose home is in Siberia. It forms a mat of rosettes of long, glabrous, undulate, strap-shaped, widely and coarsely dentate leaves, narrowed at both ends. The leaves are larger and coarser than those of *C. persicifolia* to which the present species is closely akin and from each rosette springs a stiff flower spike, up to three feet in height. The lower third of this stem is furnished with leaves similar to those of the rosette, diminishing gradually in size as they ascend, the upper part with large flat saucer-shaped flowers about two inches across in blue or white and either singly or in threes, which, being carried on very short pedicels, produce a solid and formal effect. The calyx segments are broad, ovate-acute, entire and erect and only about one half the length of the corolla. The conspicuous style is tripartite and the species is one of the small group in which the capsule dehisces near the apex.

It will grow in any soil, in semi-shade or full sun, and is easily propagated by division or by self-sown seedlings.

It is commonly grown in our gardens under the name *C. latiloba*, but the name here used, which was given to the plant by Fischer & Meyer, takes precedence.

The Award of Garden Merit was bestowed on this species in 1936 and a number of improved forms have since been introduced, the best being known as Highcliffe variety, which, like the Telham Beauty form of *C. persicifolia*, is probably a tetraploid form.

C. grossekii. A coarse wild-garden species from Hungary which may be briefly described as *C. trachelium* with appendages on the calyx. Yet it is not without attractiveness despite the unkind way in which Farrer dismisses it—'gross as its name seems to indicate'.

From a cluster of large rough ovate-cordate, dentate, petiolate leaves arise bristly angular flower stems which may reach to a height of three or four feet and are distinctly reddish. These stems bear ovate, doubly dentate and sessile leaves which, as usual, diminish in size towards the summit. The lower part of the stem is branched and in the leaf axils and terminally are short stiff penduncles each carrying two to four pendent flowers. The latter are fairly full bell-shaped, commonly of a pale lilac colour, with a line of stiff hairs on the exterior nerves and on the margins of the lobes; internally the flowers are smooth except for a certain downiness where the lobes divide. The lobes themselves are about one third the length of the corolla, pointed acuminate and not much recurved. The calyx, its segments and appendages are all bristly; the segments, which are about one third as long as the corolla, are broad at the base, becoming suddenly narrow and are distinctly revolute terminating in a hard point, almost a knob; the appendages, rather shorter than the calyx tube, are broadly triangular. The style, about the same length as the corolla, is bright yellow and correspondingly conspicuous, while the stigma is tripartite. Pollen also is bright yellow in colour. The capsule is pendent and the plentiful seeds provide a ready means of increase.

C. gumbetica. A small greyish plant from calcareous rocks in the Caucasian province from which it takes its name, forming tufts of small, reniform-cordate, crenate leaves on short petioles and giving rise to a few short decumbent stems with a few leaves which become smaller and sessile as they near the end and terminating in one or two shortly stalked flowers. The calyx is furnished with very small pointed appendages and triangular segments which are softly hairy and only a quarter the length of the deeply lobed funnel-shaped corolla. As described, it seems to be 'of botanical interest only'.

C. hawkinsiana. A species from Northern Greece, which is unfortunately very rare in cultivation.

From a central rootstock there arise numerous straggling shoots bearing small glabrous rather fleshy leaves, bluish green in colour, ovate spa-

thulate in shape with variably dentate margins and a few short bristly hairs
on both sides. These shoots are branched and soon form a tangled mat,
but the whole has an unfortunate habit of collapsing without warning just
when the grower is expecting flowers, though the habit is that of a perennial. The flowers, if and when produced, are wide open dark purple
sub-rotate bells with even darker veinings and are borne singly on slender
wiry pedicels. The flowers themselves are borne erect but the ripe capsules are pendent. The calyx is more or less hairy while the lanceolate
calyx segments are more or less reflexed and about one third the length of
the corolla. The species is ex-appendiculate and the style is trifid.

According to collectors the species grows exclusively in screes of ser-
pentine and schist, which gives some guide to its requirements; while those
who have had success with it advise the occasional pinching back of the
straggling shoots (the pinched off tips being used as cuttings) and, if grown
in pans, frequent repotting. In any case there can be no denying that the
species must be classed as 'miffy', and its hardiness is at least open to
question, so that it is undoubtedly safer to try it in the alpine house. It is,
however, such an attractive plant that it is well worth any trouble to satisfy
its fads, particularly for those growers who like to wrestle with the problems presented by 'difficult' plants. It can be raised from seed without
undue difficulty, though it is a case of 'first get your seed'; the difficulties
arise thereafter.

It received an Award of Merit in June 1932.

C. hemschinica. A biennial species, generally preferring woodlands,
from Bulgaria and the Balkans generally, which forms mats of smooth,
ovate-lanceolate, acuminate, sessile leaves without toothing and rather light
green in colour. As with many biennials these leaves die off as the flower
stems grow. The flower stems are erect, about a foot high, and carry a
number of leaves similar to the basal ones, though smaller and occasionally
slightly dentate and, as usual, becoming smaller and more widely spaced
towards the apex. The stems end in a loose cluster of fairly large flowers
carried erect on long peduncles, usually two-flowered. The filiform calyx
segments are about half the length of the corolla, not reflexed and without
appendages, but the calyx tube often bears a few glandular excrescences.
The corolla is bell-shaped with triangular pointed lobes half its length and
well reflexed. The style is trifid. The plant is glabrous throughout and
resembles a stiffer growing *C. patula*.

Seed of course provides the only means of propagation but the species
is not an easy one to grow, though showy and worth trouble, as it is very
inclined to damp off, in which it resembles its near ally *C. abietina*, and

CAMPANULA HERCEGOVINA

95

CAMPANULA HETEROPHYLLA

96

CAMPANULA HYPOPOLIA

97

CAMPANULA INCURVA

CAMPANULA ISOPHYLLA

98

the scree seems to be the only place for it, different as this is from the conditions in which it is found in nature.

A note on the relationship between this and other species appears under the description of *C. abietina* (p. 31).

C. hercegovina. A newly introduced species from the country after which it is named where it forms little bushlets in the limestone cliffs and is absolutely saxatile. The small oval, acuminate leaves have a pretty serrated edge with, as a rule, three sharp teeth on each side, and are carried on slender stalks a quarter of an inch to an inch in length. From the tuft arise a number of slender wiry erect stems, which often fall about with the weight of the flowers, bearing a few small leaves similar to the basal ones, though getting gradually narrower while retaining the characteristic three teeth each side and the slender petioles. These stems, which may reach eighteen inches in length, are freely branched and carry several deep lilac erect flowers which are large for the size of the plant, on thin hair-like pedicels. The corolla is smooth, campanulate in shape and divided to a third of its length into triangular, rather spreading lobes. The calyx segments are linear, about half the length of the corolla, more or less reflexed and without appendages. Frequently there is a small bract immediately below the flower. The white style, equal in length to the corolla, is trifid and the whole plant is absolutely glabrous. Although the flowers are borne erect, the buds and mature capsules are pendent.

The flowering period is late July and early August and the plant never exceeds four inches in height. It can be readily propagated from cuttings of the young shoots or from seed which is freely produced, and, as it is perfectly hardy, a sound perennial and does not seem to be particular as to soil, it must be said to be one of the best of comparatively recent introductions.

The species was given an Award of Merit in July 1933, and in 1946 a plant was shown and given a similar award under the name *C. hercegovina* var. *nana*—a dwarf compact plant. There is, however, considerable doubt as to the correctness of this name and the plant in question may well turn out to be a distinct species.

C. herminii. A species from stony places in the higher mountains of Portugal which may be little more than annual. The creeping root produces rosettes of smooth, long pointed-oval leaves on long footstalks, entire and sub-ciliate. From among these rise erect or ascendant, nearly leafless stems six inches or more in height, which may be branched towards the top producing a few-flowered panicle, but are more often simple with only a single flower. The few leaves on the flowering stems are linear-lanceolate and the upper ones sessile. The calyx segments are narrow or filiform, reflexed, and fully half as long as the corolla which is sub-erect and broadly funnel-shaped with well-spread triangular lobes. De Candolle says it is pale blue with a white base but this cannot be relied on as diagnostic. The trifid style is as long as, or sometimes longer than, the corolla and the capsule, which nods after fertilisation, dehisces at the top. In general appearance it is very close to *C. steveni* and possibly does not deserve specific rank.

C. hernandezi. The name has been mentioned as appropriate to a species from eastern Morocco but as no description has, so far as I can trace, ever been published the name is of no validity.

C. heterophylla. One of the most promising of recent introductions (or, perhaps, reintroductions) this species was sent home from Crete by Peter Davis in 1939.

It is a true perennial and indestructibly hardy having passed through the winter of 1944-45 as far north as Southport (where 25 to 30 degrees of frost were recorded) without protection of any kind.

It forms an evergreen tuft of rather thick, almost fleshy leaves which are perfectly smooth, light green, oblong-spathulate and entire, diminishing to a short petiole. From among these leaves numerous decumbent flower stems up to a foot in length are emitted; the stems are generally simple and clothed with ovate sessile leaves which, as the photograph shows, do not get smaller towards the ends of the stems. The funnel-shaped flowers of a rather mauvy blue shade, are carried erect on short pedicels throughout the final third of the stems. The calyx is rather conspicuous, having prominently winged angles and triangular acuminate segments about a quarter the length of the corolla but not reflexed, while the appendages are very small and pointed. The style is tripartite and exserted.

In nature a crevice plant, it appreciates a similar position in cultivation, but, if grown on the flat, insists on a good layer of coarse stone chippings to ensure the absence of excessive moisture round the crown, particularly during the winter. Another point to be noted is that the flower stems are unusually brittle so that a position in which the plant will not be subjected to strong winds after the flower stems have grown out is essential. In fact so brittle are these stems that I have had a whole batch of plants completely ruined by a heavy shower of rain, which broke all stems away from the crowns.

Seed seems to be produced rather sparingly but germinates well and provides the best, indeed the only, means of increase. Raised from seed, however, it seems to vary considerably and there is urgent necessity for some measure of selection, for I have seen plants in other gardens with flowers less than half the size of those on the plant illustrated and with flowers of a more mauvy, almost dull, colour.

C. hierapetrae is a small form of *C. calamenthifolia*.

C. hierosolymitana. A species of annual duration from rocky places around Jerusalem, greyish and rough. The six-inch stem is much branched and bears oblong entire sessile leaves while each branch terminates in two or three small shortly stalked flowers. These flowers are tubular in shape and pale violet in colour, bristly on the nerves externally and about twice as long as the calyx. The rough calyx segments are lanceolate and there are ovate obtuse appendages. The style is trifid, the capsule nodding, and dehiscence basal.

C. hondoensis. This Japanese species is allied to *C. microdonta* and is similar in general appearance to *C. punctata*, but the calyx is without appendages. The basal leaves are oblong-lanceolate, serrate and acuminate, on long narrowly winged hairy petioles. Stiff erect stems up to three feet in height bear similar leaves on the lower parts and smaller and nearly sessile ones above; these stems have short flexible branches which carry shortly stalked hanging flowers, tubular-campanulate in shape, reddish purple in colour and as much as two inches long with short recurved lobes. The calyx segments are broadly triangular, much shorter than the corolla and not reflexed, while the style is trifid and does not exceed the corolla in length.

C. humillima. A small and insignificant perennial species from Persian mountains. The leaves are rotund-cordate, with seven angular teeth and on long thin petioles. One or more smooth stems rise from the tuft and are loosely branched, the branches bearing small linear bracts and, usually, three flowers on thin footstalks. The funnel-shaped corolla is twice as long as the calyx segments which are themselves linear and erect. The trifid style equals the corolla in length.

C. hypopolia. Another Caucasian species, which is most distinct in appearance, but in many places rather shy of flowering. It produces a mass of trailing, interlacing shoots, furnished with long narrow grass-like leaves, greyish in colour and definitely downy on the undersides. A varying proportion of these shoots terminate in flower stems which are more or less branched and are curled up in their early stages and very downy. The whole tangled mass rarely exceeds four or five inches in height. The flowers are borne singly, and are nodding in the bud stage but tend to become more or less erect when open. The calyx is slightly hairy, the segments about one third the length of the corolla with revolute edges and re-flexed; calyx appendages are triangular and equal in length to the calyx tube; the corolla is rather narrowly bell-shaped with pointed lobes nearly half the total length, and the style, which is about the same length as the corolla, divides into three stigmata.

Cultivation is easy in any light stony soil in full sun and cuttings of the young growth in spring root easily. As it spreads, with decent moderation, by underground runners, it may also be increased by careful division. It appears to flower most freely in really hot dry places, with a deep root run, and is one of the species for which slugs seem to have a more than morbid craving.

C. hyrcania. An annual from Persia which is almost indistinguishable from *C. ghilanensis*. Such differences as there are must be looked for in the rather longer calyx segments (nearly as long as the corolla itself), which are carried erect instead of recurving. The corolla also is rather more deeply lobed.

C. hystricula. A Persian species with numerous flexible unbranched stems from a woody rootstock. These stems bear linear-oblong, sessile leaves, almost without toothing and terminate in solitary tubular-cam-panulate flowers, the corolla being divided to the middle into oblong lobes. The linear calyx segments are longer than the calyx tube itself but only about a third the length of the corolla while the trifid style is exserted. The species is included in the same section of the genus as *C. tridentata* and its allies.

C. imeritina. Native of the Caucasian province from which it takes its name, this species does not appear to be in cultivation. Plants (or seeds) are offered under this name from time to time but invariably turn out to be something different. The true plant grows six to nine inches high and is closely allied to *C. dichotoma* which occurs generally throughout the Mediterranean area, but is less definitely annual (in fact more often than not biennial) and has less intricately branched stems. The basal and lower stem leaves are oval-, or obovate-spathulate, drawn out into winged petioles as long as the blade; the upper ones are broadly elliptical or ovate and slightly and irregularly crenate. All leaves are thin, rough with short hairs and not above an inch long. Flowers are borne singly on erect half-inch footstalks and are campanulate in form, half to three-quarters of an inch in length, and smooth externally. The calyx segments are broadly lanceolate and rather less than half as long as the corolla, and there are appendages which are slightly longer than the calyx tube. Both calyx segments and appendages are noticeably ciliate but otherwise smooth.

Later writers have connected this species with *C. sibirica*, in fact, Trautvetter reduces it to a variety of that species, but the fact, clearly pointed out by Ruprecht in the original description, that the lower, and sometimes even the upper, flowers are opposite the leaves, shows the dichotomous character of the normal branching—a character which does not appear in *C. sibirica* despite its widespread distribution and many forms.

The references in the *Index Kewensis* to *C. brassicaefolia* and *C. caucasica* of Koch as synonyms of *C. imeritina* are questionable, as they appear to be based on the authority of writers who have grouped *C. imeritina* with *C. sibirica*, and it is probably with the last-named that these two so-called species are synonymous.

C. incanescens. 'A delightful saxatile plant from rocks of Southern Persia with grey hairy oval leaves and charming flowers varying in their shades of blue.' So says Dr. Giuseppi. The small grey and very hairy leaves have a few but large dentations and the root emits numerous thin flexible fragile branched stems, two to eight inches high. The flowers (which are rather small) may be borne singly or in few-flowered corymbs on the branches, the peduncles being fairly long; the corolla is funnel-shaped and half as long again as the calyx; the spreading segments of the calyx are lanceolate-acuminate and somewhat rough, while there are very small appendages which may be so small as to be overlooked. The basal leaves are shortly petiolate, but the upper ones, which are smaller and more acute, are sessile. It is very near *C. candida*, differing mainly in its branched stems and longer calyx segments.

C. incurva. This is the correct name of the plant sometimes offered as *C. leutweinii* and is a Grecian species which is, unfortunately, monocarpic.

A central rootstock forms one or more rosettes of long-stalked, ovate, cordate leaves, bluntly crenate, and, like the rest of the plant, softly hairy. They are of a somewhat yellowish green colour and are very characteristic; in fact I know of no other species with which they could be confused. In due time numerous prostrate and ascendant flower stems are produced which may be as much as twelve to fifteen inches long, are sparingly branched from the base, bear a number of rhomboid serrate leaves stalked in the lower part but becoming sessile above and terminate in a loose racemose panicle. The calyx is furnished with blunt short appendages while the calyx segments are broadly ovate and about three times the length of the calyx tube itself. The corolla is large (up to two inches long), broadly campanulate and noticeably bulged, making a rather clumsy, shaped flower.

It is of a rather washy lavender colour, has a few hairs on nerves and margins and only short revolute lobes. In general appearance it is not unlike a rather prostrate form of the well-known *C. medium*, but is readily distinguished by the tripartite style and three-celled capsule.

It is easily raised from seed and is one of the easiest and hardiest of the Grecian species.

It received the Award of Merit in 1937.

C. involucrata. A perennial species from Cappadocia which is in many ways an improvement on *C. glomerata* though similar in general outline. It produces rosettes of shortly petioled obovate-obtuse leaves crenulate and slightly downy, and erect channelled stems with ovate-acute sessile leaves, terminating in heads of large funnel-shaped flowers surrounded by an involucre of ample, ovate-acute bracts. The corolla is lobed to half its length and the calyx segments are linear and hairy. The calyx is exappendiculate.

C. isophylla. An Italian species, well known as a plant for hanging baskets, but not quite hardy, though it will survive quite severe weather if planted in a retaining wall so that no moisture can accumulate round the crown.

From a thickened rootstock emerge rotund or cordate, regularly dentate leaves on long petioles and numbers of much-branched trailing stems which carry similar leaves scattered along their length and numerous pedicelled rotate-campanulate, or salver-shaped, blue flowers in a many-flowered corymb. Buds, flowers and capsules are always erect. The calyx tube itself is very short, the calyx segments, about two thirds the length of the corolla, are broadly triangular, acuminate and sub-erect, sometimes with one or two small teeth on their margins and without appendages. As frequently happens with this form of corolla, the tripartite style is unusually prominent. The species varies considerably in the degree of woolliness of leaves and stems and a particularly woolly form is sometimes sold as *C. mollis*, a name which seems to have been attached more or less indiscriminately to the hairy leafed form of several species, but which should be confined to the Spanish species described on p. 135, which can readily be distinguished from the present species by the calyx appendages.

Another form, in which the foliage is variegated, is commonly known as *C. isophylla*, var. *Mayi*.

Propagation by cuttings of the young shoots in early spring before the formation of flower buds or in late August from non-flowering shoots is without much difficulty, and seed gives an alternative method, but of course, cuttings must be relied on for any particular form.

The species is closely related to *C. fragilis*, but may be distinguished by its more cordate leaves and the greater similarity between the basal and cauline leaves as well as by the absence of the dark ring at the base of the flowers which is such a feature of *C. fragilis*.

The white form was given a First Class Certificate in 1888, while var. *Mayi* received the Award of Merit in 1899.

C. istriaca. See p. 217.

C. jacobaea. A shrubby species from Cape Verde Islands which is near *C. vidalii* and, like that species, should probably be removed from the genus entirely. Its many stems, eight to ten inches high, are woody, knotted and hollow and bear numerous side branches with oval-spathulate, roughish dentate leaves, the lower ones being petiolate, and terminate in a few stalked flowers which are more or less pendent, long-tubular in shape with very short and broad lobes. The broadly lanceolate calyx segments are ciliate, not more than a third the length of the corolla and not reflexed. The calyx is furnished with awl-shaped appendages rather longer than the tube; the short style is trifid. Both purple and white forms have been reported, but the species would not, of course, be hardy in this country.

C. jaubertiana. This species from the Pyrenees appears to come between *C. linifolia* and *C. rotundifolia*. It forms a thick mat of rosettes of smooth round unequally but sharply dentate leaves, the basal ones on petioles as long as the blade, the middle ones gradually drawn out into short petioles and the upper ones narrower and sessile. Flower stems some two to four inches in height terminate in a one-sided raceme of two to four flowers which are fully campanulate with short oval mucronate lobes. They are blue in colour but yellowish at the base and are pendent both before and after flowering. The calyx segments are bluntly linear, erect and hairy, while the short style is only about two thirds the length of the corolla.

The stalked stem leaves distinguish it from *C. linifolia* and the pendant buds from *C. rotundifolia*, while it is separated from *C. stolonifera*—a species from the same district—by the fact that its stolons are all on the surface.

C. juncea, Wettst. seems to be merely a smooth form of *C. compacta*, Boiss.

C. kachethica. A species of which little is known, the name having been bestowed by the Russian botanist Kantschavelli in 1928. It is apparently indigenous to Russian Caucasus where it occurs in fissures of the rocks. It, or a very closely allied species, labelled *C. kantschavellii*, is, however, in cultivation in this country. After growing the two reputed species side by side and seeing them in other gardens I am convinced that there is only one species involved.

It forms a cluster of rosettes from which the flower stems are produced and is proving a good perennial though possibly short lived. The leaves of the basal rosette are greyish, almost circular and sub-cordate, regularly serrate and on petioles minutely winged and nearly twice the length of the blade. The flower stems, up to twelve inches in length, are more or less procumbent and furnished with a few leaves similar to the basal ones but sessile or sub-sessile, from the axils of which short simple or compound branches are produced terminating in erect deep lavender flowers of long tubular campanulate form, either singly or in clusters of threes. Various colour forms, including a pink, are reported. The calyx is ciliate with pointed segments one third the length of the corolla and not reflexed, and is furnished with small triangular ciliate appendages scarcely reflexed and not longer than the calyx tube. The corolla is only slightly hairy on the outside, lobed to about a quarter of its length and the reflexed lobes are broad at the base but suddenly acuminate. The style is somewhat shorter than the corolla and divides into three stigmata, while the capsule dehisces at the base.

Seed is probably the only means of increase, though it is possible that cuttings of young growth in spring would root if secured at a very early stage before they have started to spindle up for flower.

C. kantschavellii cannot be reliably separated from *C. kachethica* and the latter, being the older name, must have precedence.

C. karakuschensis. A small rather insignificant Persian species resembling *C. dulcis* of which in fact it may be only a local variant. It forms a mat of softly hairy leaves and a number of erect stems two to four inches high. The basal leaves are oblanceolate and sharply dentate while the very small stem leaves are linear and sessile but not amplexicaul. The stems carry only a few shortly stalked flowers, the corolla being funnel-shaped and scarcely as long as the calyx segments. These calyx segments are broader than in the other species named, while the calyx itself is hairy and has short linear appendages.

C. kemulariae. A species of comparatively recent introduction from Transcaucasia. It is a perennial with a running rootstock which soon makes a large clump of sharply pointed, broadly ovate, cordate and doubly serrate leaves on petioles longer than the blade. These leaves are hard, glabrous or even shiny and of a rather light green colour. The much-branched flower stems may be as much as a foot long and bear obovate shortly petiolate leaves becoming, towards the top, little more than sessile bracts which have one

CAMPANULA KACHETHICA

107

CAMPANULA KEMULARIAE

CAMPANULA KOLENATIANA

CAMPANULA LACINIATA

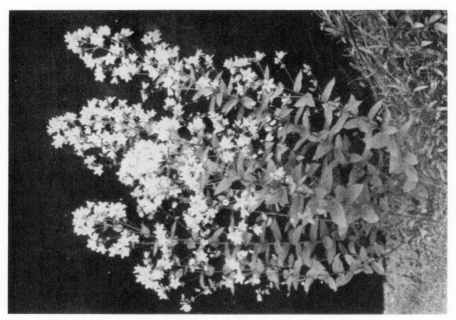

CAMPANULA LACTIFLORA

CAMPANULA LANATA

(or occasionally two) prominent teeth on each side; their general habit shows that the stems should be erect but they do not seem strong enough to bear the weight of the many flowers, with the result that the greater part of the inflorescence is hidden among the basal leaves.

The calyx is broader than the corolla tube and has triangular ciliate segments, which are not reflexed, and prominent triangular appendages with involute edges and tapering to a narrow revolute point not adpressed to, and rather longer than, the calyx tube. The corolla, an inch long and one and a half inches across, is broadly bell-shaped, twice as long as the calyx segments with broadly triangular lobes for half its length. The trifid style is much exserted and the pollen is orange rather than yellow, as in *C. raddeana*, with which it appears to be nearly akin. It is, however, a much coarser, stronger grower. The flowers are carried erect on fairly long footstalks but in many soils and strains are of a very undistinguished pale mauve colour.

Any soil and situation appear to be acceptable, though a poor stony soil checks the exuberance of the basal leaves to some extent and gives the flowers more chance to display themselves. Division of the clump as growth is starting in spring is the obvious means of increase where such is desired. The general habit suggests its use for draping the top of a dry wall where the flowers could hang over the edge.

C. ketzkhovellii appears to be indistinguishable from *C. massalskyi*.

C. kitaibeliana, R. & S. This name was given in 1819 to a plant previously called *C. microphylla* but the only description referred to the lower leaves as obovate-cuneiform, crenate; and to the upper ones as linear, entire, while the plant was said to have simple one-flowered stems. This description is, of course, quite inadequate for identification purposes and later writers regard it as a 'doubtful' species.

C. kolenatiana. A monocarpic or biennial species from sub-alpine regions of the Caucasus which in general outline resembles the better known *C. sarmatica*, though without the ash-grey leaf coloration which is typical of that species.

From a thick, almost rhizomatous, root rise a number of thickish, long-petioled leaves which are smooth, ovate-obtuse, cordate and crenate; later a number of erect or ascendant rigid stems are produced, slightly branched from the base, each branch bearing a few oblong, sessile leaves and a few flowers in one-sided racemes, the short nodding footstalks being often bracted. The calyx is wider than the corolla tube and has erect, pointed triangular, glabrous segments and bristly, sub-dentate, lanceolate appendages, recurved and longer than the calyx tube. The comparatively large

F

corolla, three times the length of the calyx segments, or up to an inch in length, is generally violet blue in colour, broadly campanulate with well reflexed lobes, smooth externally but slightly hairy within. The trifid style is sub-exserted. Fomin says that the anthers are often joined at the tip in young flowers, showing an affinity with the allied genus, *Symphyandra.*

The main differences between this species and *C. sarmatica* are in the form of the appendages, the broader calyx and the darker corolla.

Propagation, of course, is only possible from seed, which, however, is freely produced.

The species obtained an Award of Merit in 1918.

C. komarovii. Doubtfully entitled to specific rank, being too near some forms of *C. sibirica*: it has, however, larger flowers than the type of that species and calyx segments and appendages somewhat differing in shape, but *C. sibirica* itself is such a polymorphic species that it is difficult to say where it should begin or end. The present name is probably synonymous with *C. sibirica,* var. *divergens.*

The present plant forms a woody rootstock and produces a tuft of long spathulate leaves with narrowly winged petioles and a number of ascendant stems up to a foot in height, more or less rough with whitish hairs, carrying lanceolate, crenate and sessile leaves, similarly hairy, and terminating in a raceme formed of stalked flowers, each stalk usually having only one flower, though two may occur. The flowers themselves, deep violet in colour, are campanulate in shape, may be as much as two inches long with acute reflexed lobes and externally hairy on the nerves. The calyx segments are not more than a quarter the length of the corolla and are broadly lanceolate or even triangular, while the appendages are ovate. The style is shorter than the corolla, trifid and not prominent.

C. kotschyana. On the lower slopes of the Taurus Mountains this annual species grows on the edge of pinewoods. It has a rough thin erect stem, eight or nine inches high, with small ovate sessile leaves, terminating in a loose panicle of small flowers divided halfway into oblong lobes. The calyx is without appendages, has narrow segments rather more than half the length of the corolla, and dehisces near the top. The style is trifid.

C. kremeri is merely the Algerian form of the widely distributed *C. dichotoma.*

C. laciniata. A monocarpic species from Crete and other islands in the Grecian Archipelago which has a thick rootstock often continued above ground in a kind of trunk and headed by a rosette of rather light coloured and almost smooth leaves. These leaves, as much as six inches in length in mature plants, are broadly obovate and laciniate and diminish to a more or less winged petiole. The petiole lobes are generally alternate, irregular in size, and crenate, while the leaf sections are regularly and sharply dentate. The stem leaves are, as usual, smaller and are ovate-lanceolate, less nearly laciniate and sessile. The stiff flower stems, up to two feet or more in height, are smooth and bear numerous large terminal and axillary flowers in a loose panicle, the peduncles being one- to three-flowered. The calyx segments are broad, ovate-acuminate and erect and bear between them bluntly ovate appendages at least as long as the segments; both segments and appendages are entire and softly hairy. The corolla is very broadly and flatly campanulate, or cup-shaped, fully two inches across and, generally, lavender blue with a distinct white centre. The style is the same length as the corolla and divides into five (sometimes, as is not uncommon in this group, four) stigmata which roll back noticeably as the flower ages. Double (or semi-double) forms occur which can only be described as ugly and further are often of a dirty dingy colour, but such accidents cannot be avoided among a batch of seedlings.

As a monocarpic species it must be raised from seed, but this is not produced with any freedom, and so far as I can ascertain, the flowers need hand pollination, which explains the almost complete absence of this very handsome species from our gardens. It seems, too, to be rather reluctant to flower, often growing for several years and then collapsing as the flower stems begin to push up. Further, it has not proved particularly hardy and needs the protection at least of an alpine house and, indeed, probably somewhere a little warmer during the winter. It is, however, a most attractive species and, at all stages, a very conspicuous plant and well deserves all the care and attention it demands.

It received the Award of Merit in 1945.

C. lactiflora. Another native of the Caucasus, this species is one of the best dozen plants for the ordinary herbaceous border.

It forms a thick, fleshy, much-branched rootstock and is undoubtedly best from self-sown seedlings, or from seed sown where required, thinned out, but never transplanted. This is not to say that transplanting is impossible, but plants that have been moved take several years to become re-established, even if they ever attain the height and magnificence of the unmoved seedling. The basal leaves are sessile, ovate, sharply serrate and acuminate and light green in colour. A number of strong erect flower stems rise to a height of anything up to four feet, furnished with similar leaves and terminating in a loose, many-flowered, more or less umbellate, panicle, the flowers being held rigidly erect. The flowers, which are normally pale blue shading almost to white at the centre, are broadly campanulate, of medium size and generally borne in clusters of three; the corolla is lobed to about midway, the lobes being broad and pointed. The calyx tube is obconical; the segments are about half the length of the corolla, broad, acute, serrulate and not reflexed. There are no appendages. The trifid style is very short, only about one third the length of the corolla, and the capsules, like the flowers, are carried erect.

It was introduced in 1814, but long before this Parkinson had noted it as a source of cosmetics, stating that: 'The rootes beaten small, and mixed with some meale of Lupines, cleanseth the skinne from spots, markes and other discolourings. The distilled water of the whole plants, rootes and all, performeth the same, and maketh the face very splendent and cleare.'

The form of the species from Siberia, which was at one time given specific rank as *C. celtidifolia*, has rather smaller and bluer flowers.

A variety, designated *coerulea*, obtained the Award of Merit in 1901, and the type was given the Award of Garden Merit in 1926.

C. lamioides. A perennial with a creeping rhizomatous rootstock which seems difficult to distinguish from some of the many forms of *C. glomerata*. The basal leaves are described as orbicular-cordate often nearly reniform on petioles four to five inches long, and herein lies the main difference from the type. The flowers are borne in a terminal glomerule and in few-flowered glomerules in the upper leaf axils and, apart from being of a somewhat paler colour, do not differ from the type. The shape of the basal leaves alone, particularly in such a widely distributed species, scarcely seems sufficient to support specific rank.

C. lanata. A native of Northern Greece and Bulgaria, this species is another of the many species of Campanula from that part of the world which are unfortunately monocarpic. It is, however, easily raised from seed which is freely produced. It is, in nature, a crevice plant, sending its roots far down into the rocks and forming in its early life a wide basal tuft of big heart-shaped pointed grey flannel leaves, with jagged edges and long hairy footstalks which carry no lobes or lyrations. In due course there pushes up a tall well-branched pyramidal inflorescence, reaching two or three feet in height, bearing a number of leaves similar to the basal ones but smaller, and large numbers of waxy very pale yellow or peach-pink bells, in shape and carriage resembling the well known *C. medium*, though only about half the size. These flowers are terminal and in the leaf axils, usually singly, on short pedicels. The calyx is leafy and prominent and wider than the corolla; the segments are broadly triangular with undulate, ciliate edges; they are about one third the length of the corolla and not reflexed. Small acuminate appendages mark each sinus. The white, trifid style is rather shorter than the corolla. A noticeable feature is the *bright* yellow pollen. When the central stem has made some progress the plant sends out from the base a number of long stiff branches which hug the face of the rock and with their upturned flowers serve to complete the pyramid of bloom. With its woolly leaves the plant probably needs overhead protection from winter wet but otherwise presents no difficulty. It may well be tried in a vertical crevice where it can get its deep roots back into a body of rich soil and where its crown is safe from any accumulation of moisture.

C. velutina, Vel., which was at one time regarded as a separate species cannot be distinguished, and that name must now be dropped.

C. lanceolata, Lapeyr. A species from high alpine pastures throughout the Pyrenees, which produces many simple stems, eighteen to twenty inches high, which are noticeably angled and have a few white hairs on the angles. Basal and stem leaves are large, lanceolate-acute, sub-amplexicaul, serrate and ciliate, softly hairy on the undersides. The flowers are in few-flowered panicles, campanulate in form with short smooth calyces and pointed linear segments. Though still retained as a species in the *Index Kewensis* it would seem to be indistinguishable from *C. rhomboidalis* and it must be admitted that the Index is not, and in the nature of things cannot be, frequently expurgated.

C. lasiocarpa. An attractive dwarf species from Japan and the Rocky Mountains of North America which forms neat tufts of smooth ovoid or oblanceolate leaves with noticeably jagged edges tapering to a narrowly winged and ciliate petiole. From each tuft rises a stem some three or four inches high bearing a few sessile lanceolate leaves each with three or four distinct teeth on each side and terminating in a single large bell-shaped flower, sub-erect and, in the type, blue. An attractive albino has recently been introduced. The calyx segments are smooth and linear with one or two prominent teeth on each side and only an occasional bristle, though the calyx itself is hairy. These segments are half the length of the corolla and carried at right angles to it. The species is ex-appendiculate. The corolla lobes are ovate-acuminate and smooth. The style is included, blue and trifid, while the capsule is always erect and dehisces near the top.

The plant runs freely among rocks or in a loose scree, but is rather impatient of winter wet, easily rotting off. Seed is freely produced and germinates readily, forming the best means of increase but, like so many of the choicer species, slugs are very partial to the young plants.

This is the correct name of the plant sometimes referred to as *C. algida*.

C. latifolia. Occurring in the more northerly parts of Great Britain (not recorded from Ireland) and in the woods of northern Europe and central Asia, this species, with care to prevent excessive spreading, proves very useful in the herbaceous border. From basal tufts of large cordate-ovate, irregularly dentate leaves on long petioles rise tall erect smooth and unbranched stems up to three feet in height, furnished with leaves similar to those of the basal tuft though becoming gradually rather smaller and narrower and with shorter petioles and ultimately sessile. The large semi-erect long-bell-shaped flowers, lobed to about one third of their length, are carried singly in the upper leaf axils and in a terminal cluster. The smooth calyx forms an almost spherical pendent capsule and the large spreading narrowly triangular, entire segments are nearly half as long as the corolla. The triangular corolla lobes are well reflexed forming a showy open flower, sometimes bearded internally. The style is distinctly shorter than the corolla and the three stigmata markedly revolute. Apart from a certain amount of hairiness on the calyx of some forms the species is entirely glabrous.

C. eriocarpa and *C. macrantha* are but forms of this species, with minor variations in the degree of hairiness of the calyx and, in the case of *C. macrantha*, the more distinct dentations of the leaves. Neither of these forms is quite so prone to spread as the type and the form known as *macrantha* is the best, with rather larger and more spreading flowers.

All forms come readily from seed.

C. lehmanniana. A perennial from rock crevices in Turkestan which produces a number of short, more or less woody, branches from a central root terminating in rosettes of thin oblong spathulate acute, sharply denticulate greyish leaves which diminish to petioles. Only extending slightly beyond the rosettes, the flowering stems, six to eight inches long, bear a few short linear leaves and terminate in a few-flowered raceme. Calyx segments are linear and slightly longer than the spherical tube while the comparatively large tubular-campanulate corolla with ovate-pointed lobes is erect at first but later becomes pendent.

C. lepida. See p. 217.

C. leucoclada. A perennial species from rocky crevices in Afghanistan which, from a woody root, emits numerous rigid stems six inches to a foot in height covered with whitish hairs and furnished with rough oblong more or less acute and denticulate leaves becoming linear towards the ends of the stems and all sessile. The small, stalked flowers are shortly tubular and roughly hairy, while the calyx has short lanceolate-acute and ciliate segments fully half as long as the corolla and ovate-triangular appendages longer than the calyx tube. The trifid style is exserted and the mature capsule is pendent. Farrer describes it as hopeless and ugly.

C. leucosiphon. A small mat-forming species from shady rocks in the Taurus Mountains with soft thin woolly leaves which are coarsely and sharply dentate. The lower leaves are petiolate and ovate-rotund, the upper ones being sessile and triangular. The short fragile ascendant stems, which are sometimes slightly branched and may reach a height of six inches, carry the flowers in small clusters, or singly in the upper axils and form an unilateral raceme. The calyx segments are triangular acute, much shorter than the corolla and there are ovate-obtuse appendages. The corolla is small, narrowly tubular, broadening at the mouth, whitish in colour and, like the calyx, softly hairy. The style is shorter than the corolla and trifid.

C. ligularis. From rosettes of narrowly ligulate, obtuse, entire leaves rise smooth thin stems about three inches high bearing a few oblong-obtuse and ciliate leaves and terminating in a medium-sized flower carried erect. The rough calyx has linear segments and narrow recurved appendages, while the tubular campanulate corolla is more or less bearded at the edges. The style divides into three stigmata and the capsule contains three cells. It is very similar to *C. allionii* and, in fact, De Candolle is doubtful whether it can be distinguished from that species.

C. lingulata, Waldst. & Kit. A Hungarian biennial which produces its flowers in a close head. It spreads into Thrace and frequents dry, stony places. The root emits a number of erect unbranched rough angular stems about a foot high. The basal and lower stem leaves are lingulate, narrowing towards the base but sessile; those on the upper part of the stems are narrower, almost linear, and sub-amplexicaul. All are rough and bristly and crenate-undulate. The terminal flower heads are not large, generally containing only six or seven flowers round and among which are a few small ovate-acute bracts. Very occasionally smaller heads of flowers arise from the axils of the upper leaves. The calyx is rough with erect, oblong-obtuse and markedly ciliate segments and the appendages, larger and broader than the calyx segments, are pressed back on to the calyx. The tubular corolla, usually deep blue, is at least three times the length of the calyx segments, lobed to only a quarter of its length and furnished with internal hairs. The style is as long as the corolla and terminates in three well-recurved stigmata. The first year's rosette of leaves persists through the winter but dies as the flower spikes develop. There appears to be a very dwarf form with procumbent stems, not exceeding three or four inches in height and with smaller heads of flowers, which is found in Bulgaria. Farrer rightly says it is not worth growing, but it is interesting as being the only cluster-headed species which bears calyx appendages.

If wanted it must be raised from seed.

C. linifolia, Scop. This attractive plant is widely distributed, though never really common, throughout the European Alps, spreading into the Pyrenees to the west and into the Carpathians to the east. It inhabits high rocky pastures, rarely, if ever, descending below about 7,000 feet.

The growth is loosely tufted, consisting of a mass of small reniform-cordate leaves on long footstalks, and numbers of flowering and non-flowering stems which at first lie along the ground but become erect in their upper half or two thirds, ultimately reaching a height of four to six inches. The shoots bear numerous linear or narrowly lanceolate leaves, always sessile and more or less ciliate, the lowest ones sometimes very slightly toothed, and the flowering shoots terminate in a single large flower or a loose raceme of up to six flowers on long hair-like pedicels. The calyx segments are very long, often nearly as long as the corolla itself, very slender and well spread out, while the corolla is a full bell shape and of a rich purple-blue colour. A pale form may be met with from time to time but the pure white form is distinctly rare. The trifid style is nearly as long as the corolla and both buds and seed capsules are pendent.

In habit and general appearance it is difficult to distinguish it from some forms of the common *C. rotundifolia*, of which it may well be the alpine development, or prototype, but there are a number of distinguishing characters which persist when the plant is brought into cultivation and justify, in my view, the specific rank which is here accorded. The more important of these are the pendent buds, the excessively long calyx segments and style, the completely sessile stem leaves (in *C. rotundifolia* the lower stem leaves are generally reduced to a short petiole) and the decumbent nature of the lower part of the flowering stems. In addition, the corolla is more rounded at the base than in typical *C. rotundifolia* and there is rather more tendency for the root leaves to persist during the summer. With its dwarfed habit and strongly coloured flowers it is a very desirable addition to any rock garden.

A single-flowered form with calyx segments practically equal in length to the corolla was given specific rank as *C. scheuchzeri* by Villars in 1786 but this is not now generally accepted and *scheuchzeri* should be reduced to a varietal name only.

C. linnaeifolia. Occurring in swampy places along the coast of California, this does not seem to be a very attractive species. It is perennial, making a slender roughish stem four to twelve inches high sometimes

CAMPANULA LASIOCARPA

CAMPANULA LATIFOLIA

119

CAMPANULA LINIFOLIA

CAMPANULA LOEFFLINGII

CAMPANULA LONGESTYLA

121

CAMPANULA LYRATA

CAMPANULA MACROSTYLA

slightly branched at the summit and bearing ovate-oblong, crenulate leaves up to an inch long, sub-sessile or sessile and with rough hairy margins. The few solitary flowers, pale blue in colour, are about half an inch long and borne on long footstalks.

C. loefflingii. Common throughout Spain, Portugal and parts of North-West Africa, this species grows in all sandy places. From a tuft of small petiolate, ovate-spathulate dentate leaves spring numerous thin leafy much-branched stems, the leaves on which become lanceolate and sessile, or even sub-amplexicaul, towards the top. The flowers are borne on long thin branches from the leaf axils and are bright violet-blue with a white base both internally and externally; the calyx is smooth with long acuminate segments, erect at first but later reflexed. The corolla is funnel-shaped, but the well-reflexed, pointed lobes give a starry effect. The trifid style is considerably shorter than the corolla and the species belongs to that section of the genus in which dehiscence of the capsule occurs near the top. The height of the plant rarely exceeds four inches and with its free-growing habit reminds one somewhat of the well-known bedding Lobelia, and though, like all the annual Campanulas, its flowering period is short, it is one of the most attractive of the section.

The species varies considerably according to the conditions of soil, shade, etc., in which it grows. The plant known as *C. lusitanica* is now merged into this species and that sometimes seen as *C. broussonetiana* is another sub-form. The illustration is of this latter form but such differences as there are between this form and the type are of botanical interest only. Still another form, with greyish leaves, is sometimes referred to as var. *occidentalis*.

Like all the annuals it is easily raised from seed sown where it is required to bloom, and it is often better if sown in the autumn or allowed to reproduce itself from self-sown seeds.

C. longestyla. Another biennial from the Caucasus, occurring near the eastern end of the Black Sea, and closely related to *C. sibirica.*

A woody rootstock forms one or more rosettes of thick rough ovate (sometimes sub-cordate) obscurely toothed leaves, the lower of which taper downwards to a petiole while those on the stems are sessile, entire and more or less amplexicaul. The flower stems which are said sometimes to reach a height of three feet but are more usually about eighteen inches, branch loosely from the base and bear racemes of large dark blue nodding flowers, which are generally slightly hairy.

The calyx is rough and rigid with lanceolate segments which are smooth, apart from the ciliate margins and noticeably spreading, while the rounded ciliate appendages, with revolute edges, are turned down close to the calyx tube which they rather exceed in length, The drooping corolla is of full campanulate form rather longer than broad with broad reflexed lobes about a third of its length. It bulges at the base, is somewhat constricted above the middle and is smooth externally though more or less bearded within. The club-shaped style is generally sufficiently longer than the corolla to justify the specific name but there seems to be a good deal of variation in this character.

The species presents a problem in classification as there may be three, four, or five stigmata and it is difficult to say which is the normal number.

An Award of Merit was bestowed on the species in 1907.

C. lostrittii, Ten. An Italian species which, in general appearance, resembles *C. rotundifolia*, having rotund sub-cordate basal leaves on very long petioles and numerous thin smooth erect or ascendant stems with few leaves and branched in the upper part. Calyx segments are filiform and spreading and as long as the funnel-shaped corolla, which is lobed nearly halfway and carried erect, this providing the main distinction from *C. rotundifolia*.

C. lourica. A small and unimportant species from Northern Persia where it forms close mats of small rosettes of narrowly oblong, entire leaves. Short thin decumbent stems two to three inches long are dichotomously branched, bear a few oblong sessile leaves and three or four small flowers on long flexible hairlike stalks. The calyx segments are scarcely longer than the calyx tube itself and rather more than half as long as the tubular corolla. The whole plant is densely covered with grey wool.

C. luristanica. An insignificant little perennial species from rocky districts in Western Persia which produces a number of thin flexible stems about six inches high, freely branched from the base, each branch terminating in a few small flowers. The leaves are ovate-cordate with angular teeth and have thin petioles nearly as long as the blade. The calyx is without appendages and has spreading triangular acuminate segments about a third the length of the narrow funnel-shaped corolla which itself is not more than a quarter of an inch long. The style is rather longer than the corolla tube and divides into three recurved stigmata.

C. lyrata, Lam. A very ill-defined Grecian species which is said to have been introduced into cultivation as long ago as 1797.

The thick root, which according to De Candolle should be perennial but seems generally to be monocarpic, produces a rosette or cluster of rosettes of greyish tomentose lyrate leaves which are attractively crimped or undulate. The lyrations are more or less equal in size and though the terminal lobe is generally the largest there is nothing like the difference in this respect that is found in the closely allied *C. rupestris*, while the length of the lyrations is such that the full outline of the leaf is practically oblong and often as much as three inches long. Each rosette puts forth an ascendant branched stem bearing a few smaller leaves which are sessile, obovate and crenate and at flowering time becomes a long, more or less one-sided panicle of erect tubular flowers which are generally rather darker and more campanulate (or, more precisely, with spreading instead of erect corolla lobes) than in *C. rupestris*.

The hairy calyx has reflexed pointed segments broad at the base, while the pointed and reflexed appendages are small, in fact often considerably shorter than the calyx tube. The style, equal to the corolla in length, divides into five short stigmata.

Dr. Giuseppi throws doubt on its absolute hardiness, but I have carried plants of all sizes through the winter without loss, the only protection being a sheet of glass to ward off excessive rain—a precaution I consider worth while with all these woolly or hairy species, which are far more liable to rot off than to be injured by frost. There is, however, no doubt that the safest and best place for the species is the alpine house where, given a fairly rich soil, well drained by a plentiful admixture of stone (preferably limestone) chips and a good sized pot or deep pan, it will be one of the most attractive occupants of the house not only in flower but for its rosettes during earlier stages of its life.

Seed provides the only means of increase but can generally be raised without difficulty.

For the near allies of this species see p. 218.

C. macrochlamys. A rather coarse monocarpic species from Armenia which makes a tuft of ovate-rotund, entire leaves on long petioles and sends up thickish channelled stems four to six feet high, generally unbranched, covered with long hairs and furnished with numerous broadly oblong leaves which become sessile and even sub-amplexicaul in the upper part. The stems terminate in a large but close head of sessile flowers surrounded by broad oblong bracts which exceed the flowers in length. The flowers themselves have a tubular corolla more than twice the length of the lanceolate calyx segments, which are smooth apart from a margin of long hairs.

C. macrorrhiza. This species from the French Riviera, mainly in the neighbourhood of Nice, has a saxatile habit and a thick perennial rootstock which pushes itself into rock crevices. It produces a tuft of small stalked leaves which are round, more or less cordate, and dentate, and a

number of erect or ascendant smooth, sometimes branched, stems up to
a foot high. As with so many species the stem leaves differ from the basal
ones being ovate-acute and shortly petioled near the base, becoming narrower, more pointed, and sessile in the upper part. The stems are many-
flowered, the individual flowers being showy and borne singly on thin
fairly long pedicels. Buds, flowers and capsules are erect. The calyx is
smooth and without appendages and the long pointed segments are well
spread and about half the length of the broad, open-bell-shaped corolla
which has short well reflexed lobes. The style equals the corolla in length
and is trifid.

At a casual glance the species resembles *C. rotundifolia*, but, apart from
the non-running nature of the rootstock, it is readily distinguished from
that species by its habit of carrying the seed capsule, as well as the buds,
erect; the flowers too are much more nearly erect than in the better known
species. Propagation is best from seed.

C. macrostyla. The home of this species is Asia Minor where it forms
an erect, bushy plant some nine or ten inches high. The leaves are irregularly placed on the stems, are somewhat small for the size of the plant
and are ovate to lanceolate, sessile or sub-amplexicaul and slightly serrate.
The branching flower stems, like the leaves, are bristly and bear terminal
and axillary erect flowers, usually singly on stout pedicels. The calyx is
very prominent with segments nearly as long as the corolla, broad at the
base but narrowing suddenly to a point; revolute ciliate margins unite at
the base into conspicuous appendages, the edges of which roll outwards
and form a knob-like end which is almost a pouch. The large corolla (up
to two and a half inches in diameter) is very broad and open, usually white
with heavy reticulations of purple without and dull purple within; the
lobes are very broad, short and acute. The long style, which gives the
species its name, is almost twice the length of the corolla, brown and
knobbed or spindle-shaped until the three stigmata part and roll backwards on themselves. The whole flower in fact looks like nothing more
than an inverted umbrella and is really more fascinating than beautiful.
The capsule dehisces near the base. Its general appearance is, in fact, so
distinct from other Campanulas that one writer (Feer) suggested that a
new genus (*Sicyocodon*) should be created for it.

It is an annual and must be raised from seed which, however, must be
fresh or it is liable to lie dormant for a year.

C. mairei. Although recognised by some botanists as a separate
species, this plant, which is native to slopes of the Great Atlas, seems to
be no more than a Moroccan form of the Spanish *C. herminii*, from which

it differs only by its more flexible stems and its much smaller and narrower flowers.

C. makaschvilii. A Caucasian species which produces tufts of grey-green leaves, deeply cordate, acute and on petioles sometimes as much as six inches long. Erect slightly hairy stems from ten to twenty inches high spring from the tuft; they bear similar but more shortly stalked leaves, are branched in the upper half and carry narrowly campanulate flowers an inch or so long on short drooping pedicels. The lanceolate calyx segments are half the length of the corolla and there are short oblong appendages. The flower is said to be rose coloured. It resembles *C. alliariifolia* but is a smaller, less hairy, plant with shorter calyx segments and appendages.

C. malacitana, Herv. This species occurs in rocky limestone crevices in South-East Spain, forming clusters of rosettes of small oval or spathulate leaves of whitish velvet, from among which are produced the slender spreading inflorescences. These are frail and hug the surface of the rock for support; they may grow to some six inches in length, bear a few leaves similar to those of the rosette and are more or less branched. As will be seen from the illustration the flowers are freely produced and are carried erect on short footstalks; they are small, but of good bell shape with nicely reflexed lobes; after fertilisation the seed capsule assumes a more or less pendent position. The colour is generally a rather light blue with an almost white throat. The calyx is furnished with minute awl-shaped appendages while the style is trifid. This character clearly distinguishes it from the species described by De Candolle, Farrer and Col. Beddome as *C. mollis* (and illustrated under that name in the *Bot. Mag.* at t. 404) which was grouped by Linnaeus among those in which the style divides into five. There is a close relationship with *C. filicaulis*.

Minor variants have been recorded, including one from Gibraltar (var. *gibraltarica*) in which the calyx is glabrous, but I have been unable to trace any justification for the appellation 'minor' which is sometimes applied to the form in cultivation.

The species is fairly long lived in any well drained soil, though a little protection from winter wet is appreciated. Seed provides the best, if not the only, means of increase.

C. mardinensis. A small perennial plant from Mesopotamia which is covered with whitish hairs. It makes a dense mat from which fragile flexible decumbent stems are emitted. The basal leaves die off before flowering time but the stems carry broadly ovate or rotund leaves cut into two or three pointed lobes, the terminal one being much the largest. They are shortly petiolate and, as is usual, get smaller towards the top.

The stems bear short branches terminating in one to three flowers on thin hairlike stalks. These flowers are very small (much smaller than those of *C. cymbalaria* to which the species is nearly related) and of a narrow funnel shape, lobed to about a third their length. The narrowly lanceolate calyx segments are densely hairy and about half as long as the corolla.

C. massalskyi. From rocky places in the mountains of Russian Armenia, in similar situations to the closely allied *C. choziatowskyi*, this species forms a thick perennial root which spreads slowly, forming a tangle of short stiff branches which terminate in rosettes of small pubescent thickish leaves, the lower ones being ovate-rotund and petiolate. The stem leaves are ovate-cordate and shortly petiolate and all are irregularly dentate and undulate, bright green and velvety on their upper surfaces and grey tomentose below. The thin flexible trailing flower stems bear a few small axillary and terminal flowers on more or less long stalks. The calyx segments are broadly triangular, acute and velvety, while the small appendages are scarcely reflexed; the corolla, narrowly tubular-funnel-shaped, is also more or less tomentose and three or four times as long as the calyx segments. The style is trifid and shorter than the corolla tube.

C. medium. This biennial species, the ever-popular Canterbury Bell, is really too well known to need description. Its original home is generally given as Southern Europe where it occurs in stony places among calcareous rocks but it is so showy and has been in cultivation wherever there are gardens for so long that in many of its reported localities it is doubtfully indigenous. It is certainly not a Swiss species and reports of its occurrence, as a native species, in Italy may almost certainly be discounted and the probability is that it really belongs to the Eastern Pyrenees and the hilly country immediately to the north and south thereof.

In its first year it forms a large rosette of roughish, ovate-lanceolate, or lanceolate, crenate-dentate, leaves generally without distinct petioles. In its second season this develops into a strong erect, branched and leafy stem, which in cultivation in rich soil may reach a height of three feet, but in nature is little more than half this. The large bell-shaped flowers, somewhat inflated at the base and nearly two inches long, are borne terminally and in the leaf axils both on the main stem and on the branches and as the latter commence near the ground level, fall away well from the main stem and may be nearly as long as it is tall, if given sufficient room, the whole inflorescence forms a definite flowery pyramid. The flowers themselves are carried on comparatively long bracted peduncles, usually in threes, though singly in nature, and are sub-erect, though the buds are fully erect and the capsules pendent. The calyx segments are triangular-acuminate, not reflexed, and only about a quarter the length of the corolla, while the appendages are shorter but broader and reflexed on to the calyx tube. Both segments and appendages are ciliate, while the rest of the plant varies in degree of hairiness. The style, somewhat shorter than the corolla, terminates in five stigmata.

Many colour forms are available, in shades of purple, pink and white; double forms in most of the colours occur and there is an abnormal form —known as var. *calycanthema*, or 'cup and saucer'—in which an additional, flattened, more or less irregularly lobed, corolla surrounds the base of the bell. This form is also available in most of the shades. Most of these colours and forms will come very reasonably true from seed, and a number of them received Awards of Merit in 1929.

C. michauxioides. A perennial with tall erect branched stems which are leafy in the lower part but almost bare above. The lowest leaves are rotund, deeply cordate, dentate, on very long petioles, the remainder smaller, oblong and on shorter petioles. The flowers are generally solitary at the ends of the branches and, being on very short recurved stalks, the whole inflorescence takes the form of a loose hanging panicle. The ex-appendiculate calyx is shortly obconical and has narrow smooth awl-shaped segments about twice the length of the calyx tube and half that of the corolla. The latter is rotate, divided almost to the base into much reflexed narrow lanceolate lobes. The style divides into five stigmata. With its deeply divided corolla it may well be that this species should properly be included in the genus *Asyneuma* and not in Campanula at all.

C. microdonta. A Japanese species which has not, so far as I can trace, been introduced into this country. It forms a tuft of ovate acute leaves some three inches long which are smooth, membraneous, unequally crenate-dentate and on fairly long winged petioles. Smooth unbranched erect stems rise to a height of one or two feet with similar leaves becoming smaller and almost sessile near the top. The flowers are borne in small clusters on short stalks in the upper leaf axils. The smooth obconical calyx has short appendages and broadly triangular lanceolate segments not more than a quarter the length of the corolla; the latter is an inch or more in length with short triangular acute lobes. The style, which is shorter than the corolla, is trilobed. It would seem to be closely related to *C. punctata*, which is a native of the same district.

C. minsteriana. A plant from Azerbaijan which is described as having a four-parted calyx and, therefore, not properly a Campanula, though referred, doubtfully, to the appendiculate, trilocular section. Without further evidence the name cannot be accepted as valid.

C. mirabilis. A Caucasian species which, like so many, is monocarpic and unfortunately may keep us waiting several years before reaching flowering size. However, in the case of this species the reward is ample. It forms a large flat rosette eight or nine inches across, of dark green broadly oval fleshy leaves which are smooth and glossy, serrate, diminishing to a winged petiole and furnished with a row of stiff translucent hairs round the margin.

In fullness of time this develops into a flower stem up to fifteen inches in length (usually not more than nine inches) with alternate leaves similar to those of the rosette but sessile and at the extremity of the stem amplexicaul. From the leaf axils short branches are produced each carrying one to four erect stalked flowers, broadly and fully campanulate and usually of a pale lilac blue colour. The calyx segments and appendages are, like the leaves, glossy and provided with a marginal row of hairs; they are triangular in shape, the segments being about a quarter the length of the corolla and the appendages the same length as the calyx tube. The corolla is one and a half to two inches in length and when the lobes, which are about one third the length of the tube are fully recurved the open flower may measure as much as two inches across. The style is rather shorter than the fully open flower and terminates in a tripartite stigma.

Seeds of course provide the only means of propagation, but are freely produced and germinate without difficulty. Moraine treatment has been recommended, but such a starvation diet will never allow the plant to be seen at its best. A far more suitable position is in a fairly wide vertical crevice between two rocks, where it can get its roots into good rich soil behind while keeping its neck comparatively dry. It is also one of the most worthwhile species for pot culture.

The species obtained a First Class Certificate in 1898.

C. modesta differs from *C. aristata* in being generally dwarfer and more erect and in having shorter calyx segments. It would seem to be merely a local variant from the more easterly area of distribution of that species.

C. moesiaca. A biennial from sub-alpine meadows throughout the Balkans which forms large rosettes of oblong serrate leaves which are hairy above and more densely so on the lower surfaces. They diminish suddenly into winged petioles. From among these leaves rise erect, softly hairy stems terminating in a head of many flowers, while similar but smaller heads spring from the upper leaf axils. The upper leaves become gradually narrower with shorter petioles, and ultimately sessile. The individual flowers are an inch or more long and much longer than the calyx segments which are triangular-lanceolate. It appears to be very similar to *C. glomerata* and *C. transsilvanica*.

CAMPANULA MALACITANA

CAMPANULA MEDIUM

131

CAMPANULA MOESIACA

133

CAMPANULA MORETTIANA

C. mollis, L. From limestone rocks of Southern Europe and other places around the Mediterranean basin, this species has spathulate shortly petiolate leaves an inch to an inch and a half long of a velvety texture covered with silvery white hairs and forming a rosette. These leaves have entire or sub-sinuate margins as have also the stem leaves which, however, are sub-orbicular and sessile and become smaller towards the ends of the stems. Several decumbent fragile stems arise from the rosette, grow to about six inches in length, and bear, towards their ends, a few erect flowers on long stalks.

The calyx has long erect arrow-shaped segments and short awl-shaped appendages. The campanulate corolla, about half an inch across and considerably longer than the calyx segments, is of varying shades of blue but fades to white in the throat, while the nerves are outlined by an intensification of the colour. The spreading lobes, nearly half the corolla in length, are ovate-acute. The style is as long as the corolla tube and divides into five filiform stigmata.

There should be no difficulty in distinguishing this species from *C. isophylla*, some form of which has for long been in cultivation under the name of *C. mollis*. The shape of the leaves is very different and *C. isophylla* is without calyx appendages. *C. malacitana* is much closer in general appearance but has a trifid style and is, on the whole, a smaller plant. A distinction from both the species with which it is confused is that the capsule of the true *C. mollis* is fully pendent when mature.

The above relates to the plant described by Linnaeus under this name but there is considerable doubt whether in fact such a plant, with its five-partite style, actually exists. Certainly it is not, at present, in cultivation in this country.

C. monocephala. A perennial with a creeping root and numerous slightly rough, erect, unbranched and densely leafy stems four to six inches high terminating in a small head of sub-sessile erect flowers. The lower stem leaves are oblong-elliptical, obtuse or rounded at the apex and narrowing at the base though scarcely petiolate; the upper ones are narrower and sessile, while all are more or less dentate. The head of flowers is surrounded by broadly ovate amplexicaul bracts almost as long as the flowers themselves. The calyx has oblong lanceolate segments as long as the corolla which is smooth, almost an inch long, tubular-campanulate, deeply lobed and longer than the style. It closely resembles *C. involucrata* and may well be merely a local variant of that species though the calyx is said to have *very small* appendages.

C. monodiana. A new species from the Atlas which is perennial

G

and grows about six inches high. It forms rosettes of small obovate leaves narrowing at the base and more or less obtuse at the apex. These rosettes later develop into short thin erect stems which terminate in solitary erect flowers less than half an inch long. The broadly obconical calyx has narrowly lanceolate segments about half as long as the corolla and triangular ciliate appendages as long as the calyx tube itself. The corolla form is narrowly campanulate, lobed to about one third its length, the lobes being oblong acute and furnished with a few hairs at the apex. The style is rather longer than the corolla and is trifid. After fertilisation the capsule becomes pendent. It appears to be related to the Abyssinian *C. rigidipila* but is altogether a smaller plant.

C. montana. This name is mentioned only by Delarb and, as no description is given, cannot be accepted.

C. morettiana. This somewhat rare and very desirable species comes from limestone cliffs of Southern Tyrol and Dalmatia. Even there it is far from common and is always strictly saxatile, selecting almost inaccessible crevices for its home.

It forms tufts of tiny short-stemmed, ivy-shaped leaves with three dentations on each side. The stem leaves are almost circular and entire and the whole plant is grey with soft fine hairs. Short sub-erect flower stems, two or three inches high, bear usually only a single but large erect flower. The calyx segments are broad, ciliate and spreading, longer than the calyx tube and one quarter the length of the corolla; the latter is violet-blue, broadly funnel-shaped and with well reflexed lobes about one third the length of the bell. At the end of each lobe is a small tuft of hairs. The style, about as long as the corolla, is tripartite. Although one of the smallest members of the genus it is one of the most attractive and is closely allied to *C. raineri*.

Unfortunately it is far from easy to grow; a limestone crevice is its native haunt and Mr. Clarence Elliott recommends a deep hole in a tufa boulder. In any case it is not normally long lived and seed should be carefully saved and sown as soon as ripe, or cuttings taken of non-flowering shoots during late summer.

The species received an Award of Merit in 1932 and the white form was similarly honoured in 1934.

C. multiflora, Waldst. & Kit. A Hungarian species which is of biennial duration only and very similar in general appearance to *C. spicata*.

Tufts of broadly lanceolate leaves, four or five inches long and an inch broad, sessile, sinuate and hairy, prepare the way for erect, ribbed unbranched stems which may reach a height of three feet. The stems carry leaves similar to the basal ones but smaller and bract-like and sessile flowers in clusters in the leaf axils to form a compound spike. The clusters themselves are bracted and consist of a varying number of flowers, Among the clusters are ovate-acute bracts which are ciliate and externally hairy; the calyx has linear-lanceolate, obtuse segments, ciliate and erect; the tubular-funnel-shaped corolla is smooth, twice as long as the calyx segments and has ovate-acute lobes more or less reflexed. The style is rather shorter than the corolla and divides into three short stigmata. The extra number of flowers in each cluster, which is one of the characters which distinguish this species from *C. spicata*, would make it more showy and probably more worth growing, if it be admitted that any of these 'rat-tail' species merits a place in the garden, but I do not know that it is in cultivation. As a biennial, it would need to be raised from seed.

C. murrayana. This species forms a tuft of deeply cordate circular leaves on long petioles and prostrate stems up to eighteen inches long. The flowers are borne singly on long footstalks but crowded towards the ends of the stems. The flowers themselves are small, dark blue, and shortly campanulate with long narrow lobes, while the calyx also has linear lanceolate segments. It does not appear to be in cultivation and very little is known about it.

C. muscosa. Although this name appears in some books on the genus, no complete description has been published and the name cannot, accordingly, be accepted as valid.

C. mycalaea (or mykaliana). Growing on calcareous rocks in Mykali, Asia Minor, this species is said to be perennial though as it is closely allied to *C. ephesia* and others of the *lyrata-rupestris* group it is more likely to prove monocarpic. It does not, however, produce a central erect stem.

No description of the basal leaves is available (the plant is not in cultivation) but it produces a number of fragile, prostrate or ascendant stems furnished with ash-coloured leaves which are ovate-obtuse or spathulate and sinuate-dentate, the lower ones being on fairly long petioles, the upper ones sessile. Large solitary erect flowers on short pedicels arise terminally and in the upper leaf axils. The broadly oval calyx appendages are longer than the calyx tube itself; the broadly lanceolate-acuminate and ciliate segments are half the length of the corolla and not reflexed, while the corolla itself is widely campanulate, somewhat inflated at the base and has short broad recurved lobes. The style divides into five and is slightly exserted, this being the principal distinction from the nearest of the allied species.

C. myrtifolia, Boiss. A small perennial species from rock fissures in the Caucasus which is not very distinct from *C. trichopoda*. The plant is softly hairy throughout and has numerous short hairy erect and leafy stems bearing small ovate or ovate-oblong sessile leaves and three to five flowers terminally on short stalks. The tubular corolla has short blunt lobes which scarcely spread open; the calyx segments are not more than a third the length of the corolla. The whole plant seldom exceeds two inches in height.

The *Index Kewensis* makes it synonymous with *Trachelium myrtifolium*.

C. nitida. See *C. persicifolia*.

C. odontosepala. A perennial species from woods of Eastern Transcaucasia at elevations of about 4,000 feet. It has smooth, flexible but erect unbranched stems and soft smooth leaves which are ovate-oblong, acuminate, sub-cordate and petiolate. The flowers are in ones and twos on short recurved pedicels in the leaf axils. The calyx segments are linear, spreading or reflexed, denticulate and slightly ciliate, while the campanulate corolla, three times as long as the calyx segments, is lobed to a third of its length and bearded within.

C. oliveri, Rouy and Gautier. A rough, dwarf plant, probably only biennial, from the Eastern Pyrenees and not in cultivation. It has a thin, fibrous root and a very short stem on which the leaves are much congested. These leaves are oblong-lanceolate, the lower ones being gradually reduced to large sheathing petioles, while the upper ones, equally obtuse, are amplexicaul and all are crenulate and ciliate. There are one or two flowers on short rough stalks. The lanceolate calyx segments are about three-quarters the length of the campanulate corolla and there are small lanceolate appendages. It is allied to *C. alpina* and, though described as very distinct from that species, may well be only a dwarfed or local form. Bonnier, however, regards it as a sub-species of *C. speciosa*.

C. olympica. A short-lived perennial from the lower slopes of Mount Olympus, in Bithynia, which produces thin stolons ending in rosettes of elliptic, obtuse, crenulate leaves on long petioles and erect flexible unbranched stems about a foot high. These stems are furnished with oblong obtuse leaves in their lower portions and lanceolate acute ones in the upper parts, all stem leaves being sessile. They terminate in a cluster of three to five stalked flowers. The calyx is ex-appendiculate and has rigid spreading linear segments, while the shortly campanulate corolla is divided to a third its length into well-reflexed lobes. The capsule is carried erect and dehisces at the apex. It is closely related to *C. abietina* (q.v.).

C. orbelica. A Balkan species which forms a basal tuft of leaves which are linear, entire, sessile and ciliate and produces its flowers singly on longish stems up to two and a half inches long each with two or three alternate leaves similar to the basal ones. The calyx has lanceolate, acuminate, ciliate, erect segments and very small appendages closely adpressed to the calyx tube. The bell-shaped corolla has very short triangular lobes, lilac-blue in colour, smooth apart from a few hairs at the tips of the lobes and internally at the base of the bell. The style is trifid.

C. oreadum. Another of the many attractive species whose home is in Greece, this is closely akin to the rather better known *C. rupicola*; in fact, Dr. Giuseppi says 'it only differs from *C. rupicola* in having smooth edged leaves.' The leaves of the basal tuft are oblong-spathulate and obtuse, diminishing to a petiole and grey with soft hairs, while those of the trailing stems are sessile and lanceolate-acute. All leaves are without any toothing which serves to distinguish the species from most others of the group. The thin hairy flower stems with only a few small leaves often carry as many as five flowers on fairly long peduncles, though three is the more usual number, and the plant builds up a loose pyramid four or five inches high.

The calyx segments, which are not reflexed, are lanceolate and very hairy, three or four times as long as the calyx tube and, like the leaves, devoid of any toothing; they terminate in a noticeably inward-pointing hook. The appendages are also hairy, small and shorter than the tube. The corolla is large, bell-shaped (in some forms perhaps rather narrow) much longer than the calyx segments with triangular, acuminate, reflexed lobes, smooth and generally of a rich violet-purple. The style divides into three stigmata.

Another rigidly saxatile species which can only be expected to succeed wedged into a limestone crevice or possibly on a limestone scree. Seed probably presents the only means of increase but the species is now very rare in cultivation in this country. A.M. 1940.

C. orphanidea. A Grecian species of limited distribution which is akin to *C. andrewsii* and others of the *C. rupestris* aggregate.

It forms rosettes of lanceolate, somewhat undulate, leaves, broad and sub-cordate at the base, softly downy and greyish and on long footstalks. The hairs on the petioles are described as translucent. The inflorescence consists of a central spike and a number of procumbent stems radiating from the base of the rosette. All these stems bear hairy strap-shaped sessile leaves and branches, usually one-flowered, from the leaf axils. The flowers themselves are borne erect on long peduncles, are intense violet-purple in colour, tubular-campanulate in shape, and slightly hairy with well reflexed lobes half their length. The calyx segments are narrow, pointed, entire,

reflexed, and rather more than one third the length of the corolla, while
the appendages are very small, less, in fact, that the calyx tube. There
should be five stigmata, but one, or even two, frequently abort, a characteristic which, as mentioned elsewhere, is not uncommon among these
Grecian species.

The species is definitely monocarpic, but seed is freely produced and
germinates freely and the plant presents few difficulties in cultivation provided the soil is well drained and a sheet of glass is used to ward off excessive rain in winter, a precaution which most growers adopt almost
automatically with woolly leaved plants. It also makes a very good plant
for pot work, given a fairly deep pot instead of the more usual rather
shallow pan.

C. paniculata, Turra. Reported as a native of the Rhaetian and Julian
Alps, this plant is said to be perennial with smooth, lanceolate, serrate
leaves and linear, entire ones on the weak branched stems. With such a
brief description the name cannot be accepted as valid.

C. papillosa. A perennial species which inhabits limestone rocks in
various parts of Greece, forming a mat of short more or less rhizomatous
roots ending in rosettes of shortly stalked oblong spathulate and crenate
leaves. The short flower stems are single flowered and both stems and
flowers are densely covered with transparent hairs. The calyx is more or
less hairy and has bluntly oblong segments, about as long as the calyx
itself, and short appendages. The corolla, though twice as long as the
calyx, is, itself, not above half an inch long.

C. parryi. A species of comparatively recent introduction from the
Rocky Mountains, where it is said to have a very wide altitudinal range
from 5,000 to 12,000 feet. From a running root it produces small tufts of
strap shaped leaves, which are coarsely dentate, and thin trailing stems
bearing similar leaves and large lavender-blue flowers either singly or in
clusters of two or three on long pedicels in the leaf axils. The calyx segments are linear-lanceolate, entire and not reflexed, they are about the
same length as the long capsule and rather more than half the length of
the corolla. The latter is shallow campanulate or sub-rotate, lobed to nearly
half its length, the lobes being rounded acuminate. The style, which is
blue and not exserted, is trifid and the whole flower, including the calyx,
is quite smooth. Like a large proportion of American species, the capsule
dehisces near the top.

The species is still rare in cultivation, but when available should make
a good plant for hanging over a wall as it runs very freely in any light soil
and is perfectly hardy. As with so many, particularly of the rarer species,

it seems to have a remarkable attraction for slugs. Seed is freely produced and this gives the best means of increase as the long runners do not seem to take kindly to separation from the parent plant and transplant badly.

C. patula. This species, which occurs rarely in Great Britain, is common throughout Central and Southern Europe, where it grows on rough banks and in light woodland. It is of biennial duration only, forming during the first year a close rosette of smooth, oblong-lanceolate leaves, slightly dentate and sessile. In its second year the leaves of the rosette lengthen and become distinctly petiolate, while from the centre arises, to a height of eighteen inches or two feet, a slender stem (occasionally more than one), wiry, striated and much branched, generally smooth and furnished with occasional linear toothed sessile leaves and terminating in a loose panicle of long-stemmed flowers which, though actually funnel-shaped, are lobed to half of their length and have the general appearance of wide, full-rayed stars, held rigidly erect. The obconical calyx tube is generally smooth while the reflexing segments are fully half the length of the corolla and drawn out into a fine point. The style is not conspicuously long and divides into three while the capsule dehisces at the apex. The flowers are in varying shades of blue-purple (a white form is sometimes met) and the plant, which is easily raised from seed, or allowed to grow from self-sown seedlings, is both showy and graceful.

The species varies considerably within its wide geographical range and its relationship to allied species is dealt with under *C. abietina* (on p. 31).

C. pelia. A species, unfortunately monocarpic, from Thessaly which has only recently been introduced into cultivation in this country. It forms a basal rosette of regularly lyrate leaves densely clothed with grey (almost white) wool and in due time emits numerous prostrate radiating stems six to eight inches long and an erect central one about the same length. The stem leaves are sub-sessile to sessile, ovate, obtuse and sharply dentate and the flowers are carried erect, terminally and in the upper leaf axils either singly or on few-flowered branchlets. The broadly triangular spreading calyx segments are furnished with two or three prominent toothlike excrescences on each side, but the appendages are merely small pointed projections. The long tubular corolla, well over an inch long, is nearly four times as long as the calyx segments and is lobed for one third its length, the pointed lobes not being much recurved. The style is as long as the corolla tube and is trifid.

The validity of the name is perhaps doubtful. Hayek regards it as a sub-species of *C. andrewsii* (which, however, has a five-partite style), while Beauverd says it is synonymous with *C. thessala*. The name first appears on the authority of Haussknecht & Sintenis but without, so far as I can trace, any description, but the authorities of the Herbarium at Kew accept both the name and the specific rank.

Award of Merit 1950.

C. pelviformis. An endemic Cretan species (and rare even there) which, with its five-celled capsule and five-partite style, is clearly a near relation of the Canterbury Bell (*C. medium*) and, like that species, biennial.

The basal leaves are ovate-acute, serrate, and rather rough and greyish, and diminish to distinct channelled petioles which are not lyrate; the upper stem leaves are sessile but otherwise similar. A number of hairy ascendant stems, about a foot long, are produced and these are generally unbranched, bearing the flowers terminally and singly in the leaf axils, though the topmost ones are sometimes in clusters of three. The segments of the calyx are ovate-acuminate, reflexed and three times as long as the calyx tube, while the large ovate-rotund appendages are almost the same length. As will be seen from the photograph the large bell-shaped corolla, inflated at the middle, is short for its width and in fact makes a rather clumsy-looking flower. The style is about the same length as the corolla and the five stigmata are filiform and markedly revolute.

The species is not readily obtainable and care must be taken to distinguish it from a plant frequently offered under the same name which is merely a form of *C. carpatica* with flatter flowers than the type. If obtained it presents no difficulties in cultivation given the usual treatment of a biennial plant.

C. peregrina. A tall, rather second-rate border biennial from Palestine which makes rosettes of bluntly ovate-spathulate, irregularly crenate and wrinkled leaves, as much as four inches long, on short petioles. The flower stems, two or three feet high, are unbranched, dark and rather bristly and bear a number of ovate-acute sessile or sub-amplexicaul leaves and a dense spike of nearly sessile flowers in the upper half, the flowers being borne singly in each of the leaf axils.

The calyx segments are short, broad at the base but suddenly pointed, ciliate and less than half as long as the corolla; the margins are revolute and *almost* produced into appendages. The corolla itself is broad funnel-shaped, in fact rather flattish, with broad but short well displayed lobes; there is a certain hairiness inside the bell, but externally it is quite smooth and the central nerve is very prominent. It is deep violet at the centre but pales towards the margin. The style is somewhat shorter than the corolla and is deeply trifid, the lower part being white in contrast with the flower. The capsule is erect and dehiscence is apical.

CAMPANULA OREADUM

CAMPANULA ORPHANIDEA

CAMPANULA PARRYI

CAMPANULA PATULA

CAMPANULA PELIA

145

CAMPANULA PELVIFORMIS

CAMPANULA PERSICIFOLIA

146

It is closely allied to *C. primulaefolia* and, in fact, by some botanists is regarded as synonymous, but the early basal leaves and unbranched stems provide clear means of separation. A further distinction is that in *C. peregrina* the flowers are darkest in the centre, whereas in *C. primulaefolia* the deepest colouration is on the margins.

It is easily raised from seed which frequently sows itself more whole-heartedly than is desired. It is said to prefer moist positions in nature.

It received an Award of Merit in 1903 and is figured in the *Bot. Mag.* at t. 1257.

C. perpusilla. From Persia, this species is very closely allied to *C. humillima* and may, indeed, be only a form of that species. As described it differs in bearing its flowers singly and in having a cylindrical corolla and a somewhat shorter style. I cannot find that it has ever been in cultivation, nor does it seem worth introducing.

C. persepolitana seems to be another form of the foregoing.

C. persicifolia. This species, which is widely distributed throughout the whole of Southern Europe, is one of the most desirable plants for the herbaceous border, though not suitable for the rock garden. It is said to have been cultivated since 1596, when it was mentioned by Gerarde in his *Herbal.* It occurs generally in light sub-alpine woodland and shady places and the fibrous, stoloniferous rootstock forms clumps of rosettes of long, smooth, oblong or lanceolate leaves which are slightly but regularly serrate and diminish gradually to a footstalk. The erect unbranched flower stems rise to a height of two to three feet and bear throughout the greater part of their length linear-lanceolate sessile leaves and broadly campanulate flowers in the leaf axils, either singly or in short racemes of three to five with short, broadly ovate lobes. The calyx segments are narrow, pointed and entire, about half the length of the corolla and sub-erect. The style, which equals the corolla in length, is trifid almost half way; the capsule is erect and this is one of the comparatively small number of species in which the pores of dehiscence are practically at the top of the capsule.

There are numerous forms with single, double or semi-double flowers in white and varying shades of blue and some which show the development, on the calyx, of rough bristly projections. This character is far from constant, although attempts have been made to distinguish them as species under the names of *C. phyctidocalyx*, *C. cristallocalyx*, *C. sub-pyrenaica*, and others. Seedlings from these forms by no means invariably show the character and, still more important, the bristles exist on some plants of *C. persicifolia* growing in gardens where the other plant has never been grown or even heard of. *C. cristallocalyx*, so far as can be determined, is the form from Macedonia but is merely a rather stiff form, is treated by Hayek as no more than a minor variant and certainly does not deserve specific rank.

As in the case of *C. carpatica*, the species varies considerably from seed and many of these forms have been selected and named, and, in many cases, obtained the Award of Merit.

A form occurred comparatively recently, and was named Telham Beauty, which, due to a doubling ·of the chromosome content, is larger in all its parts and a stronger grower, while a pygmy form (technically a Mendelian recessive) is often referred to as *C. planiflora* or *C. nitida*.

The plant deteriorates rapidly if not frequently divided, but division is easy in autumn or spring. It is also easily raised from seed, self-sown seedlings which are not moved giving the best spikes.

As an illustration I have selected a picture of the plant growing wild in the Pyrenees in preference to one in cultivation. Under the latter conditions a much larger plant is formed.

C. petraea. A species from Monte Baldo in Lombardy which is saxatile in habit and, generally, of biennial duration only.

It produces a tuft of rough, hairy, ovate-lanceolate, crenate-dentate leaves which are green above but distinctly grey on the undersides. These leaves, which are as much as two inches long, are carried on thin, inch-long petioles. Simple, stiff, somewhat angled, erect or ascendant stems are produced, about a foot high furnished with a few sessile, lanceolate or linear-lanceolate acute leaves and terminating in a small head of yellowish or white flowers. Smaller heads are sometimes borne in the axils of the upper leaves. These heads contain, in addition to the flowers, a number of bracts shorter than the flowers themselves, while an involucre of oblong-obtuse sessile bracts, at least as long as the flowers, surrounds the whole inflorescence.

The calyx segments are linear, obtuse, erect and more or less hairy, while the corolla is about the same length as the calyx segments, lobed for nearly half its length and slightly inflated at the base. The style is prominently exserted being nearly half as long again as the corolla, and divides into three stigmata.

De Candolle says it is an attractive species, which has been unjustifiably overlooked, but later writers agree in describing it as ugly. If wanted and obtainable, seed would provide the only means of increase.

C. petrophila. A species of very recent introduction from northern slopes in the Eastern Caucasus where it grows in cool places and damp rock crevices ascending, according to Fomin, to a height of over 11,000 feet. It produces a cluster of basal rosettes of small broadly ovate leaves which are entire (or in some plants tridentate at the apex), more or less petiolate according to the way in which the plant is grown and, as is not uncommon, of varying degrees of hairiness. A number of thin prostrate flower stems grow from each rosette and bear a few sessile or sub-sessile ovate leaves, and generally terminate in a single large flower, but may carry as many as five. The calyx segments are large and leafy, triangular-lanceolate and not more than one third the length of the corolla, while the appendages are even shorter, less in fact than the calyx tube itself. Several forms are recorded, with varying shape of the pale blue corolla; in the original description this is tubular-campanulate but in some of the forms it is almost cup-shaped being at least as broad as it is deep, and the rounded lobes, bearded at the edges, are well reflexed forming a good open flower. The style is at least as long as the corolla and trifid.

It is nearly allied to the *C. tridentata* group.

It is not too easy a species to cultivate, either flowering too freely to have sufficient strength to produce new growth able to carry over the winter, or falling a prey to the attacks of slugs. It seems to do best in a deep rather rough scree.

C. phrygia. An annual species from dry pastures in Thessaly with thin, smooth, striated stems up to ten inches long which flop about and are branched repeatedly and dichotomously. The small sessile leaves are ovate-acute becoming smaller and narrower towards the extremities of the branches and, in fact, little more than bracts. The flowers are carried singly and erect on very long pedicels. The calyx is smooth, ex-appendiculate, with long linear conspicuous segments which have only a central nerve, while the funnel-shaped corolla is lobed to not quite half its length and is usually bright lilac in colour, with much darkened veinings and a white throat. Dehiscence is apical.

It is nearly allied to *C. ramosissima*, but is much less useful than that species as its flowers are considerably smaller, the corolla being only about a quarter of an inch long. Botanically it differs in having even its lower leaves very nearly sessile; a corolla less deeply lobed; and an obconical rather than a spherical capsule. Both leaves and calyx segments are without any toothing, another character in which this species differs from its near allies.

C. pilosa, Pall. A species from Alaska, the Aleutian Islands and Northern Japan which has a thickish root crowned with a small rosette of leaves and emitting short stolons terminating in similar rosettes, thus forming a close mat. The fertile rosettes throw up erect flower stems, usually about three inches high, which bear two or three small, almost bract-like leaves.

The rosette leaves may be broadly ovate or so narrow as to be almost ligulate, in any case they are smooth and crenate and diminish into a short petiole; the flower stems are downy when young and, though usually they do not exceed three inches in height, may reach as much as nine inches; they are generally single flowered, but in the stronger growing forms may be somewhat branched and carry five or six blooms; in some forms the flowers are pendent, in others, nearly, if not quite, erect; the corolla form varies from open bell-shape to quite narrowly tubular or conical, it is edged with a row of incurving bristles but is otherwise quite smooth. As with most members of the genus, the colour is rather variable, from deep purple to a rather mauvy blue with paler margins, and there was at one time a white form in cultivation. The calyx segments are ovate-lanceolate and softly hairy, particularly in bud, and not more than half the length of the corolla tube; the corolla is lobed to about half its length, the lobes being broad, acuminate and not much reflexed. Calyx appendages are small (only about half as long as the calyx tube), triangular and ciliate. The style, about as long as the corolla, is trifid; the mature capsule is pendent and dehiscence is basal.

In June 1935 an Award of Merit was given to a plant under this name which had small dark purple conical flowers, borne three on a stem, while in May 1937 a similar award was made to a plant under the name *C. dasyantha* (which Herder says is merely a variety of *C. pilosa*) in which the flowers were of more funnel shape and borne singly. In Japan there used to be considerable discussion about best forms and nurserymen there applied honorifics, such as 'elegantissima' and 'superba'. Mr. Lohbrunner. who has collected extensively in Northern Alaska which is within the recorded region for all these species or forms, tells me that he has found endless variations in the shape of the corolla and that plants with single and plants with branched flower stems grow freely together, those with branched stems being generally taller and more robust though not with larger flowers.

It is clearly a very polymorphic species, but I retain the one name until the opportunity of obtaining and examining further material from the extended native area enables decisions to be reached as to whether there is really one or more species. As described, *C. dasyantha* differs principally in being one-flowered and in having a few hairs at the base of the filaments.

It requires scree treatment and may be propagated by detaching some of the short runners and treating them as cuttings, though a safer method is by seed which germinates readily, particularly if sown as soon as ripe.

C. piperi. A North American species which, even in its native haunts, the Olympic Mountains of the State of Washington, has an extremely localised distribution and is far from common. Despite the remarks of Clay, it is really most attractive and well worth the trouble—and frankly it is a difficult species—to satisfy its needs. Growing in fissures and crannies of the hard granitic rocks, it is a prostrate plant forming small rosettes of spathulate, conspicuously toothed leaves which are smooth and dark green with a definite sheen and distinctly pointed at the end. From among the rosettes rise slender stems an inch or so high bearing one or two shortly stalked dark blue rotate or starry flowers with conspicuously scarlet anthers. The calyx segments are twice the length of the calyx tube, about half the length of the corolla and not reflexed.

It is definitely a saxatile species and is never happy unless it can nestle against a rock. It also insists on perfect drainage, a gritty soil and plenty of sunshine with ample water during the growing season. In habit, requirements and general appearance it recalls the European *C. cenisia* and, like that species, is probably rather intolerant of lime. Generally speaking it is not very long lived out of doors (though the trouble may well be slugs) but makes a good subject for the alpine house where, however, it needs a deep pan or pot, ample top-dressing with chips and repotting at least every third year. It may be divided when growth is starting in spring but is best reproduced from seed.

The Award of Merit was bestowed in 1932.

C. plasonii. A species from Macedonia bearing a superficial resemblance to *C. pyramidalis*. The root produces many erect angular stems, up to two or three feet high, frequently leafy and ending in a long leafy raceme. Basal leaves are oblong-cordate on long petioles and bluntly serrate, the small teeth being hard at the tips; upper leaves are, as usual, smaller and narrower. Flowers appear in the upper leaf axils, either singly or in clusters of as many as six; calyx may be smooth or rough with triangular acuminate segments, while the open-bell shaped corolla, nearly three times as long as the calyx segments, is lobed nearly half way and is normally of a pale violet colour. Style is exserted and trifid, while the capsule dehisces near the top. Distinctions from *C. pyramidalis* must be found in the smaller flowers with more deeply lobed corolla and in a rather less dense spike.

C. podocarpa. An annual species reported from various parts of Asia Minor which, with its thin but rigid, repeatedly branched, stems, makes a spreading plant some four inches high. The leaves are small, oblong and sessile and the small sub-sessile flowers appear at the ends of the branches. The narrow tubular corolla is scarcely expanded and not much longer than the calyx the segments of which are almost filiform. There are no appendages and the more or less erect capsule dehisces at the base.

C. polyantha, R. & S. The name given in 1819 in exchange for an earlier *C. multiflora*, of which the description mentioned only rough oblong-lanceolate, serrate leaves with flowers in a glomerate panicle. The plant was said to come from Siberia but the description does not enable it to be identified and it is generally treated as the name of an uncertain species.

C. pontica. A perennial from eastern Transcaucasia forming a tuft of slightly rough ovate-oblong leaves, which are undulate and crenate on narrowly winged petioles, from among which rise stems up to two feet in height with leaves similar to the basal ones though with shorter petioles and becoming narrower and sessile or sub-amplexicaul near the top. The flowers are borne in a loose raceme, the long axillary peduncles being generally two-flowered. The calyx tube is covered with white warty excrescences and the segments are broadly ovate but suddenly acuminate and about two thirds the length of the broadly campanulate corolla which is an inch or more across and lobed to a third its length. The trifid style has large spreading stigmata nearly half its length. Alboff says it is nearly allied to *C. phyctidocalyx* (which can only be regarded as a form of *C. persicifolia*), being distinguished by its more graceful stems, narrower leaves and broader calyx segments.

C. portenschlagiana. A native of Dalmatia, this species, known also as *C. muralis* and *C. bavarica*, forms a mass of almost woody stems, each terminating in a tuft of bright green, glabrous, rotund-cordate leaves with a few sharp dentations, resembling small ivy leaves, on fairly long petioles and evergreen. The procumbent flower stems, five to six inches long, are freely produced, bear numerous leaves precisely similar to those at the base, though becoming smaller in the upper part, and a many-flowered panicle of erect deep blue flowers, which are pedicelled and bell-shaped with oblong reflexing lobes. The calyx may be smooth or slightly hairy with awl-shaped, entire, erect segments, a quarter to one third the length of the corolla. The blue tripartite style is nearly as long as the corolla and the capsule is carried erect like the flowers.

The species seems to prefer a slightly shaded position and makes an excellent plant for a retaining wall. A variety with hairy foliage is reported but I have never seen it.

Propagation by division at almost any time of the year is easy, as it spreads freely by short underground runners.

This is one of the few dwarf Campanula species to receive the Award of Garden Merit, this distinction having been conferred upon it in 1927, as a plant which, after test, has 'proved to be excellent for ordinary use.'

C. poscharskyana. Of comparatively recent introduction from Dalmatia, this species in many ways resembles *C. garganica*, but is a stronger, more rampant grower. It has the same rotund-cordate leaves with deeply serrate margins on long footstalks and trails out stiff arms, perfectly smooth, carrying large numbers of long-stalked flowers in loose axillary racemes. The flower stems are bare except for scattered small bract-like and ciliate leaves. The flowers, which are widely expanded and star-shaped, are of a clear lavender-blue colour, but variations in the depth of colour occur in every batch of seedlings and, no doubt, we shall soon have a white form. The calyx and calyx segments are hairy, the latter being fully half the length of the deeply lobed corolla, and carried erect.

It is far too strong a grower for successful pot culture and its proper place is in a wall; in fact, on one occasion, I saw it planted at the foot of a wooden shed and its long growths had taken advantage of the shelter provided and reached a height of little less than three feet. Its propagation is of the simplest, either by division or by cuttings (seed does not seem to be produced with any freedom) and it frequently becomes a nuisance by running underground and coming up among choicer plants. It is, however, so showy that it cannot be omitted from any rock garden of any size. I have sometimes found the flower buds susceptible to damage by cold wind, which suggests that a somewhat sheltered position is desirable, particularly in exposed districts.

The species received an Award of Merit in 1933.

C. praecox. An annual from the Pyrenees which forms a rosette of smooth, shortly petiolate leaves slightly notched at the ends and a simple channelled stem not more than six inches high bearing a few leaves, the lower ones shortly petiolate but the upper ones sub-amplexicaul; these stems terminate in a loose few-flowered raceme. The calyx tube is obovate with lanceolate segments, while the pale violet corolla is funnel-shaped, lobed halfway into rather narrow lanceolate lobes. The style is short and divides into three spreading stigmata.

It seems to be very near *C. patula* and may possibly be only a form of this species.

C. prenanthoides. A rather rare species from coniferous woods and open places in California and the northern part of the Sierra Nevada.

It is a perennial which produces a tuft of rather small oblong-ovate to lanceolate leaves, smooth or slightly downy and minutely serrate, the basal ones on short petioles and the stem ones sessile. A few erect slender stems may reach a height of one or two feet though the lower figure is more usual, and terminate in a many-flowered raceme of pendent flowers on short stiff footstalks. The ex-appendiculate calyx has short spreading awl-shaped segments, about one third the corolla in length. The corolla itself, slender-cylindrical in bud, is almost five-parted into narrow lanceolate lobes which are much recurved. The trifid style is much longer than the corolla, and the thin-walled capsule dehisces at the base, which is noticeably broad.

The species seems to be nearly allied to the much more widespread *C. scouleri*, differing mainly in having more and shorter leaves (those on the flowering stems being sessile) and more erect stems. It is a small and not particularly showy species nor do I find it too hardy in this country. Seed, when obtainable, germinates readily and forms the easiest means of increase.

C. primulaefolia. A rather coarse perennial from damp shady places in Spain and Portugal, which forms a rosette of oblong or broadly lanceolate leaves, unequally crenate-serrate and softly hairy. The leaves of the rosette taper inwards to a short winged petiole but those on the flower stem are sessile. This description fails to convey the impression that the rosettes do in fact bear a very marked resemblance to those of our common English primrose, though on rather a larger scale, and the species really does justify its specific name.

The erect flower stems, two to three feet high, are branched only at the base and in the upper part bear terminal and axillary flowers on short one- to four-flowered peduncles, the stems terminating in a cluster of four or five flowers. The broadly campanulate corolla, lobed for nearly half its length, is large, sometimes as much as two inches across, and generally of a good blue colour with a white base similar to *C. pyramidalis* though the lobes are broader than in that species. The calyx segments are lanceolate, acuminate, ciliate and reflexed and there are no appendages. The style is short and filiform and divides into three stigmata and the capsule dehisces at the apex.

The species is easily raised from seed—a better and safer method of increase than division, though the latter is sometimes possible with care and gives plants somewhat sooner.

It is figured in the *Bot. Mag.* at t. 4879.

C. propinqua. A very variable annual species from sub-alpine regions

CAMPANULA PETROPHILA

155

CAMPANULA PIPERI

CAMPANULA PORTENSCHLAGIANA

157

CAMPANULA
POSCHARSKYANA

CAMPANULA
PRIMULAEFOLIA

of Persia. As a result it can only be regarded as half-hardy, but is fairly easily grown in light sandy soil when seed can be obtained. It then makes a good pot plant.

The erect stems grow to a height of twelve inches and are freely and dichotomously branched from the base. They bear obovate and more or less acute, sessile leaves with little or no notching and long-stalked terminal flowers which are reddish-purple with dark blue veins and with wide spreading lobes. The funnel-shaped corolla is glabrous or with a few hairs on the margins and the calyx is furnished with wide strap-shaped appendages which curve inwards and enclose the calyx tube while the calyx segments are linear lanceolate and half the length of the corolla. The style is tripartite and though the flowers are carried more or less erect, the seed capsule is nodding and dehisces at the base, but seed is not readily set.

The species shows very considerable variation and a particularly large form, sometimes dignified by the appellation *grandiflora*, was given an Award of Merit in 1931 under the name of *C. cecilii*.

C. pruinosa. A name sometimes found but no description appears to have been published and it cannot be accepted as valid.

C. psilostachya. This distinct species (which is sometimes referred to the allied genus, Asyneuma) comes from the shores of Cilicia and is probably monocarpic though the perennial character is often claimed for it. It produces many-leaved rosettes and unbranched erect stems up to two and a half feet in height. The basal and lower leaves are ovate-rotund, cordate, obtuse, bluntly crenate and somewhat roughly hairy. The flower stems bear similar leaves in their lower part and terminate in a long leafless more or less dense spike, the flowers being sub-sessile in three to five flowered heads with short linear-subulate bracts. The smooth, ex-appendiculate calyx has spreading subulate segments, while the small funnel-shaped corolla, little more than a quarter of an inch long, is divided for more than half its length into triangular lanceolate lobes. The trifid style is noticeably exserted and the capsule dehisces about the middle. Its nearest ally would appear to be *C. americana*. It would have to be raised from seed, but it is doubtful whether it is in cultivation in this country though plants under this name were offered before the war, and it is even more doubtful whether it is worth growing.

C. ptarmicaefolia, Lam. An Armenian species, probably biennial, which forms a thick woody root and a tuft of obtuse linear leaves which are entire and ciliate, and smooth erect stems, six to twelve inches high, unbranched and with sessile acuminate leaves and, in the upper axils, fair-sized flowers borne singly. The calyx tube is smooth and spherical

H

and without appendages, while the segments are ovate-acuminate, erect and not more than a third as long as the erect campanulate corolla. The style is trifid.

C. pulla. An attractive species from the Styrian Alps and one of the best known of the dwarf species, this plant runs freely in light but rich soil, preferably among limestone blocks, forming broad masses of rosettes of small ovate shiny leaves on short petioles. From almost every rosette arises a slender stem some two or three inches high bearing on the lower half a few ovate-acute, sessile leaves and terminating in a single pendulous bell of rich purple blue, and full rounded campanulate form, large for the size of the plant. The long narrow linear calyx segments are smooth, more than half the length of the corolla and are not reflexed. The species is ex-appendiculate. The style is fully as long as the corolla and is trifid, while the capsule is, like the flower, pendent.

Somewhat strangely it does not mind a certain amount of shade and is, accordingly, useful for the less open parts of the rock garden where many other plants refuse to grow, though it is doubtful whether it flowers quite so freely as in full sunshine where, however, a plentiful supply of moisture at the root is essential. Where happy it is rather inclined to take up more than its fair share of room and flower itself to death and it should, accordingly, be divided and replanted after flowering. If this does not provide as many plants as are needed another easy method of propagation is by cuttings of the young shoots in spring.

C. pulla, Gueldenst. Apart from the fact that another plant bears this name, no description has been published for Gueldenstein's plant.

C. punctata. The home of this very distinct species is Eastern Siberia and Northern Japan, and it would naturally be expected to prove hardy in this country. Yet experience shows that it is rarely a success except in very light soils, though whether its loss is caused by frost, damp or slugs, is uncertain. In my own garden at Bromley, where the soil may be described as sand over gravel, it was, before 1939, rapidly becoming a weed, spreading by underground runners and coming up amongst anything else in the neighbourhood. Even the centre of a clump of Golden Rod or Michaelmas Daisy had no terrors for it.

The leaves, which are on long footstalks, are large, soft, pointed oval and cordate, with sharply, coarsely serrate margins. The flower stems are thin, wiry, erect, and more or less branched, usually nine to twelve inches high, bear a few leaves similar to those at the base but smaller and sub-sessile or sessile, and, towards the top, a few large, very long, pendent, tubular, creamy bells, fully two inches long and freely speckled within with purplish dots. The calyx segments are triangular acuminate, often reddish at the ends, and are not reflexed. They are about a quarter the length of the corolla and join at their bases to form the ovate-acute reflexed appendages, which are half their length and much shorter than the calyx tube. The style is considerably shorter than the corolla and divides into three filiform stigmata.

Propagation by division of the running roots in spring is easy, while the freely produced seed germinates readily. At the Alpine Garden Society's show in September 1937, a form with pink flowers was exhibited. Although the species may not be everybody's plant, it is undoubtedly very different from all other species and is one of the parents of two hybrids—*C.* × *Burghalti* and *C.* × *van Houttei*—both of which are first-class border plants. The so-called *C. nobilis* is the same plant. It is (or was) a great favourite with the Chinese and was introduced (in 1844) from this source, not being found in a wild state until some years later.

C. pyramidalis. This species, the giant of the race, often growing five or six feet tall, is a native of Dalmatia and the regions round Venice and Verona.

It makes a thick carrot-like root crowned by a loose rosette of smooth shiny ovate-oblong and cordate leaves, slightly serrate and on long petioles. Often the crown divides, producing a number of rosettes. In fullness of time each rosette gives rise to a smooth angled flower stem, with sessile, ovate and, towards the top, lanceolate, leaves and numerous branches. The numerous terminal and axillary flowers, frequently in threes on short peduncles, build up a loose pyramidal raceme. The calyx is without appendages and the segments are narrowly triangular, half the length of the corolla, reflexed and even recurved towards their points; the corolla is large and with the long, well-displayed oblong acute lobes appears to be salver-shaped rather than campanulate. In the type, it is pale blue with a darker centre but varies somewhat and there is a pure white form. The style, which terminates in three short stigmata, is about as long as the corolla.

Although strictly speaking perennial, the species is best treated as a biennial or, where non-flowering side rosettes are produced, propagated each year from these, which should be detached after the flowering period is over and rooted in a cold frame. The species is not very satisfactory outdoors, where it seldom opens its flowers properly, meriting Farrer's condemnation, but as a pot plant for a conservatory or cool greenhouse there are few plants which make such a display with so little trouble. It requires a long period of growth and seed should be sown in the autumn as soon as ripe or early in the year (February is not too soon) in moderate warmth and grown on steadily, repotting as necessary; final potting may require eight-inch pots. It is impatient of drought and too much sunshine and will return handsome dividends for rich feeding.

It is said to have been in cultivation since 1596. One form received a First Class Certificate in 1885, and other forms secured Awards of Merit in 1892 and 1896.

C. quartiniana. A perennial from Persia which belongs rather to pastures than to mountains and is probably not hardy in this country. It produces a few oblong-elliptic, acute or lanceolate, leaves, sessile and obscurely dentate and has erect, branched, hairy stems a foot or more high. Erect medium sized flowers are borne at the ends of all branches. The calyx segments are lanceolate-acute and ciliate, while the appendages are triangular, broad at the base, acute and ciliate. The corolla is hairy externally on the nerves and has bluntish lobes. It belongs to the larger part of the appendiculate section of the genus in which the style is trifid.

C. raddeana. An attractive species from the limestone alps of Transcaucasia at about 4,000 feet which many fail to keep through an English winter. Yet it should not be difficult; the roots run freely in any light open soil (possibly lime is essential, impeccable drainage is assuredly so), forming rosettes of small, triangular, cordate, sharply dentate leaves which are glossy, distinctly veined and borne on long footstalks. From each rosette there rises a rigid branched stem about a foot high, carrying a few leaves similar to the basal ones though becoming sessile towards the top and terminating in a shower of shiny pendent deep-violet bells. The calyx is wider than the corolla, is furnished with triangular, ciliate appendages, longer than the tube and parallel to, but not adpressed on to, it; the segments, a quarter to one third the corolla in length, are triangular, ciliate and not reflexed. The corolla is lobed to about one third its length, the lobes being pointed-ovate and scarcely reflexed. The style, which is fully equal to the corolla in length, is white and trifid while the pollen is yellow or orange, contrasting strongly with the colour of the flower.

Propagation is most easily effected by division as seed does not seem to be produced with any freedom.

Award of Merit in 1908.

C. radicosa. An uncommon species from some of the Greek Islands where it grows in alpine pastures at an altitude of 6,000 to 7,000 feet.

It forms a rosette of oblong spathulate leaves, minutely toothed, diminishing gradually to a petiole and of varying degrees of hairiness. From the base of the rosette a number of flower stems radiate, pressed closely to the ground, or even penetrating under the loose shingle. These flower stems are about two inches long, bear one or two sessile, more or less rotund leaves, and terminate in a short unilateral raceme of almost sessile flowers. The flowers themselves are small and funnel-shaped and even though the pointed lobes stand wide open and are of a vivid violet colour with a startling white eye, the plant can scarcely be described as showy and it is one for the enthusiast rather than for the general grower. The calyx is without appendages and the ciliate segments are short and blunt, equal to the calyx tube in length and not more than a quarter the length of the corolla; they are not reflexed. The trifid style is roughly equal to the corolla in length.

In this country it seems to prefer half-shady scree treatment and the only means of propagation is from seed, but this does not seem to be produced with any freedom and the plant is accordingly rare in cultivation even if it still persists here.

C. radula. A perennial species which grows among the rocks in the higher mountains of Kurdistan, making a tuft of firm ovate cordate leaves, narrowing to the base, sharply dentate and crimped and one to two inches long. It produces a number of rigid, rough, erect stems, generally unbranched, set with oval leaves the lower of which are shortly petiolate and the rest sessile. The stems terminate in a panicle of narrowly campanulate, densely pubescent, flowers borne in clusters of one to three. The rough calyx has spreading triangular-lanceolate segments only about a quarter the length of the corolla and very small, almost unnoticeable, appendages. With its large flowers and stiff upstanding stems it is a promising border plant but does not appear to be in cultivation.

C. raineri. A species of very limited distribution in nature, being confined to the limestone mountains in the neighbourhood of Bergamo. Nor is it easy to secure the true plant in commerce.

The true plant runs freely in rock crevices and, from a woody rootstock, forms tufts of small ash-grey leaves which are sessile or sub-sessile, pointed oval and finely dentate, with soft hairy margins. The erect flower stems, not more than two or three inches in height, bear a few similar, but sessile, leaves and generally a single large erect flower, broadly campanulate in shape with short ovate lobes and, generally, of a mid-blue colour. A white form exists and there is a form with fully hairy leaves which is offered as *C. raineri hirsuta*. The calyx, which may be smooth or roughish, is prominent, with long erect, broadly triangular, acuminate segments half the length of the corolla and entire or slightly serrated. It is an ex-appendiculate species. The style is somewhat shorter than the corolla and is trifid.

Where a suitable crevice is not available the limestone scree is the best place for this species, but it prefers partial shade in the hottest part of the day. It is another of the species specially favoured by slugs.

Propagation is by division or cuttings in spring; I do not find it sets seed readily except perhaps when cross-fertilised.

C. ramosissima. This species which comes to us from Asia Minor is well worth the attention of all who do not bar annuals from their rock gardens. And, after all, why should they, when nature's own rock gardens contain such a large proportion of annual plants? The character of the plant itself and not its length of life should surely be the determining factor and the species now under consideration looks perfectly in place among the rocks.

It forms a much-branched bushlet from six to twelve inches high with oval, entire, sessile leaves, while each noticeably ribbed stem terminates in a single erect flower. As will be seen from the illustration, the calyx segments are broad and conspicuous, slightly but markedly serrate, acuminate and as long as the corolla, and without appendages. The corolla is large and saucer-shaped with broad prominently veined lobes. The type colour is violet-blue with a white base and, as is frequently the case, a white form is not uncommon. The style is tripartite and the whole plant, apart from the softly hairy ovary, is quite smooth. The capsule dehisces near the apex.

Seed sometimes offered as *C. loreyi* is very closely allied to the present species and may, indeed, be nothing more than a strong-growing form, though De Candolle distinguishes them by the shape of the capsule which in *C. ramosissima* is said to be obconical while in *C. loreyi* it is spherical. This difference, even if a real one, is of no importance to growers and most later authorities make the two synonymous. *C. loreyi* is an Italian plant.

The name has been used for several of the closely allied species; *C. ramosissima* of Grisebach is *C. phrygia*; of Host is *C. loreyi*; of Spruner is *C. spruneriana*; and of Willldenow is *C. loefflingii*.

C. rapunculoides. Justifiably referred to by Farrer as the 'most insatiable and irrepressible of beautiful weeds', this is a species which should be strictly confined to the wildest of wild gardens. Beautiful it undoubtedly is with its erect flower stems three to four feet high clothed for the greater part of their length with large drooping funnel-shaped flowers of a rich deep violet colour, slightly bearded within, but it runs about far too freely in almost any soil, making clumps of rough obovate acuminate leaves with coarsely serrate edges, on long petioles. The stem leaves are sessile and ovate-acuminate. The calyx is without appendages and roughish with the short segments much reflexed; the corolla is cut for about a third of its length into pointed lobes and is three times as long as the calyx segments. The style is as long as, or slightly longer than, the corolla and divides into three. In general appearance it is not unlike *C. bononiensis* but the flowers are larger and more drooping, while the reflexing calyx segments give a ready means of differentiating the two species, apart from the fact that *C. bononiensis* is only biennial.

There is no need to mention propagation for any piece of root will quickly spread into a square yard and, apparently, every one of the millions of seeds germinates. All the same in its place it is a really handsome species.

C. rapunculus. A biennial species which is common throughout Central and South Europe and is sometimes regarded as a British native. It was formerly much grown in kitchen gardens for its tuberous roots and its occurrence in the countryside in parts of Southern England may be only as an escape plant.

In its first year it forms a rosette of oblong or ovate slightly crenate and undulate leaves on footstalks as long as, or longer than, the leaf itself and in its second year throws up a number of slender but stiff, ribbed, erect stems two to three feet high bearing narrow, entire and sub-sessile leaves and long simple racemes of small flowers generally singly on short pedicels with two small bracts.

The calyx segments are awl-shaped and not reflexed, while the erect narrowly campanulate corolla, up to an inch long, is lobed nearly half way into five lanceolate lobes which, however, are not markedly recurved. The style, which divides into three stigmata, is about the same length as the corolla tube and the erect capsule dehisces by pores near the top. The species varies considerably in the degree of hairiness of all its parts (with, however, a predominance of glabrous forms) and in the extent of branching of the stems.

As a wild plant it frequents roadsides and rough pastures and when well grown a clump of ten or twelve plants set fairly closely together will not be out of place in the middle rows of the herbaceous border. Some people find the roots a useful change as a vegetable and for this purpose it is readily raised from seed.

C. raveyi. Growing in sandy stony wastes among the mountains of Caria (Asia Minor) this annual species is a weedy little plant about four inches high, its thin tangled stems, rough with stiff whitish hairs, bearing small oblong sub-sessile leaves, the upper ones being more or less deeply dentate. The small tubular-campanulate flowers with spreading lobes are confined to the ends of the branches and are about half as long again as the filiform calyx segments. There are no appendages and the capsule, which dehisces at the base, is carried erect.

C. reiseri. Another Grecian biennial species. It forms a rosette of ovate, sub-cordate, regularly serrate, roughish leaves with long petioles which sometimes bear a few pointed lobes. When flowering time arrives a semi-erect central spike, sometimes slightly branched, rises to a height of nine inches to a foot, while from the base there grow a number of closely decumbent very brittle stems which again are simple or slightly branched and often as much as eighteen inches long. These flowering stems bear a number of ovate-spathulate, dentate leaves, the lower ones being shortly petiolate and the upper ones smaller and sessile. The flowers, which are tubular-bell-shaped with short, broad and rounded lobes and a noticeably projecting style, are borne on short pedicels in an unilateral raceme. The calyx is densely hairy and is furnished with broadly-ovate (almost circular) appendages equal in length to the tube; the erect segments are triangular-lanceolate, also equal to the calyx tube in length and only a quarter to one third as long as the corolla. Both appendages and calyx segments are ciliate. The species belongs to that section of the genus in which the capsule contains five cells and, accordingly, the style is five-parted.

Both colour and fullness of form vary considerably and it would probably be well worth while to exercise discrimination in the choice of plants from which seed is to be saved; a white form has recently appeared. The seed is freely produced and germinates without difficulty.

The whole plant is softly hairy, the calyx densely so, and appears to object to overhead watering.

C. remotiflora. A perennial which produces a tuft of petiolate, cordate or ovate-rotund leaves and erect channelled stems which bear a few narrowly lanceolate leaves which become sessile near the top and are, like the basal ones, irregularly and sharply serrate. The stems terminate in a few-flowered raceme containing six to eight flowers on short footstalks. The corolla is rather narrowly campanulate, while the short smooth calyx has linear or linear-lanceolate segments, sometimes ciliate, which are as long as the corolla tube and spreading. The style equals the corolla tube in length and is trifid.

C. rentonae. A new species recently reported from Washington, U.S.A., where it was found on Mt. Stewart at an elevation of between 7,000 and 8,000 feet. It forms mats of rosettes of narrowly lanceolate or elliptical, acute, sessile leaves, entire or slightly toothed and margined

CAMPANULA PULLA

CAMPANULA PUNCTATA

CAMPANULA PYRAMIDALIS

CAMPANULA RADDEANA

168

CAMPANULA RADICOSA

CAMPANULA RAINERI

169

CAMPANULA RAMOSISSIMA

CAMPANULA RAPUNCULOIDES

170

with short white hairs. Non-flowering stems have spathulate or sub-rotund leaves drawn out abruptly into short petioles, but the flowering stems which grow to a height of four or five inches have a few leaves similar to the basal ones and terminate in solitary flowers. These are pendent, though the buds are sub-erect, violet or rose-violet in colour, paling to the base of the tube, about half an inch long and broad and lobed half way into acute spreading lobes. The calyx segments are narrowly triangular, rather less than half the length of the corolla and spreading, while the tripartite style is nearly as long as the corolla. In general appearance it is not unlike a small form of C. *lasiocarpa*, another North American species, which, however, does not occur so far south, and its apical dehiscence shows a fairly close relationship. Its running rootstock, however, and much narrower, almost untoothed leaves are sufficient to distinguish it from the better known species.

C. retrorsa. An annual species from the Lebanon which produces thin bristly stems six to eighteen inches high, generally simple but sometimes branched in the upper half. Basal leaves are rotund or obovate on thin petioles, while the stem leaves are ovate-lanceolate and sessile. The stems and branches terminate in a loose cluster of a few fairly large funnel-shaped flowers with ovate-acute reflexed lobes. The long leafy acuminate calyx segments are as long as the corolla, recurved at the ends but without appendages. The trifid style is white and short and the long narrow capsule dehisces at the top.

C. reuteriana. From Cilicia, this is an annual species which produces an erect bristly stem, dichotomously branched in its upper part and furnished with oblong sessile entire leaves, the upper ones being more or less acute. The stalked flowers are borne mainly at the ends of the branches. The rough calyx has lanceolate acuminate segments carried erect, and appendages which are short, broad and rounded. The corolla is campanulate and the nodding capsule dehisces at the base. It is nearly allied to C. *strigosa*.

C. reverchoni. An annual species from Texas which has a number of wiry branching stems, each bearing a small, narrow-throated flower with recurved lobes. The stems are slender but carried erect and attain a height of about four inches. The stem leaves are short and linear, the basal ones being spathulate and all are sparingly dentate. The corolla is lobed to about half its length the lobes being ovate-lanceolate; the narrow linear calyx segments are erect; the capsule is obovate and carried erect on thin almost hair-like stalks. The plant is said to grow only on granitic rocks and the flowers to open in succession giving an unusually long period of bloom.

C. revoluta. In its home in Macedonia this species—said to be perennial—makes a small densely tangled bushling some three or four inches high. The many much-branched stems bear leaves which are oblong-ovate on the lower part and ovate-lanceolate to lanceolate above, all being sessile, more or less crenate, and with revolute margins. A single flower on a thin footstalk terminates each branch, the small corolla being campanulate, lobed almost halfway, rather longer than the linear calyx segments and generally violet in colour. It may be nothing more than a form of the very polymorphous *C. expansa*.

C. rhodensis. From the Island of Rhodes, this annual species produces a number of branched ribbed hairy stems with entire sessile leaves and a number of erect flowers at the ends of the branches. The hairy calyx has triangular erect segments but no appendages. The campanulate corolla is only about half an inch long, somewhat inflated in the middle and is made more conspicuous by the well-recurved ovate lobes. It is very similar to *C. drabaefolia* and may, in fact, be synonymous.

C. rhomboidalis. A sub-alpine, or meadow, species common throughout Europe, which sometimes ascends to considerable elevations.

The somewhat thickened root produces a mass of pointed-ovate, crenate leaves on long slender petioles and a number of simple, erect flower stems up to two feet in height the lower parts of which are furnished, at regular intervals, with similar leaves, becoming sessile and broadly ovate-acute (or rhomboid), smooth or hairy and of a distinctly lighter colour on the under sides. The upper part of each stem forms a loose raceme of, sometimes drooping, sometimes more or less erect, purple-blue flowers on short pedicels. These flowers are lobed to about a quarter their length but the pointed ovate lobes are not much reflexed. The calyx is smooth and the short, awl-shaped segments are not much recurved and scarcely more than a quarter the length of the smooth broadly campanulate corolla; there are no appendages. The style is at least as long as the corolla tube and there are three stigmata.

The species spreads slowly by underground runners and more quickly by self-sown seedlings. In its native haunts it grows always in association with grasses and other meadow flowers and looks and does its best in such company. In other words, the proper place for it is in open parts of a wild garden where it can with confidence be left to its own devices.

C. rigidipila. A perennial from the mountains of Abyssinia with a rough stem about a foot high branched from the base. The leaves are elliptical-lanceolate, acute, sub-dentate, sessile and rough and the medium sized flowers are carried erect and singly at the ends of the branches.

Calyx segments are lanceolate-acute, ciliate and rough, as are the appendages, while the smooth corolla has well reflexed rounded lobes. The style, which is shorter than the corolla, divides into three stigmata.

C. rimarum. From rock fissures in parts of Syria, this weedy little annual species makes a tangled mass of thin branched stems about two or three inches high. The oblong-spathulate leaves are, near the base, drawn out into short petioles. The flowers are on short stalks, are very small, tubular and only shortly lobed. The calyx has triangular pointed segments and blunt ovate appendages. Dehiscence is basal and the capsule pendent. Its nearest affinity is with *C. camptoclada*, the main difference being that it is smaller in all its parts.

C. robertsonii. A perennial from crevices of limestone rocks in the Southern Shan States, Northern Burma, which is allied to the Himalayan *C. sylvatica*. It forms a thick woody root from which spring numerous erect thin flexible flower stems. The membranaceous leaves are linear-lanceolate, acute, narrowing to the base and crenate. The flowers in a few-flowered terminal panicle are on thin hairlike stalks. The calyx segments are awl-shaped and the pale blue campanulate corolla is divided for half its length into acuminate lobes. The style is the same length as the corolla and divides into three stigmata which recurve considerably. The turbinate capsule dehisces at the base. The whole plant is densely covered with whitish hairs. It appears to be an attractive plant but is not in cultivation in this country.

C. robinsiae. An annual species from grassy slopes in Florida, which is not very different from the Texan *C. reverchonii*. It grows up to six inches high and is a slender plant with branched stems which bear ovate leaves near the base and lanceolate ones in the upper part. The flowers are terminal and axillary and carried singly on short stalks; rotate-campanulate in form, the corolla is lobed to more than half its length and is four or five times as long as the lanceolate calyx segments. The style is tripartite and the capsule dehisces at the base. The whole plant is smooth, this being the clearest line of distinction from the allied species.

C. rosmarinifolia. As described this appears to be only a rather strong growing form of *C. robertsonii* with thicker leaves and a more branching habit, but the very limited amount of material available of these Himalayan species (very few have been introduced into cultivation) is insufficient to determine the claim to specific rank.

C. rotundifolia. Universally distributed throughout the temperate and even sub-arctic countries of the Northern Hemisphere, this is undoubtedly the best known species of the genus. It is the popular 'Bluebell' of Scotland and is widely distributed throughout that country and throughout the more northerly parts of England, though less common in the southern counties. Many people will, however, be interested to learn that it was reported on excellent authority to have been collected on Tooting Bec Common, in the heart of London, in 1902.

In what may be called the typical form a fibrous rootstock produces a number of rotund, petioled basal leaves, but these are generally only in evidence before the flowering shoots are produced and even then may often be described with equal aptness as ovate-cordate and so markedly dentate as to be almost ivy-shaped. Numerous short stolons soon spread into a mat. The flower stems may be only a few inches high or may considerably exceed a foot; they bear sub-sessile to sessile linear leaves and may be either one-flowered or branched repeatedly forming a loose more or less unilateral raceme; the flowers vary in size, shape and colour and in the degree to which they droop. Always, however, the buds are erect and the seed capsule droops after fertilisation. In the more common forms the corolla is lobed to about one third of its length and the lobes are pointed and well reflexed; the linear calyx segments are spreading rather than reflexed and are only about a quarter as long as the corolla.

Needless to say it presents no difficulty to the cultivator except perhaps the task of uprooting its numerous progeny from among other, and choicer, plants, for it seeds freely in all directions. The many forms and colours cannot be relied on to come true and any specially desirable form must be propagated by division. A pure white form which is sometimes obtainable is particularly attractive.

Farrer describes it not as a species but as an 'aggregate' and this question is discussed more fully at p. 223.

C. ruderalis. A small low-growing perennial from Afghanistan where it grows in rubble on hot south and west exposures at 9,000 to 12,000 feet. It produces a tuft of small, slightly rough leaves which are sub-sessile, lanceolate-oblong, obovate or orbicular, entire or very slightly denticulate and more or less crowded at the base of the stems. The latter are thin and ascendant, up to six inches in length and terminate in one to three flowers. The flowers, red-purple in colour, are shortly stalked, narrowly campanulate in form and about half an inch long with broad, rounded lobes. The species is ex-appendiculate and has a tripartite style; its affinity appears to be with *C. trichopoda.*

C. rupestris, S and S. A Grecian species of fairly erect habit which, according to De Candolle, should be perennial but seems generally to be monocarpic. It has rosettes of soft greyish, hairy, irregularly lyrate leaves, the terminal lobe being much the largest, cordate, ovate or orbicular and distinctly dentate, while those on the petiole are themselves very uneven in size. The basal and lower stem leaves are stalked but those on the upper part of the flower stems are ovate and sessile. The flower stems, of which a number spring from the one crown, are ascendant or recumbent, generally with a central one which is more or less erect; they are only slightly branched and carry a number of erect, tubular-campanulate flowers of a pretty pale lilac-blue colour in short few-flowered racemes in the leaf axils and at the ends. The calyx is covered with hairs and the calyx segments are sharply pointed with revolute margins and about the same length as the tube of the corolla. The ovate appendages are the same length as the calyx tube. The style is rather shorter than the corolla and the five stigmata are also short but revolute. While five is clearly the normal number for this species, plants (or flowers) are frequently found with only four (or occasionally three). In flower it is not easy to distinguish this plant from *C. lyrata*, but in the earlier stages of growth the basal leaves are quite distinct while the latter species is quite definitely monocarpic.

Propagation, as with all these monocarpic species, is only possible from seed. This, however, is freely produced and germinates readily.

The species is said to have been introduced into English gardens as long ago as 1788; it received the Certificate of Merit, Alpine Garden Society, in 1933, under the name of *C. andrewsii*.

For the near allies of this species see p. 218.

C. rupicola. An attractive species from high limestone cliffs of Mount Parnassus where it is reported to do equally well in rock crevices or in scree. It forms a cluster of rosettes of small oval (almost circular) dentate leaves on comparatively long petioles, usually greyish with hairs, though a glabrous form is known. The thin prostrate or decumbent flower stems bear a few small, short-petioled leaves and a few (usually not more than three) flowers, which, however, are carried erect and are large for the size of the plant, sometimes as much as two inches long and an inch across. The corolla is broadly tubular-campanulate with broad acuminate lobes about a quarter of its length and well reflexed, the central nerve of each lobe being distinctly prominent. It is generally of a blue or violet-blue colour though Dr. Giuseppi reports a pink form from Vardhousie. The calyx is smooth, the segments are broadly oblong, suddenly acuminate and ciliate, not more than half the length of the corolla and reflexed. The appendages are very small and are reflexed closely to the calyx tube.

The species is closely related to *C. oreadum*, but differs principally in having dentate leaves, fewer flowers to a stem, and smaller appendages on the calyx.

It does not seem to be one of the easiest to grow, collapsing for no apparent reason about the time the flower stems should begin to lengthen and though cuttings can be rooted fairly easily and seed germinates readily the only plants with which I have had any real success have been those derived from chance seedlings in otherwise empty pots which have never suffered root disturbance but have been potted on as soon as the roots reached the side of the pot. It should be a true perennial but is probably always short lived, though the perennial character is claimed for a form collected by Dr. Giuseppi to which an Award of Merit was given in 1937.

C. sacajaweana. A species from the Wallowa Mountains of Oregon where it grows in association with one of the American representatives of the *C. rotundifolia* group—*C. petiolata*—from which it has been distinguished by its reniform basal leaves which are sometimes shallowly lobed or toothed and by its lanceolate, rather than linear, upper leaves. Its stems bear only one or two flowers and these have broader and shorter calyx segments, not more than one third the length of the corolla which is itself broader and more shortly lobed than in the more common form of *C. petiolata*. It probably does not really deserve specific rank.

C. sarmatica. A vigorous and rather coarse species from rocky slopes of sub-alpine regions of the Central Caucasus, this is nevertheless one of the most attractive members of the genus by reason of the delicate colouring of its pale grey-blue bells seen against the downy grey-green leaves. It forms a large clump of oblong, cordate, pointed, doubly crenate and wrinkled foliage on long winged or lobed footstalks and sends up a number of sub-erect unbranched stems about a foot or eighteen inches in height furnished with a few leaves similar to those at the base, except that they are sessile, and an unilateral raceme of medium sized hanging bells which, as they are deeply cleft and have the lobes well rolled back, appear to be rather short. The nerves are strongly marked, and the flowers more or less bearded within. The calyx is rough and hairy and the broadly lanceolate acuminate segments are half the length of the corolla and not reflexed. These segments are produced backwards into short revolute appendages which curve away from the calyx tube into a kind of horn. The style is trifid and about as long as the corolla.

The plant is easily raised from seed but I have never succeeded in dividing it or in striking cuttings. Its use, of course, is for the rather rougher parts of the rock garden and it should, if possible, be planted against a background of dark evergreens, or it will do well towards the front of the herbaceous border. Generally, the whole plant is rough and almost bristly but there is said to be a glabrous form which, however, I have never seen.

C. sarmentosa. An Abyssinian species which may well be merely a variety of *C. rigidipila*. It is a perennial with a tuft of oboval-lanceolate, obtuse, sessile leaves with nearly entire but densely bristly margins. On the undersides the leaves have bristles only on the main nerves. It is stoloniferous and throws up extensively branched, cylindrical stems, each branch terminating in a few medium sized flowers. The calyx has lanceolate-acute, ciliate segments, and acute appendages, while the smooth campanulate corolla has semi-oval, acuminate, lobes. In so far as it can be distinguished from *C. rigidipila*, specific characters must be found in a more slender and more branched stem and somewhat larger basal leaves.

C. sartori. From islands of the Eastern Mediterranean, this species, like many of those from this area, is monocarpic. It forms a neat rosette of small orbicular, or reniform-cordate, coarsely dentate and slightly hairy leaves on long petioles. As usual, these leaves die away as the brittle prostrate or decumbent flower stems are produced. These stems are generally simple, but sometimes branched, and bear a few small sessile leaves, while the numerous white (or pink) erect broadly funnel-shaped flowers with broad rounded lobes are about half an inch across and carried singly in the leaf axils or on short axillary branchlets. The hairy calyx, which is without appendages, has short lanceolate and reflexed segments about a quarter the length of the corolla. The trifid style is rather longer than the corolla.

Despite its monocarpic character the species is attractive and well worth growing. Sown in crevices in the rocks the flower stems cling closely to the stone, forming a mat which is most attractive at flowering time. It is said to frequent schistose rocks and while it does not show any marked antipathy to lime it certainly seems to do better in a non-lime medium. Once obtained there should be no trouble in keeping a stock for it seeds freely and self-sown seedlings can be relied on to perpetuate the species, flowering in their second year.

It was given an Award of Merit (under the erroneous name of *C. calamenthifolia*) in 1936.

C. saxatilis. This attractive species from rock crevices in Crete forms a thick, carrot-like root which penetrates deeply into the rock. A small tuft of thick sage-green oblong spathulate leaves which are slightly but regularly crenate and diminish gradually to a simple unlobed petiole precedes the production of a number of sub-erect or ascendant flower stems bearing a few small oblong or linear-oblong sessile leaves and a loose raceme of flowers in clusters of three to five on short pedicels. The calyx is smooth and furnished with short blunt appendages, not more than half the length of the calyx tube, while the erect segments half the length of the corolla are triangular acuminate. The corolla is long-tubular with reflexed pointed lobes, of a clear pale blue with a darker bar down the centre of each lobe; the style is shorter than the corolla and divides usually into five stigmata. De Candolle groups it with *C. heterophylla* and other species having normally three stigmata, but Boissier, Halaczy and other later writers regard five as the usual number and relate it to *C. tubulosa*, though that species has winged petioles to the basal leaves.

It is a true saxatile and soundly perennial, though probably safer in the alpine house or with a little protection during the winter. Propagation is by seed, but it is certainly not an easy plant to grow.

It received the Award of Merit in 1933.

C. saxifraga. See p. 210.

C. saxifragioides. A rather remarkable species from North Africa which, on a running root, produces a number of small rosettes about half an inch across generally close together and pressed close to the ground. The leaves of the rosettes are oblong, slightly narrowed at the base and covered with short stiff silky hairs; from beneath them spring a varying number of flowering stems about an inch high, crowded in their lower part with similar but smaller leaves and each terminating in a single erect, usually pink, flower. The calyx has lanceolate segments, noticeably nerved in the middle, and very short appendages, all covered with stiff white hairs. The corolla, rather more than half an inch long and nearly an inch across is lobed to a third of its length into triangular, only slightly recurved, lobes and is about three times as long as the calyx segments. The style is much longer than the corolla and is trifid. It is allied to *C. serpylliformis*, from the same area, and it has been suggested that it is only a local variant of that species.

C. saxonorum seems to be only a hairy form of *C. propinqua*.

C. scabrella. A species from North America which, from a thick taproot, produces several leafy stems a few inches high, both stems and leaves being more or less rough. The lower leaves form a rather dense rosette; they are blue-grey in colour and obtusely spathulate in shape diminishing to a short petiole. The stem leaves are lanceolate-acute and sessile. The stems may be anything up to nine inches high and usually terminate in a single erect flower though they may bear as many as four. The ex-appendiculate calyx has linear-lanceolate segments equal to the

CAMPANULA RAPUNCULUS

CAMPANULA RETRORSA

CAMPANULA ROTUNDIFOLIA

CAMPANULA RUPESTRIS

calyx tube in length, while the narrowly campanulate violet-purple corolla, rough externally, is divided halfway into ovate pointed lobes which when reflexed form a flower nearly an inch across. The trifid style is shorter than the corolla while the erect elongated capsule dehisces near its upper edge.

It is closely allied to *C. uniflora* from the same districts but is distinguished by the shape of the capsule and by the general roughness of the plant.

C. scandens, Pall. Reported from Siberia as a species with rough ovate serrate leaves on long petioles and flexible stems a foot or more high with ascendant branches and solitary stalked axillary flowers towards their ends. No details of flower form are given beyond the statement that the calyx segments are shorter than the corolla, dentate, ciliate and spreading. Identification is, therefore, impossible and the name must be regarded as doubtful.

C. scheuchzeri. See *C. linifolia.*

C. sclerotricha. A perennial species from Persia which produces a tuft of ovate cordate leaves, coarsely dentate and on very long petioles, from among which rise erect, simple stems, rough with short hairs and shortly and loosely racemose. The stems carry a number of leaves similar in general outline to the basal ones but becoming narrower and more shortly petiolate until near the top they are lanceolate and sessile but as long as, or longer than, the flowers. The latter are few and axillary on short stalks and narrowly tubular-funnel-shaped; the calyx segments are broadly lanceolate, ciliate and equal to the corolla in length, while the calyx bears broadly ovate and more or less obtuse appendages, long enough to cover the calyx tube itself. While the flowers are borne more or less erect, the mature capsule is pendent. The style is tripartite. Closely allied are *C. grossekii* and *C. axillaris* but the present species has longer calyx segments and larger appendages. So far as I can ascertain it is not in cultivation in this country but does not seem to be worth introducing.

C. scouleri. A species from British Columbia, spreading northwards into Alaska, which runs about freely in light stony soil forming both sterile and flowering shoots. It is, however, somewhat rare in cultivation. The sterile shoots are rosettes of broadly ovate, acute, regularly dentate leaves, while in the case of the flowering stems similar leaves are distributed up the stem, those near the base tapering into a margined petiole while the upper ones become almost amplexicaul. The stems are rigid, branched and leafy, terminating, at a height of six to eight inches, in a loose panicle of a few nodding flowers, which are light blue or milky white. The

I

calyx is smooth and the narrow pointed segments are half the length of the corolla and carried at right angles to the tube. The funnel-shaped corolla is very deeply cleft and the pointed lobes fully reflexed with the result that the style protrudes nearly twice the length of the bell. There are three stigmata. The characteristic which distinguishes this species from most others is the fact that the seed capsule dehisces rather above the middle.

It can be readily propagated by division and seed is sometimes obtained, but it is not a species worth bothering about, producing more leaf than flower while the latter, so far at least as I have met them in this country, are of a very indeterminate colour. A form with violet flowers which has been reported might possibly be more worth while.

C. scutellata. A Grecian species with erect rough stems six to twelve inches high, branched dichotomously from the base and above, with oblong-lanceolate, acute, entire and sessile leaves and terminal and axillary solitary flowers, shortly pedicelled. The calyx segments are ovate-lanceolate, acuminate, reflexed and about half as long as the corolla, the latter being sub-rotate with ovate lobes somewhat hairy on the nerves externally. The calyx is without appendages and dehiscence is basal. An annual.

C. secundiflora. See page 217.

C. semisecta. An annual which closely resembles *C. dichotoma* and may indeed be only a local variant of that species. The main differences appear to be that the corolla is more deeply lobed, up to halfway, the calyx segments are much shorter (only about one sixth of the corolla) while the appendages are broader and not so long, not long enough in fact to cover the capsule even at maturity.

C. serpylliformis. An Algerian species with a large perennial woody root from which spring numerous smooth flexible much-branched stems making a dense mat. The leaves are small, elliptical, ciliate and sub-sessile while the whitish flowers also are so small as to be insignificant. The calyx segments are about half the length of the campanulate corolla and are furnished with conspicuous hooked appendages. The whole plant is more or less rough with stiff hairs.

C. setosa. A small annual species from parts of Germany which has wedge-shaped basal leaves and erect, branched stems bearing a few sessile or sub-amplexicaul, lanceolate leaves, each branch terminating in a single large flower, pendent in bud but subsequently erect. The whole plant is smooth, apart from a certain degree of hairiness of the calyx.

C. sewerzowii. A perennial species from Turkestan with a short thick woody root from which many erect flexible stems five or six inches high are produced. These stems bear a number of linear or linear-lanceolate sessile leaves, the lower ones being sharply denticulate and the upper ones entire; they are more or less angled and simply branched at the ends, the branches terminating in small solitary erect flowers. The calyx, which is ex-appendiculate, has lanceolate acute segments rather shorter than the corolla, the latter being broadly funnel-shaped and deeply lobed into lanceolate acute lobes which are not much spread. The trifid style is rather longer than the corolla.

C. shepardii. A Syrian perennial with erect or ascendant fragile stems about six or eight inches high terminating in a loose leafy raceme. The basal leaves are petiolate, obovate and crenate-dentate, the upper ones elliptic-obtuse, dentate and sessile, and all are greyish on the lower sides. The small axillary flowers, not more than half an inch long are funnel-shaped, carried on hair-like stalks and divided for two thirds of their length into lanceolate lobes. The calyx, which has no appendages, has lanceolate-acute segments equal to the turbinate tube but only about one third the length of the corolla. Allied to *C. trichopoda* it scarcely seems worth growing and, so far as I know, is not, and has not been, in cultivation.

C. sibirica. A biennial species which is more widely spread than the specific name indicates, having been reported from Hungary and even as far south as Piedmont.

It produces a tuft of rough obovate or spathulate basal leaves gradually diminishing to long petioles, entire or slightly crenate. The erect flower stems, up to eighteen inches in height, are ribbed and rough and more or less branched, and bear sessile ovate-lanceolate leaves and numerous flowers in a loose narrow panicle. The flowers are semi-pendent, of good size (nearly an inch long) and usually of a good violet-blue colour. They vary somewhat in shape, the type being narrowly funnel-shaped or cylindrical and forms with broader leaves or larger flowers—in some forms even slightly inflated have at times been given specific names, but these are now merged into the type species. Externally the corolla is smooth, though generally more or less bearded in the throat and on the margins, but the calyx segments and appendages are bristly. Both segments and appendages are triangular and sharply pointed; the appendages are reflexed against the calyx tube but the calyx segments are not reflexed and are rather less than half the length of the corolla. The style is about the same length as the corolla and divides into three filiform revolute stigmata.

As a species of very wide distribution it is not surprising to find that there are a number of synonyms and the following forms are recognised by many botanists:

elatior, with taller stems and rather large flowers.

var. *divergens*, with spreading branches and tubular-campanulate somewhat inflated flowers and larger appendages.

corymbosa, with flowers in large corymbs and very short denticulate appendages.

var. *hohenackeri*, with many ascendant multi-flowered stems and medium sized flowers.

Reference is also occasionally made to var. *eximia*, which differs from the type in being dwarfer, with narrower leaves, more branched stems and paler flowers.

The species comes readily from seed, though it is difficult to obtain the true plant or any particular form.

C. sibthorpiana. The position of this so-called species in relation to its near allies is referred to under *C. spathulata*, S & S.

C. sidonensis. A Syrian species of annual duration with thin angled stems, loosely branched and flopping, yet building up a plant as much as two feet high. The thin leaves are smooth apart from rough edges, the lower ones ovate and petiolate, the upper ones smaller and oblong. The calyx segments are broad and shortly lanceolate and about a third as long as the corolla; the latter is open funnel-shaped, up to an inch and a half across, lobed to a third of its length and carried on a long flexible stalk. It is rendered more conspicuous by its white basal zone. The spherical calyx is noticeably hairy but the rest of the plant is smooth. The species is without appendages and dehiscence takes place near the apex of the capsule.

C. silenifolia. A Siberian species with a thin creeping root producing a number of rosettes of smooth lanceolate entire leaves, two or three inches long and half an inch wide, paler on the undersides and on long thin margined petioles. From the mat rise one or more smooth erect stems, six inches to a foot in height, bearing narrower, acuminate leaves, those near the top being sessile or even sub-amplexicaul. The stems branch slightly at the top, each branch bearing few-flowered axillary and terminal clusters of stalked flowers. The erect acuminate calyx segments are only about a third the length of the corolla; the latter is comparatively large, funnel-shaped, and divided to the middle into ovate lobes which are often ciliate; the style is trifid and dehiscence apical.

It is closely related to *C. steveni* but is generally rather taller, has larger flowers and leaves without serrations.

C. singarensis. In meadows in parts of Mesopotamia this dwarf annual species does not exceed four or five inches in height. It consists of a number of decumbent or ascendant flexible stems, branched from the base, with acute angles and recurved bristles. The leaves are very small, bristly and entire, the lower ones ovate and sub-petiolate, the upper ones narrowly elliptical. The small flowers are borne on long flexible nodding peduncles and are violet with a white base though an entirely white form has been recorded. The corolla is lobed for about one third its length and is shorter than the calyx segments which are themselves lanceolate and well spread.

It is closely allied to *C. retrorsa* and *C. sidonensis* but is even smaller than these two species.

C. songeoni. A perennial species from Savoy which forms a more or less thick carroty root from which are produced numerous long thin rhizomes which terminate in tufts of small rotund-cordate petioled leaves forming a mat. Short sterile or flowering stems are produced—the latter four to six inches high—bearing ovate or ovate-lanceolate sessile leaves, crowded at the base of the stems. The few upper leaves are linear and slightly dentate and the stems end in a single nodding flower—or, rarely, as many as four—on a smooth bare footstalk. The calyx segments are awl-shaped, longer than the erect bud, not reflexed, and half to two thirds as long as the fully expanded corolla. The latter is broadly funnel-shaped divided for little more than a quarter of its length into broadly rotund, acute lobes. The trifid style is shorter than the corolla and the species is ex-appendiculate.

It is closely allied to *C. rhomboidalis*, the differences as described being found in the shorter and more flexible stems, the smaller number of flowers on each stem and in the crowding of the lower stem leaves.

C. sophiae. A species from shady meadows on Mount Pelion which is probably not worth separating from *C. spruneriana*. It forms a turnip-shaped root and rosettes of rhomboid or ovate crenate leaves on long petioles and thin erect stems, with leaves becoming gradually narrower (but scarcely linear) and sessile, and terminating in a loose raceme of flowers. These flowers resemble those of *C. spruneriana* in shape and the only noticeable differences are that the calyx segments are considerably longer, in fact exceeding the corolla itself in length, are much reflexed instead of erect, while the style is longer than in the better known species. The capsule is long and carried erect, dehiscence taking place near the top. The plant as a whole seems to be a dwarfer and weaker grower.

C. sparsa. A Grecian species of annual duration which makes a few oblong-spathulate crenate leaves which diminish into a petiole and throws up one or more angled stems sometimes as much as three inches high with sub-amplexicaul oblong or linear-lanceolate leaves and branched above the middle into a loose many-flowered panicle of large broadly funnel-shaped flowers an inch or so long, lobed to about a third their length into oblong-lanceolate lobes. The calyx segments, nearly as long as the corolla, are linear-lanceolate and more or less reflexed, but without appendages. The capsule dehisces at the apex showing close relationship with *C. ramosissima*.

C. spathulata, S and S. A perennial from Greek mountains. The root is thickened and tuberous, ovate globose or napiform; the stems angular, ascendant, smooth (or hairy in the lower part), simple or rarely paniculately branched and about a foot high. The leaves are smooth or sparsely pilose and crenate; the lower ones ovate or oblong on thin petioles, the rest lanceolate and sessile. The flowers are carried erect on long footstalks; the calyx segments lanceolate-subulate, erect, equal to, or rather shorter than, the corolla; the latter funnel-shaped, normally violet-blue and lobed half-way. A form known as var. *giuseppii* has more trailing stems and more widely expanded flowers. This form received an Award of Merit in 1933. *C. spruneriana* (and forms *hirsuta* and *lepidota*) with stems up to twenty inches tall, and *C. sibthorpiana* (and form *filicaulis*, with one-flowered stems) with stems not exceeding ten inches and calyx segments only one third to one half the corolla, are sometimes regarded as sub-species though the *Index Kewensis* accords them specific rank. Halacsy makes *C. sibthorpiana* distinct from *C. spruneriana* and says that *C. spathulata* is synonymous with *C. sibthorpiana*.

Propagation is by careful division in early spring; without this precaution I do not find the species, by any of its names, very long lived.

C. speciosa, Pourr. Generally distributed in the Eastern and Central Pyrenees and possibly in the mountain regions of Southern France, this species forms a large flat rosette of narrow linear lanceolate sessile leaves always more or less bristly and with crenate, undulate margins. The leafy flower stems, usually about a foot or eighteen inches high, form a loose pyramidal raceme of large rounded bell-shaped flowers borne singly on long peduncles. The calyx segments are linear and erect and not more than a third the length of the corolla, while the calyx itself is furnished with hairy reflexed triangular ovate appendages. The trifid style is about as long as the corolla and the capsule is nodding.

The normal corolla form is long tubular but apparently varies considerably being often less tubular and more open than in the illustration. It is interesting to note, however, that *C. affinis* and *C. bolosii* (whether or not these are separate species) are natives of the same districts and have the flatter, more open corolla and the identification may not be too certain, apart from the chances of hybridisation. Probably only cultivation of the various forms on a comparatively extensive scale from seed and careful observation can solve this problem. At first glance it is difficult to distinguish this plant from a rather dwarf form of the well known Canterbury Bell (*C. medium*). The essential difference is that the latter should have a five-pointed style, but one of the arms frequently aborts while the present species as frequently has four stigmata.

The perennial character of the species is doubtful. Farrer says definitely that it is monocarpic. De Candolle is equally emphatic that it is perennial. My own view is that it depends entirely on the extent of the flowering; if, in the second year of life the rosette is big enough to produce a strong spike, the plant dies after flowering and seeding, but if the flower spike is comparatively small, a number of basal rosettes will be produced and will carry the plant on for another year of life and another crop of flowers and seeds. I have no record of a plant repeating the process and producing still a third crop. In any case the species is easily raised from seed and though it is not so easy to bring it to the flowering stage, as it seems very liable to rot off in winter unless in very poor stony soil, it is such a handsome plant at its best that it is well worth a good deal of trouble. Award of Merit 1928.

C. spicata. A biennial species which is not uncommon in hot dry places in the Swiss Alps and the Eastern Pyrenees, but not of much interest to gardeners.

On a thick fleshy root it forms a rosette of rough oblong lanceolate leaves, undulate and slightly dentate. In its second year it pushes up a rough leafy stem reaching sometimes two feet in height furnished throughout the greater part of its length with small erect sessile purple or lilac bells in clusters of one to three, and as the leaves on the flowering portion of the stem are reduced practically to bracts, it forms a dense rat-tail spike. The calyx is rough and the segments short, broadly ovate, hairy and not reflexed. The corolla, which is funnel-shaped, half to three-quarters of an inch long, and deeply cut, is densely bearded in the throat and the lobes are but slightly reflexed and are hairy on the nerves externally. The style, shorter than the corolla, is tripartite.

Although if left to its own devices the plant is stiff and uninteresting, it can be improved by cutting off the main stem when about a foot high, a service which is often provided by goats in the wild state. A number of subsidiary spikes are then generally produced and the result is not unattractive.

C. spruneriana. A loose growing species from sub-alpine regions of Greece, *C. spruneriana* forms a mat of smooth spathulate almost entire leaves and thin stems up to eighteen inches long which try to be erect but invariably flop about. These stems are more or less branched and bear a few leaves similar to, but smaller than, the basal ones and sessile, while from the axils of these, and terminally, are produced on long stalks large erect funnel-shaped flowers divided for half their length into oblong acute lobes. The flowers are pale blue almost white at the base in the typical form but as usual there is considerably variation. The calyx segments are very long, in fact nearly as long as the corolla and filiform, with a few dentations near the base, and are carried at an angle of 45° from the corolla tube. The plant is a good perennial and is easily raised from seed or by division.

Some botanists reduce this to a sub-species under *C. spathulata* (q.v.).

C. stefanoffii. Claimed to be a distinct species this is quite clearly a near relation of *C. steveni*. It produces erect slender stems about a foot high furnished with a few small spathulate, entire leaves on short stalks and terminating, generally, in a single erect flower, though occasionally the stem is branched near the top. The large flowers are funnel-shaped, divided for a quarter their length into pointed lobes, while the erect calyx segments are narrowly lanceolate and half the length of the corolla. The species is without appendages and the capsule dehisces at the apex.

C. stellaris. This annual species inhabits rocky and sandy places by the waysides in Syria, and also occurs on the sea coast in Palestine. It is a rough hairy species with stems repeatedly and dichotomously branched from the base. The leaves are entire, the lower ones ovate to oblong, spathulate and petiolate, the others linear, acute and sessile. The plant may reach as much as a foot in height but is generally not more than half that height and bears its flowers at the ends of all the branches. The corolla is normally blue, smooth, tubular-campanulate, short and open and about half as long again as the calyx segments; the latter are rough and ciliate, lanceolate-acute and spread into a star, and there are short oblong-obtuse appendages. The capsule is nodding and dehisces at the base.

C. stellata, Thunb. Mentioned by De Candolle who, however, says: 'It is certainly not Campanula.'

C. stenocarpa. A species from the Russian Caucasus which produces six to twelve inch stems rarely branched, bearing ovate obtuse dentate leaves on long petioles, and, nearer the top, oblong and sessile ones. The stems terminate in clusters of one to five flowers. The calyx segments are narrowly awl-shaped; there are no appendages and the style is trifid. This description is far from adequate for the identification of the plant.

C. stenocodon, Boiss. From Piedmont and Dauphiny this has recently

CAMPANULA RUPICOLA

CAMPANULA SARMATICA

191

CAMPANULA SARTORI

CAMPANULA SAXATILIS

CAMPANULA SPECIOSA

193

CAMPANULA SPICATA

CAMPANULA SPRUNERIANA

194

been reduced to a form of *C. rotundifolia,* but seems to deserve specific rank, for, as Boissier says, it is 'a very distinct and easily recognised species'. It forms mats of rosettes of petiolate leaves, reniform or rotund, cordate, and coarsely crenate and gives rise to thin ascendant stems, seldom more than three or four inches high, the lower parts of which bear narrowly oblong leaves, those of the upper parts being narrowly linear and often falcate. The stems terminate in a single flower, or, may be somewhat branched near the top with four or five spreading one-flowered branches. The buds, as well as the flowers and capsules, are pendent (which should relate it to *C. linifolia* rather than to *C. rotundifolia*) and the long tubular-funnel shaped corolla with short triangular lobes is about twice as long as the smooth, awl-shaped, not reflexed calyx segments.

C. stenosiphon, Boiss. A perennial from woods in Greece with many erect or ascendant stems, hairy and leafy. The lower leaves are oblong or lanceolate gradually diminishing to a petiole while the upper ones are oblong-ovate cordate and sessile; all are minutely crenate. The stems terminate in a head of two to seven flowers and there are generally a few axillary branches carrying smaller heads. The leaf-like bracts which enclose each head are broadly ovate-acuminate, recurved and rather shorter than the flowers. The calyx segments are stiffly hairy and lanceolate; the corolla funnel-shaped, nearly an inch long, twice as long as the calyx and, in the usual form, of a violet colour. The species is ex-appendiculate and is allied to *C. glomerata* (in fact the *Index Kewensis* says they are synonymous) and of no more value than that species.

C. steveni. A mat-forming species from sub-alpine regions of the Eastern Caucasus, where it occurs at elevations from 3,500 to 10,000 feet. It is fairly closely allied to *C. abietina* and, like that species, is rather short lived unless frequently divided.

The stoloniferous root gives rise to small rosettes of smooth obovate, pointed and slightly serrate leaves on long petioles and from among these rise simple erect and leafy flower stems between six and eighteen inches high, carrying generally a single flower but sometimes a few-flowered raceme. The lilac-blue funnel-shaped flowers are of good size and the corolla lobes which are rather narrow and pointed are well reflexed giving a starry appearance and as the flowers themselves are borne erect the whole plant is distinctly showy. A characteristic of the species is the long ribbed calyx tube, the short pointed segments of which are not reflexed and it is ex-appendiculate. The style is as long as the corolla and the three stigmata divide it for half its length. It is one of the comparatively small group of species which show apical dehiscence.

There is a dwarf form usually referred to as *C. steveni nana*, which is a more desirable plant for general cultivation as the flower stems are less inclined to flop about. This form possesses the additional merit of being rather more free flowering, stems often producing five or six flowers, and obtained the Award of Merit in 1913.

Either form is comparatively easily increased by division in spring and is also easily raised from seed. It succeeds either in full sun or in partial shade, always with the proviso that the soil is on the light and well drained side.

C. stolonifera, Miége. A species much resembling *C. cochleariifolia* but with flowers nearly twice the size. As the specific name implies, it runs freely at the root, the stolons being very long and terminating in flowering or sterile rosettes. The small, stiff, almost leathery basal leaves are reniform or rotund-cordate, while the stem leaves, crowded towards the base of the flowering stems, are ovate-elliptical and obtuse becoming gradually narrower and more pointed. The ascendant stems may reach a height of six inches and terminate in a solitary pendent flower, obconical in shape with short slightly reflexed lobes.

C. stricta, L. From alpine parts of Asia Minor and spreading southwards into Palestine, this species produces, from a fleshy perennial rootstock, numerous rigid, ascendant, almost woody rough green stems, sometimes reaching a height of two feet and simple or slightly branched. The basal leaves are stiff, ovate-oblong, acute, entire or slightly dentate, and diminish gradually to a petiole; the upper ones are sub-amplexicaul and gradually become linear-lanceolate. The flowers, sessile, erect and generally solitary in the leaf axils, form a fairly long spike. The calyx has narrowly oblong segments and ovate-obtuse appendages just long enough to cover the capsule. The tubular-funnel-shaped corolla, deeply lobed with ovate-obtuse reflexed lobes, is twice or three times as long as the calyx segments. The style is short and tripartite. The type is an erect compact plant but there is a form, sometimes given specific rank as *C. libanotica*, of a dwarfer and looser habit and with smaller flowers, and another, referred to as *C. jasioniaefolia*, which appears to come between the two extremes.

C. strictopedunculata. Although often accorded specific rank, this is nothing but a form of *C. barbata* in which the flowers instead of nodding are carried erect. It frequently occurs mixed with the normal form and cannot be relied on to reproduce the erect-flower habit from seed.

C. strigosa. Another annual species from Syria and the Lebanon, a district from which a very large number of the annual species hail, which produces an erect branched stem six to eight inches high with a few rough sessile lanceolate-acute, entire leaves and solitary terminal and axillary pendent flowers which are large for the size of the plant. The calyx segments are smooth and awl-shaped and join into ovate appendages about half their length pressed back on to the calyx tube. The campanulate corolla is divided for nearly half its length into lanceolate well-recurved lobes. The style is the same length as the corolla and divides into three stigmata while the capsule is pendent and dehisces at the base. The whole plant is covered with stiff hairs.

C. suanetica. This species which inhabits rocky but wooded regions of the Eastern Caucasus is perennial and very closely allied to *C. autraniana* though it is a larger plant throughout. It differs specifically mainly in carrying the mature capsules erect and in having branchlets which carry several flowers. The whole plant is quite smooth and the thin ascendant leafy stems branch at the top into a few-flowered corymb, the terminal and axillary branchlets each carrying up to five flowers. The basal leaves are reniform or ovate-cordate on long petioles; the stem leaves ovate, more or less deeply cordate and shortly petiolate. The flowers are of medium size on long thin footstalks which remain erect even when the capsule is mature. The calyx segments are smooth, linear and spreading; the tooth-like appendages are much shorter than the calyx tube, and the broadly funnel-shaped corolla, with bearded lobes one third its length, is twice or three times as long as the calyx segments. The trifid style is rather longer than the corolla.

C. sub-idaea is only a small form of *C. tubulosa*.

C. sulphurea. A native of Palestine of annual and rather frail lax habit which grows about a foot high. It is worthy of interest if only from its colour, which is a clear sulphur yellow. Its thin stems are sparsely furnished with amplexicaul obovate pointed leaves, almost entire and, as usual, diminishing in size towards the ends of the stems. From the upper leaf axils single flowers on long pedicels are produced. These flowers are of medium size and good broad funnel shape; the broadly triangular ciliate calyx segments, with noticeably revolute edges, are about half the length of the corolla, carried erect and continued backwards into horn-like appendages. The style is trifid and dehiscence is basal.

C. sylvatica. A Himalayan species with the general appearance of *C. rotundifolia* though without the rotund basal leaves of that species. De Candolle says that the whole plant is roughly hairy; that the campanulate corolla is twice the length of the calyx segments while the style is slightly longer than the corolla tube. The general hairiness of the plant is the main, if not the only, distinguishing feature.

C. takesimana. A reported species from Korea, but as the name only is given without description it cannot be accepted as valid.

C. taranensis. A Balkan species which I have never seen and which is not, I believe, in cultivation. It is placed by Hruby between *C. balcanica* (which is a form of *C. rotundifolia*) and *C. hercegovina* and is described by him as having circular or heart-shaped basal leaves and a number of ascendant stems six to twelve inches high, furnished with lanceolate, sharply-toothed, leaves, rather crowded in the lower part, and terminating in a loose panicle of two to six flowers, resembling *C. patula*. The calyx segments are a third to one half the length of the corolla and the buds, like the flowers are carried erect on rather long footstalks.

C. telephioides. A small perennial species from moist alpine meadows in Anatolia at 8,000 to 9,000 feet, which forms rosettes of long oblong ciliate leaves which diminish gradually to a petiole and are usually slightly notched at the tip. Short decumbent flower stems bear ovate sessile leaves and small sub-sessile flowers almost hidden in the axils. The calyx is without appendages; the segments are smooth but ciliate, shortly triangular-acute, shorter than the calyx tube and half the length of the corolla, which is lobed to a third its length. The style is shorter than the corolla which is given as the main distinction between this species and *C. radicosa*.

C. teucrioides. A rare species whose natural range is limited to a small district in Western Asia Minor, but not sufficiently showy to appeal to any but the enthusiast. It rambles about in schistose screes producing rosettes of greyish ovate leaves which are deeply dentate or pinnatifid, cuneate at the base, undulate and bristly, seldom more than half an inch long, the lower leaves being on short petioles, the remainder sessile. The flower stems are more or less prostrate, bear a few leaves even smaller than the basal ones, and terminate in a small unilateral spike of one to five small funnel-shaped flowers, in varying shades of blue or lilac, twice or three times the length of the calyx. The segments of the latter are sharply triangular-lanceolate and fringed with hairs, while the somewhat inflated appendages are longer than the calyx tube itself. The style is tripartite and the seed capsule nodding after fertilisation.

Propagation should be by division, for seed does not seem to be produced with any freedom, while the scree is clearly indicated as providing the appropriate conditions for successful cultivation—and a not over rich scree, or the plant will go coarse. Overhead protection is essential in winter and I do not feel very satisfied as to the hardiness of the plant (though it is a true perennial) and at least until it is more readily obtainable, some protection should be given. Recent inquiries fail to show that it is in cultivation in this country at the present time.

C. thessala. A perennial from calcareous rocks of Thessaly which has oblong basal leaves cut into narrow lobes and drawn out at the base into short petioles. There are numerous decumbent flower stems, sometimes shortly branched, bearing oblong-obovate, sessile leaves and terminating in a loose raceme of flowers on short stalks. The calyx has triangular-lanceolate segments with a few small teeth and more or less hairy and very short appendages, while the tubular funnel-shaped corolla, twice to three times the length of the calyx segments, has short acute lobes. The style is trifid.

In general appearance it is said to resemble *C. calamenthifolia*, but its deeply lobed leaves, longer calyx segments and larger flowers enable it to be distinguished.

C. thyrsoides. The only perennial European species with any pretensions to be called yellow. It is widely distributed over the limestone Alps and forms a rosette of many very long lanceolate leaves which, like the rest of the plant, are rough with a covering of stiff hairs. The inflorescence is a thick stocky spike, rarely more than a foot high, of closely packed sessile rather long tubular bells, lobed to a third their length, carried erect rather than drooping, and of a pale straw colour. Actually they are borne singly in the leaf axils, but the internodes are much compressed and the leaves reduced to bracts. The calyx tube is smooth, but the segments, half the length of the corolla and not reflexed, are ciliate. The style is exserted and divides into three filiform stigmata. It is very nearly allied to *C. spicata*.

As an exception in a family whose general character is grace, it can only be described as stiff and clumsy. Fortunately it is only monocarpic, but anyone who, having once grown it, wishes to do so again, can easily save and raise seed.

C. tillishii. An annual species which seems to differ from the widely distributed *C. phrygia* only in having rather broader and slightly notched basal leaves.

C. tommasiniana. The home of this attractive little species is Istria, though even here it is of very local occurrence. Similar in many ways to *C. waldsteiniana* it makes a thick perennial root from which arise numbers of thin wiry stems which reach a height of four to six inches and carry a few rather thick, linear-lanceolate, serrate leaves with almost horny tips. These stems have a branching habit and bear numbers of pendent flowers of a pale lavender blue colour. The smooth calyx has short, filiform, entire segments which are reflexed and not more than about one sixth as long as the corolla. The latter is long, narrowly tubular with short pointed and reflexed lobes about one fifth of its length. The style, shorter than the corolla and trifid is the same colour as the flower in its lower part but white towards the apex.

It must be admitted that the bells are rather too long and narrow and perhaps their drooping habit renders the plant less showy than *C. wald-steiniana*, but it is none the less well worth growing and succeeds in either sun or semi-shade in any open soil. It shows no tendency to run, but can be propagated from seed or from cuttings of the flowerless shoots in early spring or in August.

C. trachelium. One of our British species which also extends through-out Western Europe and Russian Asia. It makes a tuft of bristly leaves which are ovate-cordate, deeply and doubly dentate and acuminate, the basal ones on long petioles. The flower stems, furnished with a number of lanceolate, sessile or sub-sessile leaves which, like the basal ones, are rough and sharply serrate, rise to a height of three to four feet. They are angular and frequently much branched and the axillary, shortly pedicelled flowers, borne singly or in threes, and nearly erect, build up a loose raceme. The calyx, often so dark as to be almost black, is stiffly hairy. It has hairy broadly lanceolate acuminate segments, not much reflexed, and is without appendages. The corolla is large, fully campanulate, at least three times the length of the calyx segments with well displayed lobes about one third the length of the tube; externally the main nerves are ornamented with a line of stiff hairs and the corolla is more or less bearded within. The style is tripartite and the capsule is distinctly pendent.

Both blue and white forms occur and there are also double forms in each colour, the white being the more common on granitic rocks. This species is the old English Throatwort and possibly the original Canterbury Bell, though the latter name is now attached to *C. medium*.

The plant known as *C. urticifolia* is only a variant of this species and well deserves its name from its very close general resemblance to the common stinging nettle.

The species is of course suitable only for the wild garden, though in such surroundings, growing through rough grass or against a loose hedge, it can be quite effective.

It is, as one would suppose, easily raised from seed.

C. transsilvanica. A Bulgarian biennial from alpine pastures with simple erect stems which are softly woolly in the upper parts. The leaves are slightly woolly, the lower ones oblong-spathulate diminishing to a petiole, the upper ones lanceolate and sessile or sub-amplexicaul, all finely serrate. The flowers are sessile and form a many-flowered head. The calyx segments are lanceolate, with a fringe of wool; the corolla about an inch long, more than twice as long as the calyx segments. In general appearance it resembles *C. glomerata*, but being biennial does not run at the root like that species and is dwarfer.

C. triangularis. A species from Persia very similar to *C. michauxioides*, but with broader and longer calyx segments which are softly hairy rather than smooth. Like the better known species it should probably be transferred to the genus Asyneuma.

C. trichopoda. A small species recently introduced from the Lebanon where it grows in fissures of shaded rocks. It makes a rosette of a few leaves which are spathulate, petiolate, entire and softly hairy. From these rosettes a few short thin flexible and procumbent stems are produced bearing a few similar leaves and single tubular whitish flowers terminally and in the leaf axils on thin stalks. The ex-appendiculate calyx is densely hairy with spreading ovate segments longer than the calyx tube and about half the length of the corolla. The style is trifid.

Post suggests that this is merely an alpine form of *C. euclasta* and *C. damascena* which, he further says, are too much alike to be separated.

C. tridentata. A species (or collection of species) very widely distributed throughout the Caucasus which, at the top of a thick, rather carrot-like, root, forms clusters of rosettes of spathulate leaves which diminish to a footstalk, are more or less hairy and more or less dentate. These rosettes throw out a number of simple, decumbent flower stems bearing a few rather small obovate sessile leaves and terminating in a single large erect flower. The calyx itself is generally smooth, but the segments, broad at the base and sharply acuminate are often more or less ciliate and vary considerably in length and in the extent to which they are reflexed, while the ovate-acute appendages are generally edged with a line of fairly stiff hairs. The corolla is bell-shaped, or broadly funnel-shaped, with the lobes well spread, and is of some shade of blue with, invariably, a conspicuous white base. In some forms it is noticeably hairy externally, particularly on the nerves. The style is seldom as long as the corolla and is divided into three stigmata. The capsule is pendent.

The species is deep rooting and requires careful treatment in well drained situations; the scree is generally too dry. It is a sun lover, but often not very free flowering, especially if grown near a town; it is one of the earliest flowering species, being at its best in May or June. It is not difficult to raise from seed which, in fact, provides the only means of increase.

Under this name a plant received the Award of Merit in 1935.

For the near relatives of this species see p. 210.

C. tubulosa, Lam. A most attractive species endemic to Crete whose only fault is that it is biennial, or perhaps more correctly, monocarpic. In its first year it forms a rosette of thickish, lanceolate, deeply crenulate and more or less hairy greyish leaves which diminish to a petiole. Subsequently the rosette throws out a number of decumbent only slightly hairy stems, clothed with small lanceolate leaves the lower ones petiolate and the upper ones sessile, from the axils of which short stems arise which are frequently branched and, on the short branches, bear medium sized erect flowers either singly or in groups of three. The calyx is bristly and the segments lanceolate acuminate and ciliate and about half the length of the corolla and not reflexed, while the appendages are small, ovate and obtuse. The corolla justifies the specific name being tubular in outline and is generally of a transparent blue colour. The style is as long as the corolla and it is one of the small section having five stigmata.

It is closely allied to *C. corymbosa*, Desf., in fact some authorities regard the two as synonymous, treating *C. tubulosa* as merely a small form of the other species. Gandoger, however, says that *C. tubulosa* is much the more common so, if they are not to be regarded as distinct, it would seem to be more logical to treat *C. corymbosa* as the larger form and group both as *C. tubulosa*. The *Index Kewensis*, however, treats *C. corymbosa* as synonymous with *C. pelviformis*.

The plant is a true saxatile, being found in crevices of limestone rocks, always in rather shady places, and requires a similar situation if it is to be a success in cultivation. It would, of course, require to be raised from seed.

The species received an Award of Merit in 1933.

C. turbinata can only be regarded as a form of *C. carpatica* with single-flowered stems and a rather flatter form of flower (see p. 212).

C. tymphaea. A species from alpine and sub-alpine meadows of Greece which is generally smooth, though slightly downy forms have been reported. It produces a number of leafy stems varying from four to twelve inches in height from rosettes of oblong-spathulate, petiolate leaves which persist throughout the flowering period. The stem leaves are oblong or ovate-lanceolate, sessile or sub-amplexicaul, and bright green, while the flowers are in terminal heads each composed of four to seven flowers, In strong plants subsidiary but smaller heads are sometimes produced in the upper leaf axils. Each head of flowers is surrounded by ovate, shortly acuminate bracts which are often denticulate and ciliate. The calyx segments are ciliate and rather longer than the smooth calyx tube while the smooth corolla is funnel-shaped and two or three times the length of the calyx segments.

CAMPANULA STEVENI

CAMPANULA THYRSOIDES

CAMPANULA TOMMASINIANA

204

C. uniflora. Despite Col. Beddome's description of this species as 'a beautiful little plant' the interest must be mainly botanical. It has probably the most northerly distribution of any member of the genus, being found in Northern Sweden, North Russia and across Greenland and the Rocky Mountains where it occurs at an altitude of 12,000 to 14,000 feet. From a garden standpoint, however, it is of little importance for besides that the flowers are comparatively insignificant, they never seem to open properly. It has a rather thick fleshy perennial rootstock with a few stalked oblong-oval, obtuse leaves and produces numerous stolons, leafy, and ending in thin flexible stems one to two inches high, bearing small ovate-lanceolate leaves on short petioles. Many of the stems are sterile and on these the leaves are entire, but on the flowering stems the upper leaves become crenate. Leaves, stems and calyces are all slightly velvety. The flowers are always borne singly and more or less horizontally; they are small, narrowly tubular in shape with lobes that do not reflex at all and their only merit is their colour which is a good mid blue. The pointed calyx segments equally are not reflexed and are almost as long as the corolla which they seem to hug and prevent it expanding; the capsules are much longer than the flower and dehisce at the top. The species spreads in much the same way as *C. allionii*, and would probably be equally difficult to propagate except from seed.

C. vajdae appears to be only a one-flowered form of *C. abietina* though described as having longer and narrower calyx segments, characters which would scarcely entitle it to specific rank.

C. valdensis is merely a hairy form of *C. linifolia*.

C. vandesi, G. Don. This name appeared in Loudon's *Hortus Britannicus* but as no description was given it cannot be regarded as valid.

C. vayredae. From Monserrat in north-eastern Spain, this need not be distinguished from *C. affinis* from the same area. The only distinctions shown by the description are that the calyx segments are shorter than in typical *C. affinis* being only the same length as the appendages and only half the length of the corolla, while the inflorescence contains fewer flowers, said not to exceed eight.

C. velata. An insignificant and little-known species from Algeria which is described as perennial with rosettes of very small lanceolate and shortly petioled leaves and small pale blue flowers. The calyx has very small, scarcely noticeable appendages. Somewhat similar to *C. malacitana*, it is clearly too small to be of even the smallest interest.

C. velenovskyi. A perennial from alpine meadows of Stara Planina and probably other parts of the Balkans whose fibrous root with numerous

K

thin and much branched stolons soon forms a close mat of rosettes. The leaves are generally smooth, elliptic or elliptic-oblong, obtuse, very slightly crenulate and drawn out into long petioles. Numbers of short ascendant stems, smooth and sharply angled, some eight to twelve inches high, bear linear-lanceolate, obtuse, almost entire and sessile leaves and terminate in two or three flowers on long footstalks. The smooth obconical calyx has long linear segments somewhat broadened at the base, almost as long as the corolla tube and carried erect. The corolla is broadly funnel-shaped, divided to halfway into oblong-lanceolate lobes.

Its affinities are with *C. patula*, *C. hemschinica* and *C. steveni*. Its perennial character is sufficient to distinguish it from the first two, but it might well be merged in the last, the only differences described being its larger basal leaves, its two- or three-flowered stems (*C. steveni* is usually one-flowered) and its broader corolla.

C. verbenaefolia, Sieb. Reported by Sieber as a plant from Japan, but as his description and plate refers to a plant with its leaves in whorls it clearly cannot be accepted as a Campanula.

C. veronicifolia. From the neighbourhood of Canton, this does not seem to be distinguishable from the very variable *C. colorata*.

C. verruculosa. A tall biennial common in most parts of Spain and Portugal, which the *Index Kewensis* says is the same as *C. rapunculus*. There are, however, many points of difference which should entitle it to specific rank. The main distinctions are that the upper part of the stems is much more profusely branched; the flowers too are on much shorter pedicels and are held erect, while the calyx is bristly, more angled and longer than in the better known species.

C. versicolor. Another Grecian species which grows on cliffs in the lower wood region. From a thick, almost tuberous root it forms rosettes of a few smooth, oblong, sub-cordate, noticeably serrate leaves on long footstalks, and pushes up a number of rather lush, leafy stems to a height of perhaps four feet. The flower stems are unbranched, but bear in each leaf axil a rather loose spike of from one to five erect, stalked flowers. The calyx is without appendages and the spreading calyx segments are narrow, almost linear, acuminate and half the length of the corolla. The flowers are campanulate-rotate, or saucer shaped and are cleft to about three-quarters of their length, and as the lobes tend to be revolute at the edges the effect is almost of a star-shaped flower. The coloration, from which the species derives its name, is deep blue at the centre, shading to a paler tint, and almost white at the edge. The style is exserted, that is, longer than the corolla, and is trifid. The type plant is wholly glabrous, but there is a hairy form, known as var. *tomentella,* in which leaves and stems are covered throughout with soft hairs. This form is smaller in all its parts than the type and less certainly perennial and apparently it cannot be depended on to come true from seed, a proportion of any batch of seedlings being of the stronger, glabrous, type.

Propagation is generally from seed, but when, in later years, the crown produces a number of rosettes some of these can be carefully detached and used as cuttings. It is also said to be possible to reproduce it from root cuttings.

It is closely allied to, and similar in general outline to, *C. pyramidalis,* but is more nearly perennial in character and, the inflorescence is rather looser and less formal.

A hybrid between the two species (known as *C. × pyraversi*) shows the merits and demerits of both parents and does not really seem to be wanted.

The type received an Award of Merit in 1932.

C. vidalii. A perennial species whose home is in the Azores and which, accordingly, cannot be regarded as hardy in this country. Unlike any other member of the genus it is of a shrubby habit, the stems, branched from the base, persisting from year to year. These stems are glossy and grooved and more or less clammy to the touch; they are furnished with thick fleshy oblong-spathulate leaves which are three or four inches long and coarsely serrate, becoming smaller towards the upper part of the stems. The flowers, on short thick pedicels, are borne in loose, few-flowered, terminal racemes. The thick triangular calyx segments are about a quarter the length of the corolla, while the latter, up to two inches in length, is pendent, fully tubular, inflated at the base, yellowish in colour and has a ring of orange at the base.

It is in so many respects different from all other Campanulas that it may well be doubted whether it should rightly be included in the genus at all. A Swiss botanist, Feer, did in fact suggest this course as long ago as 1890 and proposed a new monotypic genus to which he gave the name Azorina, but the suggestion appears to have been overlooked or ignored by later writers.

C. vincaeflora, Pau. A form of the annual *C. loefflingii* which is stronger growing generally and has rather larger flowers.

It received a First Class Certificate from the Royal Horticultural Society in 1895.

C. violaefolia, Lam. A plant under this name, said to have been imported from Siberia, was in cultivation in Paris in 1765 but I can find no trace of it at the present time. According to description it has a thin running rootstock which at intervals emits tufts of ovate-rotund, cordate, crenate leaves on petioles about the same length as the blade, resembling in general outline those of *Viola canina* and softly hairy on the undersides. Later, erect hairy stems some three or four inches high are produced which bear a few oblong-ovate, dentate leaves and terminate in two or three large pendent flowers on short footstalks. The calyx segments are erect, lanceolate, ciliate and long acuminate and nearly as long as the corolla which is full-bell shaped but not inflated and has short lobes bearded at the edges. There are ovate-acute appendages and the style is about two thirds the length of the corolla. It is clearly a close ally of *C. punctata* and is said to differ only in the length of the calyx segments.

C. violiifolia, Pau. (an unfortunate similarity in naming) is a form of the Persian *C. humillima*. It does not appear to deserve specific rank, but a definite pronouncement on this point is impossible in the absence of material.

C. visiani is the name given by Reichenbach to a form of *C. waldsteiniana* with much more bell-shaped flowers.

C. vulgaris, Gueldenst. A name published without any description and, therefore, not valid.

C. waldsteiniana. A native of Dalmatia, this species occurs in rocky crevices wherever the soil is sufficiently rich, yet light and well drained. Here it forms a thick root which increases yearly in size and produces a number of erect wiry stems four to six inches high, sparsely furnished with leaves which, like those at the base, are smooth, lanceolate, sessile and about an inch long with a few conspicuous teeth. Each stem terminates in a loose cluster of three to five erect, shortly tubular-campanulate, almost star-shaped, flowers, the much reflexed lobes being at least half the length of the corolla and blue-violet in colour.

The calyx tube is glabrous and the segments are not more than a quarter the length of the corolla; they are awl-shaped, pointed and reflexed. There are no calyx appendages and the trifid style is rather shorter than the corolla. It bears considerable relation to *C. hawkinsiana*, one of the main differences being that the latter species has a hairy calyx. It is, however, much more amenable to cultivation than that species, presenting few difficulties if given a sunny spot in rich gritty soil.

It is one of the latest to flower, being at its best towards the end of August and is a very neat, tidy little plant. Increase is from seed or by cuttings of the young growth early in the season before the shoots have begun to spindle up for flower.

The Award of Merit was bestowed on this species in 1916.

C. wilkinsiana. A North American annual species which has a number of prostrate few-flowered stems, with an occasional one fairly upright and from three to six inches high. The small light green leaves are oblong lanceolate and toothed only at the apex, while the stems terminate in one to three fair-sized flowers which face upwards on slender footstalks. The calyx segments are lanceolate, longer than the calyx tube and carried erect, while the deep blue-purple, funnel-shaped corolla is cut halfway into moderately spreading lobes.

Its distribution in nature is very restricted, being confined to Mt. Shasta, California, and even there it is far from being a common plant.

C. zoysii. An Austrian or North Italian species whose home is in the almost inaccessible crannies of the Karawanken.

It forms tufts of small roundish shiny leaves with short stalks and entire but hairy margins and produces short stalks about three inches high each carrying a few shortly stalked obovate lanceolate or linear leaves and terminating in anything up to six pale blue stalked flowers which have been well described as 'soda water bottle' shape. At least the shape is so characteristic that anyone who has once seen the plant in flower or a good illustration is unlikely to mistake it for any other, and Feer, in 1890, went so far as to suggest the creation of a new genus under the name Favratia. The spreading calyx segments are awl-shaped and only about a quarter the length of the corolla. The trifid style is shorter than the corolla and the species is another of those in which dehiscence of the capsule takes place near the apex.

It does best in a rich limy crevice or perhaps in cultivation even better in a scree, watered from below; in any case it is almost the first species to fall a victim to any marauding slug, and often flowers so freely that it has no strength to make new growth to carry over for another year; in other words it often dies after flowering, so that seed should be carefully collected, or care should be taken to secure cuttings of the young shoots in the early part of the year. It is certainly not one of the easier species to grow and, particularly, to keep alive from year to year though definitely perennial, and it is probably most satisfactory in the alpine house in a rich limy scree mixture.

It was given an Award of Merit as long ago as 1924.

CHAPTER V

GROUPS OF SPECIES

IN addition to the species considered and described in the previous
pages there are many Campanulas which some botanists regard as distinct species but in which the differences are of a minor and essentially
botanical character and not such as will appeal to the practical grower nor
such as can be distinguished in a photograph.

They fall into groups around very definite species and are so treated
in the following pages.

(1) tridentata group

This group includes species referred to as *C. ardonensis, aucheri, bellidifolia, ciliata, saxifraga,* and, more indistinguishable still, *adami,* Bieb., *alpigena, argunensis, biebersteiniana, bornmuelleri, kryophila, ledebouriana,
pubiflora, ruprechtii, stenophylla, dzaaku, circassica, anomala,* and
besenginica.

The *Index Kewensis* (followed by Farrer) reduces the group considerably, regarding *adami,* Bieb. as synonymous with *bellidifolia, biebersteiniana*
as synonymous with *tridentata,* of which also *stenophylla* is regarded as
merely a dwarf high alpine form, while *ruprechtii* is treated as synonymous
with *saxifraga,* and *kryophila* as a form of *ardonensis. Alpigena, argunensis*
and *pubiflora* are regarded as synonyms for *aucheri,* while *ledebouriana* is
only a small form of *saxifraga.* A number of even less known names can
be found; *affinis,* Fisch, *fallax,* Rupr., *hygrophila,* Rupr., *mayeriana,* Rupr.
are all synonymous with *aucheri; bithynica,* D.C., and *tridens,* Rupr. are
tridentata; gilanica, Rupr. is *saxifraga*; and *hispida,* Spreng, is *ciliata.*
Finally, we have two invalid uses of the name *bellidifolia,* first by Frivaldski,
where it is synonymous with *orphanidea,* and second by Lapeyrousse,
whose plant has been identified as *patula.*

We are thus left with a considerably reduced list, in addition to *C.
tridentata* itself, which has been adopted as the group name as it appears
to be the oldest. This is fully described on p. 201.

All are from the Caucasus district or Asia Minor.

C. ciliata is the most distinct for it produces only a single stem from
each rosette, instead of a number as in all the others. Distinctions have
been framed on the varying degree of hairiness of stems, leaves, and flowers,

saxifraga being the most hairy while *ardonensis* and *bellidifolia* are practically without hairs. Again, distinctions have been sought in the length of calyx segments relative to the corolla, the segments of *bellidifolia* being one third, and those of *tridentata* and *saxifraga* one half the corolla length; or in the colour of the flowers, *ardonensis* being described as rich violet-blue, *aucheri* as violet-blue (apparently not 'rich'), *saxifraga* as deep amethyst, *tridentata* as deep Tyrian purple and *bellidifolia* as intense deep purple, but there are few, if any, botanists who will base specific differences on colour alone, particularly in a genus like Campanula where colour variations are the rule rather than the exception. By others, differences have been remarked in the width and dentations of the basal leaves. We are told that *aucheri* has the leaves scalloped all the way round, that *saxifraga* confines its scallops to the upper half of the leaf (or dispenses with them altogether), while *tridentata* has merely three notches (some botanists admit five!) at the extreme top. *C. bellidifolia* is not particular about scallops. Distinctions based on the number of leaf serrations are not, however, in my view, to be relied on. On almost any plant you can find at the same time all possible variations; further, a plant showing the, so-called, characteristic tridentations of its name species in the seedling stage may entirely lose this character with age, and as far as I can see a safer line (if any discrimination is necessary) is to say that *aucheri* has the broadest leaves of the group (they are about twice as long as broad), in *saxifraga* the length is at least three times the breadth, *bellidifolia* has smaller leaves than the others and nearly round, while in *ardonensis* they should be very narrow and almost grass-like. The leaves of *tridentata* are more greyish green in colour than those of its relations. The position is, in fact, well summed up by Mr. Ingwersen who has collected extensively in the native haunts of these Campanulas and, in a paper read before the Royal Horticultural Society some years ago, refers to 'the confusing group containing *C. bellidifolia, saxifraga, tridentata* and *ardonensis, all grading into each other to a bewildering extent*' (the italics are mine) and, elsewhere, to 'Campanulas of the *C. saxifraga* persuasion endlessly variable with paler or darker bells and deep or shallow ones'. Farrer too falls into an error in comparing them with *C. allionii* which differs fundamentally in producing underground stolons, apart altogether from the shape and carriage of the flowers which, in *C. allionii*, are long and sub-pendent whereas those of *C. tridentata* and its group are at least as wide as deep and carried erect.

Finally, distinctions can be based on the length of the calyx appendages and if any reader is anxious to pursue these small botanical differences, the following 'key' may prove useful:

A. Appendages longer than calyx tube.

{Corolla bell-shaped, pubescent   *aucheri*

{Corolla bell-shaped, not pubescent

    Leaf margins crimped   *saxifraga*

    Leaf margins not crimped

        Corolla two or three times as long as

            calyx segments   *tridentata*

        Corolla four or five times as long as

            calyx segments   *bellidifolia*

{Corolla narrow bell-shaped   *kryophila*

{Corolla broad bell-shaped

    appendages long   *anomala*

    appendages very long   *argunensis*

AA. Appendages equal to calyx tube

    Single flower stems   *ciliata*

    More than one flower stem

        corolla bell-shaped   *circassica*

        corolla narrow bell-shaped   *ardonensis*

AAA. Appendages shorter than calyx tube

    Leaves coriaceous   *dzaaku*

    Leaves glabrous   *besenginica*

(2) carpatica group

C. carpatica is one of the most variable species when raised from seed, as is manifest from the number of forms which have been given garden names, e.g. *Isobel*, *White Star*, *Riverslea*, etc., and new names are added almost yearly. All these are probably only seedling forms selected by nurserymen and vary not only in colour and size of flower but in height and hairiness; yet the possibility of a hybrid origin cannot be disregarded for *C. carpatica* is one of the comparatively few species which succumb to the blandishments of the hybridist. So it is not surprising that attempts have been made to accord specific rank to some of these variants.

The most noticeable is that known as *C. turbinata*, which by description should be dwarfer than the type, never exceeding six inches, and softly hairy in all its parts, stems, leaves and calyx tube, and should only carry a single flower on each stem, while the flower itself is more cup-shaped.

Another form is frequently offered as *C. pelviformis*—a sad trap for the unwary, for the true *C. pelviformis* is an entirely different plant and closely related to *C. medium*. The *C. carpatica* form under this name differs from the type in having smaller and *flatter* flowers.

213

CAMPANULA TUBULOSA

CAMPANULA VERSICOLOR

214

CAMPANULA WALDSTEINIANA

C. dasycarpa, Schur. and *C. oreophila*, Schur. are not to be distinguished from *C. carpatica* type; while the plant sometimes listed as *C. reuteriana* also belongs to this group and is without any very clear distinguishing features. (It is to be noted that there is also an annual species under this name.)

(3) garganica group

Names which come within this group are *C. acutiloba, adsurgens, barbeyi, cephallenica, debarensis, fenestrellata, istriaca, lepida, secundiflora,* and, possibly, *elatinoides*.

C. acutiloba—the Persian relative—has been separately described.

C. adsurgens is the Spanish representative. It is sometimes said to be of biennial duration only. Its flowers are more restricted to the ends of the branches which are longer than those of other members of the group. The basal leaves, too, have longer petioles, but it does not seem to be in cultivation.

C. barbeyi is a looser grower than the type with thicker leaves and has more mauve in its flower colour, while the peduncles are shorter.

C. cephallenica carries looseness of growth even further but compensates for it to some extent by having larger flowers and is indeed the most distinct of the group. The flowers of this form are slightly hairy externally.

C. debarensis, also from the island of Cephallonia, seems to be nothing but a more generally hairy form of the last named.

C. istriaca seems to differ only in being a hairy form, leaves, stems and calyx being covered with short, soft hairs, a character which is more fully developed in *C. elatinoides* which is so densely clothed as to be more adequately described as woolly or downy. It—*C. istriaca*—is the most robust of the group, and is identical with the plant often offered as *C. g. hirsuta*.

C. lepida has small and more clustered flowers.

C. secundiflora belongs to this group but has more rounded basal leaves and is a stronger and more upright grower than the type.

Probably the best form in the group is *C. fenestrellata* which is a neat, compact-growing plant with smaller leaves and shorter stems but with the same bright starry flowers which are, as a result, more conspicuous, especially as, though possibly not so widely open as those of some of the others, they generally have longer footstalks which lift them well clear of the foliage.

Feer points out that *C. garganica* type and *barbeyi* are natives of Mount Gargano which is isolated from the other Italian mountains and might well have been connected in earlier periods with the opposite Illyrian coast

which is the home of the other species, with *C. cephallenica* furthest from
the centre.

(4) lyrata group

(5) rupestris group

These two groups must be considered together, partly because they
are difficult to separate, but more particularly because they are inextri-
cably mixed. Between them they present the greatest nomenclatural
problems of the whole genus.

All are natives of Greece and the surrounding islands; all are monocarpic or nearly so (claims have been made for the perennial character of
C. ephesia and *C. rupestris* S. & S., but though an occasional plant may
survive to flower a second time this is not the usual experience); all have
a five-partite style and a five-celled capsule; all have greyish-tomentose
basal leaves which are more or less lyrate or laciniate with long lobed or
winged petioles; and all produce long, many-branched, many-flowered
prostrate flower stems, sometimes with a more or less erect central stem,
the flowers being funnel-shaped though varying somewhat in width.

Names within the groups are *anchusiflora, andrewsii, appendiculata,
betonicaefolia, calamenthifolia* (of Aucher), *celsii, ephesia, eriantha, erucifolia, hagielia, laciniata* (of Andrews), not to be confused with *laciniata* (of
Linnaeus), *lanuguinosa, lyrata, lyratella, mycalaea, rupestris* (of many
authorities), *sporadum, stricta,* S. & S., *tomentosa* (also of many authorities)
and *topaliana.* So great is the confusion that, according to the *Index
Kewensis, rupestris,* of Sibthorp and Smith, is *tomentosa*; while *rupestris,*
of Adams, is *bellidifolia*; *rupestris,* of Bieberstein, is *biebersteiniana* (syn.
tridentata); *rupestris,* of Spruner, is *rupicola*; *rupestris,* of Host, is *waldsteiniana*; and *rupestris,* of Risso, is *macrorrhiza*—all very distinct species.

Again, the *Index Kewensis* says, *andrewsii, appendiculata, calamenthifolia,* Auch., *eriantha,* and *laciniata,* Andr. are all synonyms of *tomentosa,*
and, at one remove, the same applies to *ephesia, hagielia, lyrata,* Bourg.,
and *stricta,* S. & S., while Feer says *erucifolia* is *laciniata,* L. Boissier
regarded most of them as forms of *tomentosa,* Vent., his form *brachyantha*
being the *rupestris* of De Candolle and his form *bracteosa* the *celsii* of De
Candolle. Nevertheless he retained as distinct species, *anchusiflora, lyrata*
and *hagielia.*

Doubtless, as many forms (or, if you like, species) could be found as
there are islands in the Greek Seas or mountains on the mainland, but for
practical purposes they can be reduced to the two names mentioned at
the head of this section. Between these there are fairly clear distinctions

in the form of the basal leaves (which, however, die off as the flower spikes are produced).

The first group, which I here call *C. lyrata* is based on the *C. lyrata* of Lamarck and contains those species, or pseudo-species, in which the lobes of the basal leaves are more or less similar in size, forming a leaf whose full outline would be a long oval with deeply jagged edges. Generally, too, these leaves are crimped or undulate. Other names in this group would be *lyratella*, an inland form characterised by stronger stems, smaller and more numerous flowers, and a generally duller grey in the leaf colour; *sporadum*, Feer, which, from the original description shows considerable variation in form of leaf and shape and size of flower, depending on the position in which it happens to be growing; *topaliana* which may be distinguished by its sharply dentate calyx segments which are nearly as long as the corolla, and by its exserted style.

In the second group the terminal lobe of the lyrate basal leaves is very distinctly larger than the rest—in fact the lyrations are frequently little more than teeth—and the leaf as a whole is generally flatter. In this group would come, as names recognised as species by the *Index Kewensis*, *andrewsii*, *celsii* and *anchusiflora*, such differences as there are being found mainly in the appendages and calyx segments. It is also stated that *tomentosa* has more spreading of the corolla lobes than the others, while *anchusiflora* has specially narrow and specially blue flowers. *C. celsii* is the doubtful one of the group, with its basal leaves often deeply dentate rather than lyrate, and it may well be regarded as a link between the two groups.

The choice of a name for this group presents considerable difficulty. The earliest description is that of Ventenat in 1800, as *tomentosa*, but, unfortunately, that name had been used by Lamarck several years earlier for an entirely different species, a species, in fact, which was described as ex-appendiculate and was reported as a native of Asia Minor. The next description is that of Sibthorp and Smith in 1806 under the name *rupestris* but Boissier prefers *tomentosa*, Vent. and the *Index Kewensis* says *rupestris* S. & S. is synonymous with *tomentosa*. This, however, leaves us with two quite distinct plants, those of Lamarck and Ventenat, bearing the same name and it seems preferable to follow still later authorities (e.g. Halacsy, 1902 and Hayek, 1928) and accept *rupestris*, S. & S. as the group name. Halacsy retains *anchusiflora* and *celsii* as distinct species in addition to *rupestris*, but Hayek says there are only two true species, though he admits a number of sub-species and varieties under the shadow of *rupestris*. His separation, though it produces the same result as that here proposed, is based not on leaf form but on the general habit of the plant, *C. rupestris* and its sub-forms having prostrate, ascendant stems whereas those of *C. lyrata* are erect. While, no doubt, this is broadly correct, it is equally true that most of the forms grouped under *rupestris* tend to throw a central, almost if not quite erect, stem, while *lyrata* and its kin produce, in addition to the central stem, others which spread more or less horizontally. The fact that the basal leaves disappear before flowering time makes the problem of naming a difficult one, but, if anyone wishes to pursue these small differences, the following key may be of assistance; but it must be stressed that the characters on which differentiation is based are very difficult to assess with any real certainty and may well be largely caused or masked by geographical or cultural conditions, while, when all is said and done, the two groups are practically identical from the gardener's point of view.

A. Appendages longer than calyx tube:

    (*a*) Corolla more than twice calyx segments:

        (*i*) Calyx segments triangular lanceolate   *andrewsii*

        (*ii*) Calyx segments ovate lanceolate   *betonicaefolia*

        (*iii*) Calyx segments long acuminate $\left\{\begin{array}{l}\textit{mycalaea}\\\textit{breueri}\end{array}\right.$

    (*aa*) Corolla not more than twice calyx segments $\left\{\begin{array}{l}\textit{lyrata}\\\textit{lyratella}\\\textit{sporadum}\\\textit{lavrensis}\end{array}\right.$

B. Appendages not longer than calyx tube:

    (*b*) Corolla more than twice calyx segments:

        (*i*) Calyx segments triangular lanceolate   *anchusiflora*

        (*ii*) Calyx segments ovate lanceolate   *celsii*

        (*iii*) Calyx segments long acuminate $\left\{\begin{array}{l}\textit{ephesia}\\\textit{hagielia}\end{array}\right.$

    (*bb*) Corolla not more than twice calyx segments:

        (*i*) Calyx segments triangular lanceolate $\left\{\begin{array}{l}\textit{rupestris, S. \& S.}\\\textit{tomentosa, Vent.}\end{array}\right.$

        (*ii*) Calyx segments dentate   *topaliana*

Reference must here be made to a number of species which bear a very strong resemblance to these two groups, but in which the style is only tripartite and the capsule trilocular. They cannot be grouped in the same way as those dealt with above and have accordingly been separately described in preceding pages. The principal names coming within the group are *calavrytana*, *constantinii*, *pelia*, and *thessala*. It must be pointed out, however, that at least one Swiss botanist has argued that all species within the botanical section Medium (i.e. those which have appendages on the calyx) vary from plant to plant, and even from flower to flower on the same plant in having the style divided into three, four or five stigmata. This seems to be going too far, for although, as stated elsewhere, a species which normally has five stigmata will frequently abort one of them, while a species whose normal complement is three may occasionally produce a fourth, I have never met the more extreme case of interchangeability between five and three.

(6) Himalayan group

Apart from a number of well defined species which have already been described, there are, in the Himalayan mountain block, a number of so-called species (and many more names) which are only to be distinguished by minor botanical differences and for all practical purposes quite a few names would suffice.

Indeed, it may well be that here, on one of the most recent land elevations, we are in the presence of the gradual development of what we call species from an earlier universal type, the differences being caused mainly by elevation and general environment.

Amongst names that will be met with from time to time are *alphonsii, alsinoides, anomala, aprica, argyrotricha, benthami, cana, canescens, capernioides, cashmiriana, colorata, evolvulaceae, himalayensis, hoffmeisteri, integerrima, mekongensis, moorcroftiana, nervosa, pallida, pasumensis, ramulosa, stricta,* Wall., *sylvatica, tenuissima, tibetica,* and *xylopoda.*

Of these, *anomala, himalayensis, hoffmeisteri, moorcroftiana, nervosa, pallida, pasumensis, ramulosa* and *tibetica* are synonyms, or forms, of *colorata,* with *ramulosa* as a rather erect growing form. *Alphonsii* is a very dwarf and often one-flowered form but otherwise indistinguishable from *cana; benthami* is the same as *canescens* (which itself is *cana); evolvulaceae* is *cashmiriana; mekongensis* and *xylopoda* are *alsinoides; tenuissima* is *argyrotricha;* while *integerrima* and *capernioides* are *sylvatica,* as is also *stricta,* of Wallich (distinct from *stricta,* of Linnaeus).

But that is not the end; Hooker, in *Flora of British India,* groups a large number of these so-called Indian species into a common aggregate, in the same way as many botanists collect the many local forms of *C. rotundifolia,* and groups *cashmiriana* and *evolvulaceae,* and many other more or less perennial species, under *C. cana,* saying (he is writing of *C. cashmiriana):* 'The fully developed form of this species with zigzaggy stems and very large brilliant flowers is *C. cana;* the middle form with flexuose stems and medium flowers is *C. cashmiriana*; the weak form with smaller flowers, half inch by one fifth inch, less hairy without, is *C. evolvulaceae.*' All the others in the above list, being definitely annuals, would then be grouped as *C. colorata*, while the plant referred to as *C. aprica*, Nannf. also belongs here. Clay goes even further and says '*cana* embraces everything from large flowered and desirable plants to coarse and half-shrubby weeds', while '*canescens* is a further step down in the same series'. Personally I have yet to find a campanula in this group which can be described as large flowered or half-shrubby.

On the other hand, the distinctly tubular corolla, with well reflexed lobes, of *C. argyrotricha*, would seem to entitle the latter to specific rank, but the extent to which the group varies is very well shown by the illustration in Hay's book, *Plants for the Connoisseur*, his plant referred to as *C. argyrotricha* having very distinctly cup-shaped flowers.

All these Himalayan species are characterised by a rather leafy calyx which is wider than the base of the corolla, a tripartite style, a capsule which dehisces at the base, and the bad habit of frequently producing cleistogamous flowers. They are annuals, or at least very short lived perennials, generally lax and weedy in habit and with flowers that are not distinguished in either size or colour.

The most distinct and worth while of them have been described in earlier pages: *C. alsinoides* on p. 36, *C. argyrotricha* on p. 41, *C. cana* on p. 55, *C. cashmiriana* on p. 57, *C. colorata* on p. 66, and *C. sylvatica* on p. 196.

This would seem to be the most appropriate place to refer to several plants from this part of the world which, though commonly classed as Campanulas, have only two stigmata and, accordingly, do not appear to be really within the genus. They are nearer Phyteuma, in which in fact Blatter (*Beautiful Plants of Kashmir*) includes at least one of them but the absence of the joined petal tips which is so characteristic of better known members of that genus may be diagnostic and further observations (so far as I know none of them is in cultivation) may well lead to the establishment of an entirely new genus.

C. chanetii, Levl. makes a tangled bushling of many much-branched stems with greyish sessile leaves which are linear-lanceolate and jagged with irregular but deep dentations. Calyx segments are linear, reflexed and hairy but only a quarter the length of the fairly large corolla. The style is long, exserted, dilated at the apex and bilobed.

C. griffithii occurs frequently in rocky crevices of Baluchistan and Afghanistan and forms a thick root emitting numerous sub-erect stems, six to nine inches high, which are dichotomously branched and furnished with small greyish oblong-lanceolate dentate and sub-sessile leaves rather less than half an inch long and roughly hairy. The shortly stalked pendent flowers, half an inch long, form a panicle. The rough calyx has short ovate segments and small appendages, while the corolla is broadly campanulate and hairy. The long style is twice as long as the corolla and is much exserted and divides into two or three stigmata.

C. khasiana. In height and general habit this is said to resemble *C. rapunculoides.* The stout erect stems rise to a height of three feet and bear obovate acuminate serrate and sessile leaves and terminate in a long raceme which is sometimes compound. The smooth, medium-sized nodding flowers up to three-quarters of an inch long, are broadly funnel-shaped with short lobes while the globose calyx has narrowly lanceolate segments about half the corolla length. The thin style is about the same length as the corolla and divides into two short stigmata.

C. thomsonii. A plant from temperate woods in the eastern part of the Himalaya which makes a woody perennial root with erect stems, nine inches to two feet high, generally quite smooth and slightly branched. These stems are furnished with ovate-acute, cordate leaves, irregularly serrate, one to two inches long on thin petioles and terminate in a long loose panicle containing sometimes as many as forty small flowers carried erect on thin stalks. The smooth calyx is shortly turbinate and has thin hairlike segments, while the broadly campanulate corolla, not more than half an inch across, is divided for more than half its length. The long thickish clawed style has two short stigmata.

(7) Rotundifolia group

This is undoubtedly the largest and most disputable section in the whole genus. A plant resembling in general appearance the Linnaean *C. rotundifolia* is widespread throughout the greater part of the area in which any member of the genus is found, being absent only from Southern Greece, Southern Italy and North Africa. The *Index Kewensis* seems to accept *rotundifolia,* L., *linifolia,* Scop., and *scheuchzeri,* Vill. as foci around which most of the names can be grouped, giving some 60 synonyms for *rotundifolia,* 20 for *linifolia* and 10 for *scheuchzeri,* but in addition it includes a large number of names which are really only minor variants of the same theme and even the three main names referred to are not reliably separable. Much of the confusion arises from the fact that the original descriptions are very short and contain no reference to characters later regarded as specific. De Candolle, in 1830, was, so far as I can trace, the first writer to draw attention to the fact that the plant which he identifies as *C. linifolia* has pendent buds, whereas those of *C. rotundifolia* are carried erect, the peduncles only arching as the flowers expand. He points out that this characteristic is not easily ascertainable from herbarium material, which may well explain why published descriptions so often fail to refer to it. Another clear and important distinction between these two species is that the lower stem leaves of *C. rotundifolia* are *shortly* petiolate, whereas those of *C. linifolia* are always sessile. *C. scheuchzeri* resembles *C. linifolia* in having sessile stem leaves and pendent buds but the flowers, generally borne singly, are nearly if not quite erect. So we have *C. rotundifolia* with erect buds and pendent flowers; *C. linifolia* with pendent buds and pendent flowers; and *C. scheuchzeri* with pendent buds and more or less erect flowers; all have pendent capsules. The remaining combination is erect buds and erect flowers and the earliest name I can trace for this is *C. lostrittii*, Ten. (1831). Typically all these have smooth leaves and stems, but forms occur in which both leaves and stems are softly grey hairy and the name *C. valdensis* has been applied by many authorities, with no apparent reference to the distinctions pointed out above.

So much for the only species mentioned by the earliest authors, but much critical analytical work has been done since then and much more material collected from all parts of the world. Naturally, variants have been found and the only question is how many of these should be raised to specific rank. Farrer refers to it as an 'aggregate' in which he includes some twenty names. Witasek, at the other extreme, finds differences which are regarded as justifying splitting the type *rotundifolia* into three series and 32 species or sub-species and other botanists follow his example. And, though the gardener may adopt Farrer's view, botanically the question is of considerable importance for there are other quite easily recognisable differences which, provided they remain constant despite environmental conditions, whether in the wild or in cultivation, and are also repeated in plants raised from seed, certainly deserve specific rank. Which differences should be so recognised is, however, a question for the trained botanist and, more important, it is a question on which botanists should be expected to agree among themselves. That investigations must be on an extensive scale and carried on for a considerable time is admitted by the work which has been done and is continuing but, unfortunately, too much of the work is carried on independently and each worker has produced his own set of names based on his own views of the distinctions which are important. Thus we have one set of names based primarily on variations in the corolla shape, this ranging from the full campanulate form with rounded, and sometimes almost square, base, to the funnel shape or even tubular form of *C. stenocodon* which some botanists now regard as merely a variety of *C. rotundifolia*. Another line of classification rests primarily on the length and carriage of the calyx segments relative to the corolla, some plants having the segments almost as long as the corolla and well spread out—and correspondingly conspicuous—while in others they are quite short and either recurved or hugging the base of the bell. These variations, too, seem to arise in any of the four main groups referred to above, while still another break occurs, possibly confined to the *rotundifolia* and *lostrittii* sections, where the flowers are much shallower, in other words where the corolla is practically as broad as it is long. Sometimes a particular form is predominant (or even exclusive) in a particular area, but does not retain its characters (or all of them) when transferred to different conditions. On the other hand, plants showing many of the differences mentioned can be collected during a morning's ramble in many areas where plants of the group are at all common. This is not the place, however, to go into such a complicated question in detail—a whole volume would be needed to deal with the matter adequately—enough has been said to give the reader an idea of the problem involved. Some of the most distinct have been described in previous pages but it will be of interest to anyone contemplating the acquisition of a new Campanula to append a list of names which, while not as yet accepted generally as synonyms (see pp. 233-255) are yet somewhere within the present group.

The names involved, apart from those included in the accepted lists of synonyms on pp. 233-255, would include: *adscendens, alpicola, apricornis, arctolinifolia, bohemica, borbasiana, bracteata, camtschatica, cinerea, consanguinea, exul, frondosa, hegetschweileri, hirta, hispanica, latifrons, luxurians, mixta, moravica, nevadensis, ovalifolia, paenina, papillifera, perfoliosa, perneglecta, polymorpha, pourrettii, praticola, pseudo-stenocodon, pygmaea, scabriuscula, scheuchzeriformis, silvicola, sudetica, susplugasii, nmbrosa, xylorrhiza.*

CHAPTER VI

HYBRIDS

For a genus of this size, hybrids, whether of natural or garden origin, are distinctly uncommon and it is an interesting subject for speculation why this should be so, for species overlap to a considerable extent in nature and more so in gardens.

On the garden side, it may be, of course, that horticulturists have been fully satisfied with the diversity provided by the genus itself, though this seems scarcely likely in these days when the craving for novelty is almost morbid, and it is a safe guess that efforts have been made without success. Examination of the parentage (or alleged parentage) of all the garden hybrids I have been able to trace, which are briefly described in the present chapter, may provide the explanation. It shows that, apart from a very few which have had only a very ephemeral existence, almost all have as a parent (on the pollen or seed side) one of only three or four species, viz. *carpatica*, *cochleariifolia*, *rotundifolia*, or *isophylla*, which supports a hypothesis that most of the species are incompatible and will not set seed with the pollen of other species. In the case of a species which *does participate* in the production of hybrids, the various forms appear to be equally effective and there seems to be little difference, so far as the production of fertile seed is concerned, whether the species is used as the pollen or seed-bearing parent.

In the following notes the known hybrids are grouped on this basis.

(1) Hybrids with *C. carpatica*.

pulloides (*turbinata* × *pulla*) tends to the running root habit of *C. pulla* but has larger, brighter and more erect flowers and normally reaches a height of six or eight inches.

G. F. Wilson (*pulla* × *turbinata*)—the reverse cross—is nearer *C. carpatica*, with flowers almost upturned. There are, or were, two forms, one with normal green foliage and the other with leaves of the yellowish-green colour which is characteristic of many hybrid Campanulas. The latter is much dwarfer and less vigorous and requires more care (and particularly sharper drainage) in cultivation.

pseudo-raineri (probably *carpatica* × *raineri*) really shows very little influence of *C. raineri* except for a certain greyness in the leaf.

Fergusonii, *hendersonii*, *tymonsii* (*pyramidalis* × *carpatica*) may be grouped together as they are almost indistinguishable. They show little of the *C. pyramidalis* character for they are only four to six inches high and have stiffly branched stems bearing wide-mouthed, rather shallow and almost erect bell-shaped flowers.

innesii (*carpatica* × *pyramidalis*)—the reverse cross—is one of the best of the hybrids, producing numerous spreading and freely-branched stems up to at least a foot in length furnished with quantities of open starry flowers much resembling those of *C. pyramidalis*. It is an easy reliable plant in any soil and position, never spreading or seeding itself into a nuisance but propagated without difficulty either by cuttings or by division.

haylodgensis (*cochleariifolia* × *carpatica*) has yellowish foliage and showers of double bluebells on slender more or less trailing stems some six or eight inches in length.

Warley White (*syn. Warleyensis*) is a white-flowered seedling from the last. These two succeed best with a northerly exposure, thereby ensuring winter dormancy.

Stansfieldii (probably *carpatica* × *tommasiniana* or the reverse) is a very valuable plant of which the parentage is obscure as it appeared as a chance garden hybrid. It spreads slowly into a mat from which rise numerous ascendant branched stems about five inches high with somewhat hairy foliage and numerous widely open semi-pendent violet cup-shaped flowers. Spring cuttings root without difficulty or the plant may be divided as growth is beginning.

Riverslea, *Profusion* (*carpatica* × *isophylla*) are very much alike and resemble *C. carpatica* except for rather flatter and more starry flowers. The hybrid origin is shown by a certain yellowness in the foliage; and the presence of *C. isophylla* blood leads to an inclination to trail, to continuity and lateness of flowering, and to a certain degree of tenderness.

Avalon (*raineri* × *turbinata*), *Iseult* (*raineri* × *turbinata alba*) are attractive hybrids (if still in existence) in which the influence of *C. raineri* is shown by the size of the large cup-shaped flower and the dwarf habit.

Spetchley, *Abundance* (*rotundifolia* × *carpatica*) see page 229.

The quality of fertility persists into further generations as shown by:

Brookside (*turbinata* × *stansfieldii*) a dwarf compact plant, seldom more than two or three inches high, the stems being clothed with ovate-lanceolate leaves and terminating in two or three soft violet-blue flowers with pointed lobes. Award of Merit, 1933.

Woodstock (*Profusion* × *arvatica*) where the influence of the latter parent is seen in the form of the light violet coloured flowers, while the freedom of flowering and erect sturdy habit are characteristic of the other parent, the six-inch stems carrying six to nine flowers each.

Norman Grove (possibly *isophylla* × *stansfieldii*) resembles the latter parent but is rather stronger growing, carries its flowers erect and is of a lighter shade of blue.

Still another generation gives us:

Enchantress (*Norman Grove* × *waldsteiniana*) a gem of six inches with pale blue starry flowers, upturned as in *C. waldsteiniana*.

Peter Pan (*Norman Grove* × *turbinata, White Star*).

(2) Hybrids with *C. cochleariifolia*

Clarence Elliott (*cochleariifolia lilacina* × *isophylla mayi*) approaches the latter parent in habit and flower characters, having trailing branched stems each branch bearing one or two wide cup-shaped lavender flowers.

hallii (*cochleariifolia* × *portenschlagiana*) is fairly intermediate between the two parents though the wide-open semi-erect white flowers are usually borne only singly on two-inch stems.

R. B. Loder (*cochleariifolia* var. *Miss Willmott* × ?) is possibly not a hybrid at all but a seedling form with double (hose-in-hose) flowers. It is otherwise similar to *C. cochleariifolia*, the only suggestion of hybrid origin arising from the yellowish coloration of the leaves. A.M. 1922.

Gremlin (*isophylla*—the nurseryman's *mollis*— × *cochleariifolia*) has branched hairy stems four to six inches tall bearing a profusion of open bell-shaped lavender flowers and leaves which have glabrous blades but hairy petioles. Award of Merit, 1946.

justiniana, Smithii are two now unknown plants mentioned by Farrer as chance hybrids of garden origin. The parentage suggested by him is *cochleariifolia* × *rotundifolia* for the first named and *fragilis* × *cochleariifolia* for the latter.

haylodgensis (*cochleariifolia* × *carpatica*) see page 227.

(3) Hybrids with *C. rotundifolia*

rotarvatica (*rotundifolia* × *arvatica*) is a valuable and attractive plant which combines the constitution and ease of cultivation of *C. rotundifolia* with the bright starry flowers, on four- to six-inch stems, and dwarf running habit of *C. arvatica*. Award of Merit, 1935.

Lynchmere (*elatines* × *rotundifolia*), one of the latest introductions, has the foliage and growth of *C. elatines*, in its hairy form, but shows the influence of the second parent in the shape and carriage of the flowers. It is too early to say anything of its behaviour in cultivation but it is certainly showy and appears very promising. Award of Merit, 1948.

Spetchley (*syn. jenkinsae* or *jenkinsonii*—both forms of this name occur) (reputedly *rotundifolia* × *carpatica alba*) has been described as an improved white Harebell. It has stiff erect flower stems about a foot high terminating in a loose shower of six or eight snow-white flowers larger and more cup-shaped than in *C. rotundifolia*. As the buds are sub-pendent it should be referred to *C. linifolia* rather than to *C. rotundifolia*.

Abundance (*rotundifolia* × *carpatica*) shows greater affinity with the latter parent though the flowers are generally smaller and more numerous than in that species.

(4) Hybrids with *C. isophylla*

balchiniana (*isophylla* × *fragilis*) is very near the seed parent, *C. fragilis*. The raiser admitted at the time of introduction (1897) that he might have applied pollen of *C. turbinata* as well and added that he could not see that either *isophylla* or *turbinata* had had any obvious influence on the result. It received the Award of Merit in 1896.

wetherbyi (*isophylla* × ?) though a trailer has a compact branching habit, the branches being short and each terminating in a single large purple-blue flower. The influence of *C. isophylla* is shown in some lack of hardiness except in warm well-drained situations. I have not seen it for many years and it may not still be in existence.

Gremlin (*isophylla* × *cochleariifolia*) *see page* 228.

(5) Other garden hybrids

kewensis (or *Phyllis Elliott*) (*excisa* × *arvatica*). Originating as a chance seedling at Kew, the cross was repeated by Mr. Clarence Elliott, the progeny being indistinguishable from the Kew plant. It runs rather readily underground and produces numbers of erect threadlike stems some three inches high terminating in clusters of violet flowers which are carried horizontally and whose corolla lobes are acutely pointed and waved. It is a most attractive plant and the Award of Merit was given (to *Phyllis Elliott*) in 1937.

pyraversi (*pyramidalis* × *versicolor*). As in the case of the *C. carpatica* hybrids, the influence of *C. pyramidalis* is not very marked. Growing to a height of about three feet, the leafy stems bear a profusion of flowers of much the same shape and size as those of *C. versicolor*. It is not now readily obtainable though it survives at Kew, but does not really seem to be needed.

burghaltii (possibly *latifolia* × *punctata*) has been so long in cultivation that its origin is lost and can only be guessed. It produces a number of thin branching stems sometimes as much as three feet high terminating in loose clusters of long narrow deep purple buds which develop into pale lavender hanging bells three or four inches long. It shows a slight tendency to run underground like *C. punctata*, though not to the same extent. I have never known it to set seed (some evidence of hybrid origin) but it can be increased by careful division in spring. It seems to prefer a slightly shaded situation.

Van Houttei (possibly *punctata* × *latifolia*—the reverse cross to *burghaltii*) takes generally after *C. punctata* but is more tufted and smoother. The flowers too are similar in shape and size but deep rich purple in colour.

walla (*waldsteiniana* × *pulla*).

wockii (possibly *pulla* × *waldsteiniana*—the reverse cross to *walla*) has dangling pale blue bells on neatly tapered spires.

Ladhamsii (*garganica* × *poscharskyana*).

Birch hybrid (*portenschlagiana* × *poscharskyana*) is a showy plant but does not seem to be very different from a major form of *C. portenschlagiana* which is in cultivation. A.M. 1949.

Natural hybrids have been reported from time to time from many districts, forms having been found which differed to a greater or less extent from the prevailing type. Their parentage must be very largely a matter of opinion or guesswork, for few, if any, of them have been brought into cultivation and perpetuated and many, if not all, may be nothing more than aberrant forms or chance variants. The following list is as complete as possible and it may be assumed, in the absence of any fuller description, that the plant named is more or less intermediate between the two suggested parents.

arrecta (*primulaefolia* × 'other varieties'). A biennial with the foliage of *C. primulaefolia* and more or less branched stems two feet or more high but with flowers the size and shape of *C. pyramidalis* and deep blue-purple in colour.

besseana (*bononiensis* × *glomerata*) has leaves intermediate between the parents, though on longer footstalks than those of *C. glomerata*, while the flowers are longer though less open than those of *C. bononiensis*.

chevalieri (*trachelium* × *rapunculoides*). A form from Andorra which is apparently much the same as *lundstroemii*, described as the reverse cross. It is, however, clearly impossible to determine which is the seed, and which the pollen, parent in the case of these so-called natural hybrids.

cottia (*stenocodon*, Boiss. × *cochleariifolia*) as described comes midway between the parents, but *stenocodon*, Boiss. is regarded by many authorities as a dwarf, narrow-belled, form of *C. rotundifolia*.

christii. See *murithiana.*

digenea (*barbata* × *glomerata*). From the Tyrol, lacks the basal rosette of *C. barbata* but has clear indications of appendages on the calyx. The stems branch from the base and terminate in small clusters of flowers which are sessile and erect in bud but later become shortly stalked and more or less pendent. The corolla is tubular with long acute lobes scarcely recurved but, like *C. barbata*, is densely hairy within. The calyx segments are much shorter than in typical *C. glomerata*. It does not, according to the reports, set seed.

gisleri. See *ursaria.*

glomeratiformis (*spicata* × *glomerata*) has been reported from the Brenner Pass district. The habit is, in general, like *C. glomerata* but the flowers are darker, shorter and more cylindrical.

lundstroemii (*rapunculoides* × *trachelium*). A hybrid origin is claimed here on the strength of a somewhat modified shape of the capsule and the existence of hairs within the corolla.

murithiana, christii (*rhomboidalis* × *scheuchzeri*). Described as plainly intermediate between the parents and distinguished from one another by the broader and more dentate leaves of the latter. A similar hybrid, for which the softly hairy grey-leaved variety of the latter parent (var. *valdensis*) may be assumed to be responsible, has also been reported and named var. *incana.*

murii. See *semproniana.*

pechlaneri (*glomerata* × *spicata*) is said to be the reverse cross to *glomeratiformis* with the habit and form of *C. spicata* but with shorter basal leaves and considerably larger and more bell-shaped flowers.

rhomboidalis × *rotundifolia*. A whole range of intermediates between these two species crop up everywhere, but as both species vary considerably, the existence of a true hybrid is not so certain. In a communication to the Royal Horticultural Society in 1899, Wolley Dod said that, in his garden, 'the two species are united by imperceptible gradations, all of which are fertile' and suggested that *C. rotundifolia* may be a species which is gradually evolving into new species which are not yet sufficiently defined. (See also *murithiana.*)

schroeteri. See *ursaria.*

semproniana (*cochleariifolia* × *scheuchzeri*). From various parts of Canton Valais. It has the basal leaves, habit of growth, and corolla form of *C. cochleariifolia* but is considerably taller with longer stem leaves and calyx segments which are longer and more erect than in that species. It differs from the second parent in having rather broader stem leaves and a shorter and more broadly campanulate corolla. The buds are reported as being generally carried erect, in which case the second parent would be some form of *C. rotundifolia*. The name *C. × murrii* was originally given to this hybrid, but was not properly published and is, therefore, not valid.

truedingeri (*cochleariifolia × rotundifolia*) does not appear to be distinguishable from the last named.

ursaria (*scheuchzeri × rhomboidalis*). Both the glabrous and hairy forms of *C. scheuchzeri* are reported as being involved in the hybrids between these two species, and, apart from that, two distinct forms of the hybrid occur, possibly depending on which is the seed parent. The first (*gisleri*) is the smaller plant, eight to ten inches high, but has larger flowers and broader leaves than the other, the lower leaves being almost ovate and the corolla nearly an inch long. In general appearance it may be described as a dwarf form of *C. rhomboidalis*. The other (*schroeteri*) is twelve to fifteen inches in height, with lanceolate leaves and smaller flowers more like those of *C. scheuchzeri*.

APPENDIX

SYNONYMS

THE genus is very badly overloaded with synonyms. That this should be so is probably due in large measure to the fact that the majority of the species come from those parts of the world which have for a long time been settled, are more or less easily accessible and, accordingly, have been fully explored by botanists and others interested in plants, who, however, until comparatively recently, have not correlated their finds but, working independently, have followed their individual lines in the matter of nomenclature. This has led naturally to great confusion and with the increased intercourse of recent times the synonymity has largely come to light. Many of these difficulties have been dealt with in Chapter V and in the following lists all other known synonyms have been included. It is to be hoped that this will do something to resolve the complications and at least enable a grower who acquires a plant under an unknown name to ascertain readily whether it has previously been referred to under one of the recognised names in the genus.

Part I consists of names which are synonymous with other names still within the genus, while Part II contains names which, in the light of later botanical research and knowledge, belong to plants in other (generally closely allied) genera. In cases where the same name has been used by different authorities for different plants the name of the authority follows the name of the plant, in accordance with the general practice of botanical nomenclature, but where a name has been used only once it has not been thought necessary to add the name of the authority.

The importance of these lists to the grower can scarcely be overrated. Nurserymen are busy people and, generally speaking, have neither the time nor the opportunity to check the names under which they receive consignments of plants or seeds from abroad, their main interest being in propagation and distribution. No doubt there are exceptions, but the difficulties are immense, particularly in view of the ever increasing number of species and genera with which they have to deal, to say nothing of hybrids, and *caveat emptor* is a sound legal maxim. Even with the lists there will often be uncertainty, for the same name may have been used for different plants, for example, the name *hispida* may represent *C. lactiflora, persicifolia, morettiana,* or *ciliata,* or *Microcodon glomeratum*; and *lanceolata* may mean *C. steveni, persicifolia,* or *rotundifolia* in addition to the species which

233

correctly bears this name. Or, to look at the problem in another way, a purchaser of *C. alaris, cernua, divergens, gundelia, hohenackeri, lanuguinosa, pannonica, parviflora, racemosa,* or *undulata* would get nothing distinct from *C. sibirica,* while *C. lychnitis, mirantha, obliquifolia, ruthenica, simplex, tenuiflora,* or *thaliana* would merely be adding to the stock of *C. bononiensis.* As for the names which represent very minor variations of *C. rotundifolia* their name is legion, and *C. rapunculoides* and *C. glomerata* are also well provided with aliases.

PART I

acuminata, Michx.	americana
acutangula	arvatica
adami, Bieb.	bellidifolia
adami, Willd.	lasiocarpa
adhaerrens	retrorsa
affinis, Fisch.	aucheri
affinis, Reichb.	portenschlagiana
afganica, Pomel.	atlantica
afra	dichotoma
aggregata, Willd.	glomerata
alaris	sibirica
alaskana	rotundifolia
albanica	rotundifolia
albiflora	sarmatica
alexeenkoi	andia
algida	lasiocarpa
allionii, Lapeyr.	speciosa
allophylla	rotundifolia
alpestris, All.	allionii
alpigena	aucheri
altaica, DC.	pilosa
altaica, Ledeb.	steveni
amabilis	phytidocalyx (persicifolia)
americana, Mill.	persicifolia
amygdalifolia	persicifolia
andina	gumbetica
angustifolia	linifolia
antirrhina	caespitosa; rotundifolia
arctica	rotundifolia
arcuata	rotundifolia

argaea spicata
argunensis aucheri
aspera, Donn. aparinoides
asperifolia glomerata
asperrima ajugaefolia
asteroides americana; persicifolia
athoa trachelium
attenuata persicifolia
attica ramosissima
azurea rhomboidalis

baicalensis silenifolia
baicalensis, Pall. pilosa
balcanica rotundifolia
baldensis ramosissima
barbata, Lapeyr. speciosa
barbata, Spreng. glomerata
barrelieri fragilis
baumgartenii linifolia
bavarica portenschlagiana
beckiana linifolia
bellardii cochleariifolia
bellidifolia, Frivald. orphanidea
bellidifolia, Lapeyr. patula
bertolae linifolia
betonicaefolia, Biehl. sarmatica
betonicaefolia, Gilib. glomerata
bicaulis speciosa
bicolor camptoclada
biebersteiniana tridentata
bielzii rotundifolia
billardieri, DC. cymbalaria
biserrata lactiflora
bocconi, J. F. Gmel. rhomboidalis
bocconi, Vill. caespitosa
bithynica tridentata
boissieri, Sprun. radicosa
bosniaca pseudo-phrygia
brachiata, Salzm. dichotoma
brachiata, Siedl. patula

brachysepala	cenisia
brassicifolia	imeritina
bravensis	jacobaea
breynina	rotundifolia
brodensis	patula
brotherorum	sarmatica
broussonetiana	loefflingii
brunonis	latifolia
bulgarica	rotundifolia
burgalensis	rotundifolia
calaminthifolia, Griseb.	orphanidea
caldesiana	medium
californica	linnaeifolia
calycantha	pilosa; silenifolia
calycina	rapunculus
canescens, Biel.	sibirica
capitata, Schur.	cervicaria
capitata, Sims.	lingulata
cariensis	betonicaefolia
carnica	linifolia
cassandrina	ramosissima
castellana	rapunculus
catinensis	dichotoma
caucasica, Bieb.	sibirica
caucasica, C. Koch.	imeritina
cavolini	fragilis
cecilii	propinqua
celtidifolia	lactiflora
cephalantha	glomerata
cephalaria	cervicaria
cephalotes	glomerata
cernua, Hort.	sibirica
cerviana	cervicaria
cervicarioides, DC.	glomerata
chaberti	rapunculus
cichoracea	lingulata
ciliata, Patr.	silenifolia
coarctata	rapunculus
cochleariifolia, Vahl.	fragilis

commutata	sarmatica
compacta, Hegets.	rotundifolia
confertifolia	rotundifolia
congesta	glomerata
conglomerata	glomerata
contracta	rapunculoides
cordifolia, C. Koch.	rapunculoides
coriacea	radula
corymbifera	pelviformis
corymbosa, Desf.	pelviformis
corymbosa, Ten.	versicolor
costae	patula
crassa	expansa
crassifolia	fragilis
crassipes	rotundifolia
crenata	rapunculoides
cristallocalyx	persicifolia
dahurica	glomerata
dalmatica, Tausch.	cervicaria
dasyantha, Bieb.	pilosa
dasycarpa, Kit.	persicifolia
decipiens	dichotoma
declinata	americana
decloetiana	rotundifolia
decumbens	loefflingii
decurrens, Linn.	patula; persicifolia
decurrens, Thore.	rapunculus
decurrens, Zucc.	peregrina
delicatula, Jord.	caespitosa
denticulata, Boiss.	betulaefolia
diffusa, Vahl.	fragilis
dilecta	rotundifolia
dissoluta	retrorsa
divergens	sibirica
diversifolia, Dum.	rotundifolia
drabaefolia, Friv.	scutellata
drabaefolia, Steud.	fastigiata
drabaefolia, S. and S.	ramosissima
dubia	rotundifolia

dumetorum

duriaei

echiifolia

elatina

elatines, Bout.

elatines, Petag.

elatines, Poll.

elatior

elliptica

elongata, Port.

erinoides, Cav.

erinoides, Muhl.

eriocarpa

esculenta, Salisb.

euboea

euxina

fallax

farinosa

farinulenta

fastigata, S. G. Gmel.

ficarioides

filiflora

filiformis, Gilib.

filiformis, Moretti.

firmiana

flaccida, Dalle Torr.

flagellaris, Hal.

flexuosa, Michx.

flexuosa, Walds. and Kit.

floribunda

florida

foudrasi

frigida

frivaldskyi

garganica, Vis.

gautieri

gieseckiana

gilanica

rapunculoides

loefflingii

cervicaria

elatines

specularioides

garganica

elatinoides

rapunculus

glomerata

rapunculoides

loefflingii

aparinoides

latifolia

rapunculus

erinus

rotundifolia

aucheri

glomerata

rotundifolia

rapunculus

linifolia

prenanthoides

rotundifolia

morettiana

barbata

patula

tymphaea

divaricata

waldsteiniana

isophylla

medium

caespitosa

pilosa

expansa

fenestrellata

linifolia

uniflora

saxifraga

glabricarpa	rapunculoides
glandulosa	rapunculus
glareosa	caespitosa
glaucophylla	glomerata
gracilis, Jord.	caespitosa
graminifolia, Willern.	glomerata
grandiflora, Lam.	medium
grandiflora, Pourr.	speciosa
gummifera	sarmatica
gundelia	sibirica
gypsicola, Costa	macrorrhiza
halacsyana	hawkinsiana
hauryi	rotundifolia
hellenica	rotundifolia
herminii, Bory and Chaub.	spruneriana
heterodoxa, Boug.	rotundifolia
heterophylla, S. F. Gray	rotundifolia
hirsutissima	peregrina
hispanica	rotundifolia
hispida, Fisch.	lactiflora
hispida, Lejeune	persicifolia
hispida, Port.	morettiana
hispida, Spreng.	ciliata
hispida	glomerata
hispidissima	propinqua
hochstetteri	caespitosa
hohenackeri	sibirica
hoppeana	cochleariifolia
hornungiana	linifolia
hortensis	rapunculoides
hostii	linifolia
humilis, Schur.	persicifolia
hungarica	lingulata
hygrophila	aucheri
illinoensis	americana
imbricata	caespitosa
inconcessa	linifolia
infundibuliformis	rapunculoides

longifolia	speciosa, Pourr.
longifolia, Schloss.	cervicaria
longipes, Coss.	loefflingii
loreyi, A. Blanco	loefflingii
loreyi, Poll.	ramosissima
lunariaefolia, Riechb.	rapunculoides
lusitanica	loefflingii
lychnitis	bononiensis
macedonica, Boiss.	scutellata
macedonica, Boiss. and Orph.	multiflora; macrostachya
macrantha	latifolia
macrocalyx	pulla
macrophylla	alliariifolia
macrostachys, Panz.	rapunculoides
macrostachys, Willd.	multiflora
malyi	rotundifolia
marchesettii	rotundifolia
mathonetii	caespitosa
matritensis	loefflingii
mauritanica, Pomel	trachelium
mayeriana	aucheri
mayi	isophylla
medium, Lapeyr.	speciosa, Pourr.
mentiens, Witas.	rotundifolia
micrantha	bononiensis
microphylla, Cav.	mollis (? malacitana)
microphylla, Kit.	kitabeliana
minor, Honck.	caespitosa
minor, Lem.	rotundifolia
minuta, Savi	rotundifolia
modesta, Schott	caespitosa
molineri	sibirica
monantha	linifolia
monanthos	linifolia
morifolia	rapunculoides
multicaulis	linifolia
multiflora, Hort. ex DC.	bononiensis
multiflora, Willd.	polyantha, R. and S.
muralis	portenschlagiana

M

muricata	stricta
musarum	rupicola
myosotidifolia	argentea
nana, Lam.	allionii
napuligera	rotundifolia
neglecta, Bess.	rapunculoides
neglecta, R. and S.	patula
nemerosa	rapunculoides
nicaeensis, Risso.	macrorrhiza
nicaeensis, R. and S.	glomerata
nitida	(see p. 148)
nobilis	punctata
notata	caespitosa
numidica	mollis (? malacitana)
nutans, Lam.	rapunculoides
nutans, Vahl.	sibirica
obliqua	americana
obliquifólia	bononiensis
oblongata	glomerata
oenipontana	rapunculoides
oligosantha	trachelium
orientalis	peregrina
pallasiana, Vest.	pilosa
paniculata, Pohl.	sibirica
pannonica	sibirica
parviflora, Lam.	sibirica
parviflora, St. Lag.	erinus
parvula	caespitosa
patens	patula
patula, S. and S.	spruneriana
pauciflora, Des.	spruneriana
paui	rotundifolia
pelviformis, Lam.	corymbosa
pennica	rotundifolia
pennina	rotundifolia
perpentiae	raineri
pestalozzae	propinqua

petiolata	rotundifolia
petraea, All.	glomerata
petraea, Habl.	bononiensis
petraea, Kotschy.	involucrata
petraea, Zanted.	elatinoides
phyctidocalyx	persicifolia
pinifolia	rotundifolia
planiflora	(see p. 148)
planiflora, Engelm.	parryi
planiflora, Lam.	pyramidalis (or nitida)
planiflora, Willd.	versicolor
plicatula	trachelium
podanthoides	rimarum
porcii	linifolia
portensis	erinus
praesignis	rotundifolia
pratensis, Lapyl.	rotundifolia
pratensis, Reut.	trachelium
precatoria	lanceolata
prostrata	linifolia
pseudo-carnica	rotundifolia
pseudo-carpatica	carpatica
pseudo-lanceolata	linifolia
pseudo-pulla	pulla
pseudo-valdensis	rotundifolia
pubescens, Reichb.	rotundifolia
pubescens, Schmidt.	caespitosa
pubiflora	aucheri
pulchella, Jord.	caespitosa
pulcherrima	rapunculoides
pulla, Baumg.	linifolia
pulla, Parol.	morettiana
pumila, Curt.	caespitosa
pumila, Schmidt	persicifolia
pusilla, Haenke	caespitosa
pyramidalis, Gilib.	bononiensis
pyramidiflora	rapunculoides
pyrenaica, Hecht. and Willd.	rhomboidalis
racemosa, S. G. Gmel.	sibirica

racemosa, Opiz.	rapunculoides
racemosa, Witas.	linifolia
ramosissima, Griseb.	phrygia
ramosissima, Sprun.	spruneriana
ramosissima, Willd.	loefflingii
rapuncula	rapunculus
rapunculoides, Pall.	bononiensis
rapunculiformis	rapunculoides
rapunculus, O. F. Muell.	rotundifolia
re	linifolia
reboudiana, Gren. and G.	rotundifolia
reboudiana, Pomel.	filicaulis
recta	linifolia
redowskyi	pilosa
redux	linifolia
reflexa, Hausm.	linifolia
reflexa, Schur.	caespitosa
regina	mirabilis
reniformis	carpatica
reyneri	raineri
rhodensis	ramosissima
rhodii	linifolia
rhomboidalis, Gorter.	rapunculoides
rhomboidea, Endr.	rhomboidalis
rigescens	silenifolia
rigida, Gilib.	rapunculoides
rochelii	steveni
roezlii	prenanthoides
rohdii	linifolia
romanica	rotundifolia
rosani	versicolor
rosulata	cenisia
rotunda	rotundifolia
rotundifolia, All.	rhomboidalis
rotundifolia, Boiss.	macrorrhiza
rotundifolia, Ledeb.	linifolia
rotundifolia, Pall.	adscendens
rubra	rhomboidalis
ruprechtii	saxifraga
ruscinonensis	linifolia

russeliana	strigosa
ruthenica	bononiensis
sabatia	macrorrhiza
sajanensis, Fisch.	pilosa
sajanensis, Spreng.	lasiocarpa
salviaefolia	glomerata
sancta	rotundifolia
sanensis	pilosa
sardoa	macrorrhiza
scheuchzeri, A. Gray	parryi
scheuchzeri, Lodd.	rotundifolia
schleicheri	linifolia
secunda	rapunculoides
semiamplexicaulis	linifolia
seminuda	steveni
serotina	glomerata
serratifolia	trachelium
sessiliflora, C. Koch.	grandis
sessiliflora, Vukot.	raineri
setosa, Fisch.	rapunculoides
simplex, Lam.	bononiensis
simplex, Stev.	steveni
solstitialis	rotundifolia
spathulaefolia	ramossisima
spathulata, W. K. Plant.	sibirica
spathulata, Ehrenb.	trichopoda
spathulata, S. and S.	spruneriana
spathulata, Waldst. and Kit.	sibirica
speciosa, Gilib.	persicifolia
speciosa, Hornem.	glomerata
specularioides	loefflingii
sphaerothrix	expansa
spicata, Geners.	cervicaria
spiciformis, Boiss.	rapunculus
spruneri	spruneriana
stelleri, Steph. ex. Herd	lasiocarpa
stelleri, Rad.	pilosa
stenophylla, Witas.	rotundifolia
stenosiphon, Reichb.	rotundifolia
steveniana	steveni

styriaca	linifolia
suaveolens	persicifolia
subramulosa	caespitosa
subulata, Beauv.	americana
sub-pyrenaica	persicifolia
subuniflora	linifolia
symphytifolia, All.	glomerata
syriaca, Ehrenb.	stellaris
syspirensis, C. Koch.	stricta, L.
tauscheri, A. Kern	bononiensis
tenella, Jord.	caespitosa
tenella, Lange.	rotundifolia
tenorii	versicolor
tenuiflora, Schur.	bononiensis
tenuiflora, Ten.	lingulata
tenuifolia, Hoffm.	rotundifolia
thaliana	bononiensis
thomasii	versicolor
tommasiniana, Koch.	waldsteiniana
trachelioides, Bieb.	rapunculoides
trachelioides, Munby.	trachelium
trachelium, Brot.	peregrina
trachelium, Ball.	rapunculoides
trachelium, Thunb.	punctata
trachyphylla	glomerata
trilocularis	allionii
tridens	tridentata
tubiflora	glomerata
tyrolensis	caespitosa
ucranica	rapunculoides
umbellifera	pyramidalis
undulata, Moench.	sibirica
uniflora, Georgi.	silenifolia
uniflora, Gorter.	rotundifolia
uniflora, Honck.	cenisia
uniflora, Schult.	caespitosa
uniflora, Vill.	linifolia
urticaefolia, All.	latifolia

urticaefolia, Gilib.	bononiensis
urticaefolia, Turra.	rapunculoides
urticifolia	trachelium
variifolia	rotundifolia
velebitica	rotundifolia
velutina, Desf.	mollis (? malacitana)
velutina, Velen.	lanata
venosa	rhomboidalis
venusta	caespitosa
verticillata, Guss.	versicolor
vesula	persicifolia
vollanii	caespitosa
violae	violaefolia
virgata, DC.	rapunculus
virgata, Rafin.	divaricata; linifolia
visiani	waldsteiniana
vitinghofiana	steveni; persicifolia
vlachovae	glomerata
volubilis	lactiflora
welandii	expansa
wightii, Gamble.	ramulosa, Wight, non Wall
willdenowiana	versicolor
witasekiana	linifolia

PART II

adpressa	Wahlenbergia adpressa
agrestis	Wahlenbergia gracilis
albicans	Trachelium albicans
alburnica	Phyteuma amplexicaulis
alliariaefolia, Reichb.	Symphyandra pendula
alopecuroides	Phyteuma sibthorpiana
alpini, Linn.	Adenophora liliifolia
alpini, Pichl.	Phyteuma amplexicaule
altiflora	Prismatocarpus altiflorus
americana, Hort ex Streud.	Phyteuma canescens
amplexicaulis, Boiss.	Phyteuma amplexicaule
amplexicaulis, Michx.	Specularia perfoliata

anagalloides	Cephalostigma hirsutum
androsacea	Wahlenbergia androsacea
angulata	Specularia perfoliata
anticensis	Specularia perfoliata
arborescens	Hamelia ventricosa
arida	Wahlenbergia linarioides
armena	Symphyandra armena
arvatica, Lag.	Wahlenbergia hederacea
arvensis	Specularia speculum
aspera, Boiss.	Phyteuma asperum
asperuloides	Trachelium (Diosphaera) asperuloides
aurasiaca	Asyneuma aurasiaca
aurea	Musschia aurea
axillaris, Oliver	Campanumoea axillaris
axilliflora	Adenophora axilliflora
banksiana	Wahlenbergia banksiana
bergiana	Prismatocarpus subulatus
biflora	Specularia biflora
boissieri, Vatke.	Phyteuma asperum
bracteata	Roella bracteata
brevibracteata	Microcodon glomeratum
brodensis	Adenophora infundibuliformis
buchii	Wahlenbergia pilosa
canariensis	Canarina campanulata
candolleana	Prismatocarpus candolleanus
canescens, Roth.	Phyteuma canescens
capensis	Wahlenbergia capensis
capillacea	Wahlenbergia capillacea
capillaris	Wahlenbergia gracilis or multicaulis
cappadocica	Phyteuma cappadocica
carnosa	Peracarpa carnosa
caudata, Vis.	Wahlenbergia dalmatica
celebica	Campanumoea celebica
cernua, Thunb.	Wahlenbergia cernua
cervicina	Wahlenbergia cervicina
chalcidica	Trachelium chalcidicum
chilensis, Bert.	Wahlenbergia hirsuta, or reflexa
chilensis, Molina.	Wahlenbergia linarioides

chondrophylla	Wahlenbergia chondrophylla
cichoriformis	Phyteuma cichoriforme
ciliaris	Roella ciliata
ciliata, Thunb.	Lightfootia tenella
cilicia	Phyteuma amplexicaule
cinerea	Lightfootia grisea
circaeoides	Peracarpa circaeoides
clivosa, Banks.	Wahlenbergia angustifolia
clivosa, Herb. Roxb.	Wahlenbergia linifolia
coa	Specularia pentagonia
coccinea	(not Campanula, but genus not determined)
coloradoense	Specularia lindheimeri
controversa	Phyteuma rigidum or Asyneuma lanceolata
cordata, Tausch.	Adenophora cordata
cordata, Vis.	Specularia speculum
coronata	Adenophora marsupiiflora
coronopifolia	Adenophora coronopifolia
cretica	Symphyandra sp.
crispa, Banks.	Prismatocarpus crispus
cylindrica	Wahlenbergia cylindrica
dalmatica, D. Dietr.	Wahlenbergia dalmatica
debilis, D. Dietr.	Wahlenbergia debilis
dehiscens	Wahlenbergia gracilis
denticulata, Burch.	Lightfootia capillaris
denticulata, Spreng.	Adenophora tricuspidata
denudata	Wahlenbergia denudata
diffusa, Banks.	Wahlenbergia nudicaulis
diffusa, D. Dietr.	Microcodon lineare
diversifolia, D. Dietr.	Wahlenbergia diversifolia
dracunculifolia	Phyteuma rigidum or lanceolatum
dunantii	Wahlenbergia dunantii
ecklonii	Wahlenbergia ecklonii
elongata, Banks.	Wahlenbergia nudicaulis
elongata, Willd.	Wahlenbergia capensis
ensifolia	Heterochaenia ensifolia
ericoides	Prismatocarpus paniculatus

erysimoides	Adenophora gmelini
exilis	Wahlenbergia exilis
expansa, Rudolph.	Wahlenbergia homallanthina
falcata	Specularia falcata
fasciculata	Lightfootia fasciculata
fernandeziana	Wahlenbergia fernandeziana
filiformis, Ruiz and Pav.	Wahlenbergia linarioides
firma	Phyteuma aucheri
fischeri	Adenophora communis
fischeriana	Adenophora coronopifolia
flaccida, D Dietr.	Wahlenbergia flaccida
flagellaris, H.B. and K.	Specularia perfoliata
fontanesiana	Phyteuma lanceolata
fruticosa, Banks.	Prismatocarpus fruticosus
fruticosa, Hill.	Prismatocarpus paniculatus
fruticosa, Linn.	Lightfootia subulata
gentianoides	Platycodon grandiflorum
ghilanensis, Pall.	Specularia ghilanensis
glabrata	Wahlenbergia undulata
gmelini, R. and S.	Adenophora marsupiiflora
gmelini, Spreng.	Adenophora gmelini
gracilis, Boiss.	Phyteuma lobelioides
gracilis, Bert.	Wahlenbergia berteroi
gracilis, Sims.	Wahlenbergia gracilis
graminifolia, Host.	Wahlenbergia tenuifolia
graminifolia, Linn.	Wahlenbergia graminifolia
graminifolia, W. and K.	Edraianthus graminifolius
grandiflora, Jacq.	Platycodon grandiflorum
hastaefolia	Canarina campanulata
hederacea	Wahlenbergia hederacea
hederaefolia	Wahlenbergia hederacea
hesperidifolia	Phyteuma lobelioides
heterophylla, Baumg.	Symphyandra wanneri
hilsenbergi	Wahlenbergia hilsenbergi
hirsuta, Guss.	Specularia speculum
hirta	Specularia speculum
hispida, Eckl.	Microcodon glomeratum

hispidula, Link.	Microcodon glomeratum
hispidula, Linn.	Microcodon depressum
homallanthina	Wahlenbergia homallanthina
humilis, D. Dietr.	Wahlenbergia humilis
hybrida	Specularia hybrida
inconspicua	Wahlenbergia lobelioides
indica	Wahlenbergia indica
intermedia, R. and S.	Adenophora communis
intermedia, Engelm.	Specularia biflora
interrupta	Prismatocarpus interruptus
jacquini, DC.	Trachelium jacquini
japonica	Phyteuma japonica
javanica	Campanumoea javanica
juncea, D. Dietr.	Lightfootia juncea
juncea, Hort., ex DC.	Wahlenbergia lobelioides
juncifolia	Wahlenbergia lobelioides
kitabelii, DC.	Wahlenbergia kitabelii
krebsii	Wahlenbergia zeyheri
lamarckii	Adenophora lamarckii
lancifolia, Roxb.	Campanumoea celebica
larreinii	Wahlenbergia fernandeziana
lavandulaefolia	Wahlenbergia gracilis
leptocarpa	Specularia leptocarpa
leptopetala	Phyteuma rigidum
liliflora	Adenophora communis
lilifolia, Lam.	Adenophora lamarkii
lilifolia, Linn.	Adenophora communis
limonia	Phyteuma limonifolium
limonifolia	Phyteuma limonifolium
linarioides	Wahlenbergia linarioides
linearifolia	Prismatocarpus campanuloides
linearis	Microcodon lineare
liniphylla	Adenophora marsupiiflora
linoides	Wahlenbergia linarioides
littoralis	Wahlenbergia gracilis
lobelioides, Linn.	Wahlenbergia lobelioides

lobelioides, Spreng.	Wahlenbergia nutabunda
lobelioides, Vatke.	Phyteuma lobelioides
longebracteata	Treichelia longebracteata
longirostris	Prismatocarpus crispus
ludoviciana	Specularia biflora
lunariafolia, Willd.	Phyteuma campanuloides
lycia	Phyteuma lycium
lyraefolia	Michauxia campanuloides
macrocephala	Wahlenbergia tenuifolia
madagascarensis	Wahlenbergia oppositifolia
marginata	Wahlenbergia gracilis
marschalliana	Phyteuma campanuloides
marsupiiflora	Adenophora marsupiiflora
massonii	Wahlenbergia massonii
microcodon	Microcodon glomeratum
mikoi	Adenophora mikoi
minae	Phyteuma amplexicaule or Asyneuma trichocalycina
minuta, Agardh.	Jasione foliosa
monadelpha	Adenophora coronopifolia
montevidensis	Specularia biflora
multicaulis, Boiss.	Asyneuma persica
myrtifolia	Trachelium myrtifolium
nudicaulis	Wahlenbergia nudicaulis
nutabunda	Wahlenbergia nutabunda
nutans, Sieber.	Symphyandra cretica
ossetica	Symphyandra ossetica
ottoniana	Lightfootia oxyococcoides
ovata	Wahlenbergia ovata
paniculata, Linn.	Wahlenbergia paniculata
paniculata, Sm.	Wahlenbergia banksiana
paniculata, Wall.	Cephalostigma paniculatum
parnassica	Edraianthus parnassi
parviflora, Salisb.	Wahlenbergia lobelioides
peduncularis	Wahlenbergia peduncularis
pedunculata	Wahlenbergia paniculata
peirescifolia	Adenophora latifolia

pendula	Symphyandra pendula
pentagonia	Specularia pentagonia
pentagonophylla	Wahlenbergia hederacea
pereskia	Adenophora latifolia
pereskiaefolia	Adenophora latifolia
perfoliata	Specularia perfoliata
periplocifolia	Adenophora periplocaefolia
perpallens	Adenophora perpallens
persica	Asyneuma persicum
phyteumoides	Phyteuma limoniifolium
pichleri	Phyteuma amplexicaule (or Asyneuma trichocalycina)
pilosa, Less.	Adenophora tricuspidata
plicata	Prismatocarpus crispus
polymorpha	Wahlenbergia gracilis
pomponiifolia	Adenophora gmelini
porosa	Salmolus porosus
postii	Trachelium postii
preissii	Wahlenbergia gracilis
prismatocarpus	Prismatocarpus nitidus
procumbens	Wahlenbergia procumbens
pulchella, Boiss.	Phyteuma pulchellum
pulchella, Salisb.	Specularia speculum
pumilio	Wahlenbergia pumilio
punduana	Campanumoea parviflora
purpurea	Codonopsis purpurea
pygmaea, D. Dietr.	Microcodon glomeratum
pygmaea, Lam.	Borago laxiflora
rabelaisiana	Adenophora gmelini
redowskiana	Wahlenbergia homallanthina
repanda	Phyteuma limonifolium
repens, Hort, ex Steud.	Wahlenbergia procumbens
rhomboidea, Murr.	Adenophora communis
richteri	Adenophora richteri
rigida, Boiss.	Phyteuma rigidum
riparia, Boj.	Wahlenbergia eminensis
riparia, Leprieur.	Wahlenbergia riparia
roelloides	Prismatocarpus paniculatus
rubioides	Microcodon lineare

sajanensis, Fisch.	Adenophora marsupiiflora
salicifolia, Boiss.	Phyteuma canescens
salicifolia, Boiss. and Kotschy.	Phyteuma amplexicaule
salicifolia, Juss.	Adenophora coronopifolia
saxicola	Wahlenbergia saxicola
schimperi	Cephalostigma hirsutum
serbica	Wahlenbergia serbica
serpyllifolia	Edraianthus serpyllifolius
sessiliflora, Boiss.	Podanthum brachylobum
sessiliflora, D. Dietr.	Prismatocarpus campanuloides
sessiliflora, Linn.	Lightfootia longifolia
sessilis	Prismatocarpus sessilis
setacea	Wahlenbergia capillacea
sibthorpiana	Phyteuma sibthorpianum
sieberi	Wahlenbergia gracilis
silenifolia, Host.	Wahlenbergia pumilio
sinai	Phyteuma lanceolatum
sinensis	Adenophora sinensis
sparsiflora	Microcodon sparsiflorum
speculum	Specularia speculum
spinulosa	Wahlenbergia spinulosa
spreta	Adenophora communis
spuria	Specularia hybrida
st. helenae	Wahlenbergia linifolia
stellarioides	Wahlenbergia stellarioides
stenanthina	Adenophora marsupiiflora
stenophylla, Boiss. and Held.	Phyteuma linifolium
stylidioides	Phyteuma lobelioides
stylosa, Bess.	Adenophora communis
stylosa, Lam.	Adenophora stylosa
suaveolens, Gilib.	Adenophora communis
subulata, Spreng.	Lightfootia subulata
subulata, Thunb.	Prismatocarpus subulatus
swellendamensis	Wahlenbergia swellendamensis
syngenesiflora	Adenophora marsupiiflora
syriaca, Willd.	Specularia falcata
tauricola	Phyteuma rigidum or Asyneuma lanceolatum
tenella, Linn.	Lightfootia tenella or thunbergiana

tenerrima	Prismatocarpus tenerrimus
tenuifolia, W. and K.	Wahlenbergia tenuifolia
tetraphylla	Adenophora verticillata
thalictriflora	Codonopsis thalictrifolia
thomsonii	Phyteuma thomsonii
thunbergii	Lightfootia ciliata
trichocalycina	Phyteuma amplexicaule (or Asyneuma trichocalycina)
tricuspidata	Adenophora denticulata
trigona	Specularia speculum
triphylla	Adenophora triphylla
truncata	Campanumoea celebica
umbrosa	Adenophora communis
undulata, Linn.	Wahlenbergia undulata
unidentata	Lightfootia unidentata
uzemurae	Adenophora uzemurae
verticillata, Pall.	Adenophora verticillata
vincaeflora, Vent.	Wahlenbergia gracilis
virgata, Labill.	Phyteuma limonifolium (or Asyneuma virgatum)
viridis	Codonopsis viridis
wanneri	Symphyandra wanneri
wettsteinii	Edraianthus wettsteinii
wildenowii	Phyteuma lobelioides
zeyheri	Wahlenbergia zeyheri

ADDENDA

Since completing this book information has been obtained concerning four additional species as follows:

C. baileyi. From mountains in Trinity Co., California, and nearly related to *C. linnaeifolia*, this species produces slender simple erect stems from a creeping perennial rootstock, each stem terminating in a single flower, pendent in bud but erect when open. The lower leaves are obovate, with a few teeth at the apex, those on the stems being elliptic-lanceolate and sharply serrate. Calyx segments are triangular acuminate and about two thirds the length of the bell-shaped corolla which is lobed to rather more than halfway. Dehiscence is apical.

C. cypria. A small annual species recently reported from Mt. Troodos, Cyprus, with thin slightly downy stems three to four inches high bearing small oblong spathulate sessile leaves, densely covered with fine ash-green hairs, and terminating in a crowded but few-flowered corymb, the flowers of which are borne erect on short stalks. The calyx has linear segments but no appendages and the narrowly tubular-campanulate corolla, three times as long as the calyx, is very shortly lobed and sometimes more or less bearded. The style is exserted and the capsule carried erect, the last-named character serving to distinguish it from *C. delicatula* and *C. podocarpa*; while *C. raveyi*, otherwise similar, has more hairy leaves and flowers more than twice the size.

C. macdougalii. A smooth slender perennial, some fifteen inches high, from Idaho, with noticeably thin leaves. The basal and lower stem leaves are broadly ovate, coarsely dentate and petiolate, the upper ones being lanceolate or linear and entire. The corolla, about three-quarters of an inch long, is much the same shape as that of *C. rotundifolia* and the narrow awl-shaped calyx segments about three-quarters the length of the corolla. The style is exserted which distinguishes it from that species.

C. stylocampa. A perennial species from Dawson, U.S.A., which has slender simple erect stems about eight inches high, furnished with oblanceolate to linear-acuminate sessile leaves with undulate margins. The narrow awl-shaped calyx segments are smooth and about half the length of the corolla which is divided almost to the base into narrow lobes. The species is remarkable for its long exserted style which, while erect at the base, is 'curved like a sickle downwards'.